Advanced praise for *Belly of the Beast*

"The annals of war chronicle the depths of human suffering, and the heights to which men soar, for love of country. Judith Pearson explores these extremes in the Pacific theater of World War II, where Estel Myers and his fellow American prisoners endured unspeakable deprivation as the shadow of Imperial Japan cast Asia into darkness. Most of the prisoners were lost, their cause ennobled by their sacrifice. Those who emerged from the "Belly of the Beast," and the souls of the departed who marched home with them, merit the recognition Pearson offers in this searing tribute to the honor they brought America during her bleakest hour, and in her greatest victory."
—Senator John McCain

"An inspiring look at one of World War II's darkest hours."
—James Bradley, author of *Flags of Our Fathers* and son of Navy corpsman John Bradley, an Iwo Jima flag raiser

"*Belly of the Beast* captures an experience almost too terrifying for words. To follow one man's ordeal in a Japanese torture ship is to travel through the bowels of hell."
—Iris Chang, author of *The Rape of Nanking*

"By the time the island fortress of Corregidor fell to the Japanese in May 1942, more Americans were prisoners of war than at any other time in our history. For these unfortunate men and women, the real ordeal had barely begun. In *Belly of the Beast,* Judith Pearson chronicles the experience of Estel Myers, a Navy hospital corpsman who not only lived through starvation and disease in Manila's notorious Bilibid Prison, but who also survived a cruel and heartrending voyage aboard the Japanese 'death ships.' How one man clung to his humanity despite deprivation and the unspeakable misery all around him is the real story."—Jan K. Herman, historian of the Navy Medical Department

continued . . .

"The events described in *Belly of the Beast* are so real that they brought back memories of those awful days when I was a POW. Judy Pearson has captured the torment and pain of men and women taken prisoner by the Japanese at the fall of Bataan. Her description of the events was so real I could hear and feel the crying out of the suffering. Her story brings out the barbaric events that accounted for so many American lives during World War II. Thank you, Judy, for sharing your research and writing skills in describing how prisoners of the Japanese lived and died."

—Lester Tenney, former POW survivor and author
of *My Hitch in Hell: The Bataan Death March*

"Immensely readable. From the professional historian's and archives director's points of view, I appreciated how skillfully [Judith Pearson] put the individual POWs' experiences in context. Most important, [her] careful exposé of this type of ordeal clearly and forcefully reflects . . . a remarkable, faithful picture of what these brave men and women had to endure. I think it was particularly important that [she] described the judicial and personal aftermath of the horrific war in the Pacific. Most Americans do not know how few Japanese perpetrators of these crimes had to pay for them, or how lingering were the effects of their cruelty upon the survivors."

—Dr. William O. Oldson, director, Institute on
World War II and the Human Experience,
Florida State University

BELLY OF THE BEAST

---★---

A POW's Inspiring True Story of Faith,
Courage, and Survival Aboard the Infamous
WWII Japanese Hell Ship *Oryoku Maru*

JUDITH L. PEARSON

NEW AMERICAN LIBRARY

Published by New American Library, a division of
Penguin Putnam Inc., 375 Hudson Street,
New York, New York 10014, U.S.A.
Penguin Books Ltd, 27 Wrights Lane,
London W8 5TZ, England
Penguin Books Australia Ltd, Ringwood,
Victoria, Australia
Penguin Books Canada Ltd, 10 Alcorn Avenue,
Toronto, Ontario, Canada M4V 3B2
Penguin Books (N.Z.) Ltd, 182–190 Wairau Road,
Auckland 10, New Zealand

Penguin Books Ltd, Registered Offices:
Harmondsworth, Middlesex, England

Published by New American Library, a division of Penguin Putnam Inc.

First Printing, October 2001
10 9 8 7 6 5 4 3 2

🅝🅐🅛 REGISTERED TRADEMARK—MARCA REGISTRADA

LIBRARY OF CONGRESS CATALOGING-IN-PUBLICATION DATA:
Pearson, Judith, 1953–
Belly of the beast : a POW's inspiring true story of faith, courage, and survival aboard the
infamous WWII Japanese hell ship Oryoku Maru / Judith Pearson.
p. cm.
Includes index.
ISBN 0-451-20444-1 (alk. paper)
1. Myers, Estel Browning, 1920-1973. 2. Oryoku Maru (Prison ship) 3. World War,
1939–1945—Prisoners and prisons, Japanese—Biography. 4. Prisoners of war—Biography.
5. World War, 1939–1945—Atrocities. 6. War crimes—Japan—History—20th century.
I. Title.

D804.J3 P43 2001
940.54'7252—dc21   2001032628

Printed in the United States of America
Set in Adobe Garamond
Designed by Leonard Telesca

BOOKS ARE AVAILABLE AT QUANTITY DISCOUNTS WHEN USED TO PRO-
MOTE PRODUCTS OR SERVICES. FOR INFORMATION PLEASE WRITE TO PRE-
MIUM MARKETING DIVISION, PENGUIN PUTNAM INC., 375 HUDSON STREET,
NEW YORK, NEW YORK 10014.

The beast, which you saw, once was, now is not, and will come up out of the Abyss and go to his destruction.
—Revelation 17:8

Contents

Acknowledgments

Constructing *Belly of the Beast* was very much like assembling a complex jigsaw puzzle. Locating the pieces and finding their exact position in the story would never have been possible without the help of many individuals who graciously gave me their time and assistance. These brief acknowledgments are only a token of my heartfelt gratitude.

Thanks first to military antique maven Larry Stewart, whose insistence on recognition for Estel Myers was the book's foundation. And thanks, too, to Ken and Evelyn Myers, Estel's brother and sister-in-law. I am grateful for the friendship that developed between us as we worked on this book as well as for their stories that helped me come to know Estel better.

The inspiration, as well a great deal of the material for *Belly of the Beast,* was gleaned from WWII veterans themselves, including brave survivors of Bataan and Corregidor. In addition to my thanks to them, we all owe them a great deal for their service and sacrifices: Malcom Amos, Ernie Bales, Art Beale, Chuck Charleston, Clyde Childress, Martin Christie, Ed Foster, Duke Fullerton, Pat Hitchcock, Ernie Irvin, Dave Johnson, Ben Lohman, Leo Padilla, Frank Sacton, Gap Silva, Les Tenny, and Hilda Osborn and Viola Wright, widows of veterans.

Recognition is also due to those who help keep history alive and who assisted me with my research: Jan Herman, historian of the Naval Bureau of Medicine and Surgery, Washington, D.C.; Jeff Hunt, curator of the Admiral Nimitz Museum of the Pacific War, Fredericksburg, Texas; and Rick Padilla, curator of the Bataan Museum, Santa Fe, New Mexico.

I am equally indebted to those who share my love for writing and telling a good story: my agent, Peter Rubie, who was most patient as he guided me through the business of writing; my editor, Dan Slater, whose urging for me to write from the gut paid off; and my writers' group for their support and painstaking copyediting during this project: Cindy Goyette, Wanda McLaughlin, Val Neiman, Gary Ponzo, and Rich Schooler.

And lastly, my deepest gratitude goes to my husband and sons, who allowed me to spend two years living in the 1940s. Their love and support gave me the strength and courage to tell this story.

Preface

While visiting a Phoenix area antique shop, the owner, an acquaintance of mine, shared with me his most recent find: items belonging to a World War II veteran. Among the collection was a series of newspaper clippings, now browned with the passage of time. My friend was very moved by the story told in the clippings and asked if I would consider writing a tribute to this veteran, a naval corpsman and former POW, who had been so brave amid so much suffering. Thus the story of Estel Myers found me, an unusual twist for a writer who is usually the one finding stories.

For those of us who were not there, the unspeakable horrors Myers and his comrades endured during the war are impossible to imagine. And while a great deal is known about the European Theater of Operations of World War II, very little is discussed about the Pacific Theater. Americans know that their war began and ended in the Pacific Theater, with Pearl Harbor and the atomic bombs, respectively. But the vast middle of the war in the Pacific is often overlooked. And so, too, are the innumerable acts of bravery and examples of the indomitable human spirit.

Theories explaining the scarcity of Pacific war materials vary. The United States government was strongly allied with Great Britain, a nation threatened by Hitler's advances in Europe. Thus the U.S. developed a "defeat Germany first" attitude. But even more to the point, the Pacific Theater consisted of more than six thousand square miles, most of it ocean, dotted with islands relatively unknown to the average American. It was foreign and uncharted territory in 1941, and to a certain extent is still considered that way today.

I learned from Myers' death certificate, included in my friend's collection, that he had died in Phoenix in 1973. Detective work at the library produced his obituary and the fact that he had a brother living in the area. When I contacted Ken Myers, he had no idea that his brother's effects had left the family's possession and was even happier than I was to have them make their way back to where they belong. Then with Ken's help, I embarked on this journey through history.

Belly of the Beast is factual and historically correct. It is not, however, *just* Estel Myers' story. It is the story of many men, a mosaic of remembrances gathered from interviews with more than three dozen veterans, along with Myers' experiences as we know them to have happened. Rather than a collection of memoirs or a historical review, *Belly of the Beast* is a biographical narrative. There are no footnotes or annotations that might interrupt the flow of the story. The extensive bibliography at the end gives credit to all of those researchers who compiled information before me and to the veterans themselves.

As our nation reflects back upon the twentieth century, I wrote this book in the hope of accomplishing several things. First and foremost, I want to bring to light the tremendous sacrifices made by the men and women who served in the Pacific Theater during World War II. To them, our nation is eternally grateful. Secondly, I hope this book will educate Americans of all generations about a fact that seems so obviously lacking in history books: While the United States was so resoundingly defeated on that fateful day in December 1941, the country pulled together to rally to become victorious over the enemy.

Lastly, it is my hope that this book will serve as a warning to future generations. Evil exists throughout the world. It is like a beast: it knows no race, religion, or national origin. It exists among the peoples of all nations. Left unchecked, this evil will surely produce suffering and destruction and death. We must, therefore, never forget what history has taught us, so that it is never repeated.

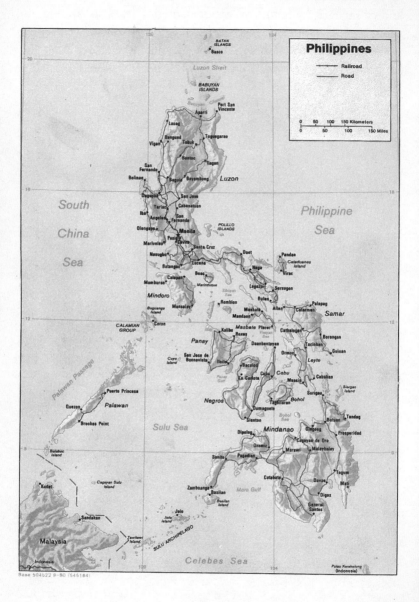

Philippines

Railroad
Road

| 0 | 50 | 100 | 150 Kilometers |
| 0 | 50 | 100 | 150 Miles |

BATAN ISLANDS
Basco

Luzon Strait

BABUYAN ISLANDS

Port San Vincente
Aparri

Laoag

Bangued
Vigan
Tabuk
Tuguegarao

Bontoc

Ilagan

San Fernando
Bolinao
Baguio
Bayombong

Luzon

Dagupan
San Jose
Tarlac
Cabanatuan
Iba
Angeles
San Fernando
Olongapo
Pasig
Manila
Mariveles
Cavite
Nasugbu
Santa Cruz
Batangas
Lucena
Boac
Calapan
Mamburao
Marinduque

Mindoro
Buguanga Island
Coron

CALAMIAN GROUP

POLILLO ISLANDS

Daet
Naga
Virac
Pandan
Catanduanes Island

Legazpi
Sorsogon

Sibuyan Sea
Romblon
Bulan

Masbate
Meshate
Mandaon

Palapag
Allen
Catarman
Samar

Panay
Kalibo
Roxas
Masbate Placer
Visayan Sea
Daanbantayan
Calbayog
Borongan

Cuyo Island
San Jose de Buenavista
Iloilo
Bacolod
La Carlota

Cebu
Ormoc
Tacloban
Guiuan
Leyte

Negros

Maasin
Cebu
Bohol
Tagbilaran
Surigao
Cabalian
Siargao Island

Palawan Passage

Puerto Princesa
Quezon
Palawan

Brookes Point

Sulu Sea

Dumaguete
Siaton

Bohol Sea

Butuan
Tandag
Gingoog
Prosperidad

Dipolog
Mindanao
Ozamiz
Cagayan de Oro
Maramag
Malaybalay

Balabac Island

Cayagan Sulu Island

Siasi
Pagadian
Cotabato
Davao
Tagum
Mati

Kudat
Zamboanga
Basilan
Basilan Island
Maro Gulf
General Santos
Digos

Sandakan
Jolo
Jolo Island
SULU ARCHIPELAGO

Tawitawi Island

Malaysia

Indonesia

Celebes Sea

Pulau Karakelong (Indonesia)

South
China
Sea

Philippine
Sea

Prologue

At 1100 hours on December 13, 1944, the temperature was already well over eighty degrees. Sixteen hundred and nineteen filthy, gaunt men were forced to march four abreast through the dirty streets of Manila on the Philippine island of Luzon. The men staggered, barely able to shuffle one foot in front of another, as they were prodded along by the bayonets of armed Japanese guards. Behind them, they left three years of life as prisoners of war, spent most recently at Bilibid Prison Camp. They left behind fellow prisoners who were too sick to travel and doomed to certain execution.

From dingy windows and along the litter-strewn sidewalks, Filipinos, who had lost friends and relatives at the hands of the Japanese Imperial Army, watched the sorry parade. Some cried openly, others surreptitiously flashed the "V for victory" sign. The Americans had originally come to help establish independence in the Philippines. The Filipinos hoped to encourage the prisoners of war without inciting the barbarous Japanese guards. This brutality was never more evident than on the faces and bodies of the brave servicemen stumbling before them.

Every single man was emaciated to the point of resembling a walking skeleton. Rib cages were clearly defined on bare chests; arms, shoulders, and legs were completely lacking in visible musculature. Vicious, badly healed scars abounded on backs, having come from beatings with barbed wire or jabs with bayonets. Some of the men were being led by fellow prisoners, as blindness was a frequent affliction. Without proper nutrition, the body begins to shut down essential functions, including eyesight. Those who could still see stared dully straight ahead, their eyeballs sunk deeply in bony sockets.

The vast majority of this shabby group, almost two out of every three men, were officers. The senior officer from Cabanatuan Prison Camp, Lieutenant Colonel Curtis Beecher, was among them. So were most of the other combat commanders who led the attacks on Bataan and Corregidor. A large number of them were dedicated Army and Navy doctors and corpsmen, including Pharmacist's Mate Second Class Estel Myers.

As the hot, midday sun bore down on Myers' back, the rope from his pack of belongings cut into his bony shoulders. That makeshift backpack contained the sum total of his worldly possessions: a canteen, some extra rations, a mess kit, and the fork he'd made from a piece of scrap tin, all of it tied in a shoddy scrap of blanket. It only weighed a few pounds, but after three years of continual malnutrition, it might as well have weighed a hundred.

Even in his exhaustion, Myers was conscious of how sad and desolate Manila had become. Manhole covers, iron scuppers, trolley tracks, streetlights, and anything else made of metal had been removed and sent to Japan to be melted down and made into instruments of war. He was conscious, too, of the humming truck engine occasionally grinding to a stop behind the columns of prisoners. Its purpose was to pick up the men who could not finish the forced march. Myers knew they would surely suffer the same fate as those who had remained at the prison.

The grueling march continued for five miles and ended around 1400 hours at the waterfront, which also lay in shambles. Pier 7, once proudly known as the Million Dollar Pier, was badly damaged from bombing runs. Myers took note of the cruel irony: nearly four years earlier, he'd left from Pier 7 off the San Francisco coast. He and the other prisoners stumbled their way through rubble to get to the dock.

There, skulking in the dirty water, sat the *Oryoku Maru,* a 7,300-ton combination passenger vessel and freighter. Beyond her floated a collection of seven other vessels, including transports loaded with Japanese troops hooting loudly from the decks, a cruiser, and several destroyers. They were obviously assembled to accompany the *Oryoku Maru* on her impending journey.

Already overheated, the prisoners were ordered to wait without shade while Japanese soldiers and equipment were unloaded. That completed, the ship's other fares, about seven hundred well-dressed Japanese citizens, largely women and children evacuees, boarded to occupy the available cabin space topside. Also on board were one thousand Japanese seamen, survivors of ships sunk in Manila Harbor, a hundred crew members, and thirty Japanese guards. The ship was badly overcrowded.

The prisoners did not talk during the wait. Escape wasn't even considered. The feeble men wanted only to survive this new trial. Finally, at around 1700 hours, the POWs were loaded into one of the three cargo holds under the scrutiny of Japanese General Koa, in charge of all POWs held in the Philippines, and Lieutenant Nogi, Japanese director of the hospital at Bilibid.

Nogi was small in stature and had studied medicine in Germany. He spoke little English, although he wrote it fairly well, and had even spent time in the U.S. before the war. He had been the Japanese medical officer on both Bataan and Corregidor before his stint at Bilibid. Although he was an Imperial officer, Nogi had a streak of compassion not often exhibited by the other prison personnel. He had occasionally tried to alleviate the prisoners' conditions at Bilibid, although he was relatively unsuccessful in his attempts.

Nogi and the American commander at Bilibid, Thomas Hayes, had an odd mutual respect born out of the understanding that both were serving their countries to the best of their abilities under difficult conditions. As the loading began, the two shook hands as a final acknowledgment of this shared regard.

The Japanese filled the aft hold first, separating the five hundred highest-ranking American officers from the group and prodding them toward the hatch. The prisoners crept down a twelve-foot wooden ladder into the gloomy hold. Once they reached the bottom, they were met by Sergeant Dau and a band of guards. As had been the case throughout the war, the Japanese used individuals from the bottom rung of their social structure to manage the POWs: their own prison internees, the mentally dysfunctional, and those unfit to hold any other position. Dau and his group fell into this category, cruelly forcing the American officers back into the darkness by beating them with brooms.

Around the perimeter of the hold were double-tiered stalls, each about three feet high. They resembled the berths in a Pullman train car, but were square in shape rather than long and narrow. The hold might have comfortably held two hundred men. The Japanese were intent on filling it with eight hundred.

The sunlight outside had been harsh, and the prisoners' eyes had not yet adjusted to the hold's dim light. They were moving too slowly to suit the Japanese guards, so the guards shoved them roughly, filling first the upper stalls, and then the lower stalls. The three-foot-high compartments forced the men to sit, and as they were crowded in so closely, extending their cramped legs was an impossibility. Instead they sat hugging their knees or with their legs folded under them.

Once the stalls were filled, guards drove men into the center of the hold, insisting that the new arrivals not even try to sit, but stand packed together like vertical sardines. The Japanese forcibly crowded in as many men as was physically possible, pushing those who had arrived first even farther back into the airless gloom.

The guards beat the last men down the hold's ladder with rifle butts. Looking through the hatch from the deck above, they saw a pit filled with eight hundred men staring back up at them with terrified eyes as they struggled to breathe. The most senior officers in the back had begun to faint almost immediately from the intense heat and the lack of air circulation created by so many bodies. The hatch was slammed shut and the men were immersed in a sea of complete and forbidding darkness.

At the same time that the aft hold was being filled, six hundred more men were packed into the forward hold. Within minutes, the air there, too, became thin and foul. Despite senses that had been numbed from years of physical and mental abuse, these men realized that their current situation was more life threatening than anything else they had previously been through.

The remaining 219 men were jammed into the hold amidships, the only one that was fully ventilated. Pharmacist's Mate Estel Myers was one of the last to be shoved at bayonet point down into that hold.

The *Oryoku Maru* cast off around 1900 hours. One thousand six hundred and nineteen men had been swallowed by this immense steel beast. For them, the closest thing to hell on earth had begun.

CHAPTER ONE

★

Sentimental Journey

Spring in San Francisco is an uncertain season. Some years, the fog locks the city in for weeks, streetlights glowing yellow twenty-four hours a day. People hurry by on the sidewalks, eagerly seeking shelter from the cold, damp air. Other years, the warm spring sun rises over Oakland Bay, burning off the early morning mist and conferring the promise of another summer on the bay.

The spring of 1941 was a little on the rainy side, but mild for the most part. In Hollywood, Mickey Rooney and Ava Gardner were engaged. Twelve-year-old Shirley Temple was earning $50,000 for her role in *Kathleen,* the latest picture she had just begun shooting. Bing Crosby and Helen O'Connell were topping the country's record charts. And Glenn Miller's "Chattanooga Choo Choo" could be heard from the Brooklyn Bridge to the Golden Gate.

But despite the sunny, lighthearted optimism, a fog heavier and bleaker than any that had ever been seen before was settling over the city. News from Europe suggested that Hitler was preparing to launch heavy military campaigns, as he had done the previous spring. If these new marches were as successful as the others had been, hundreds of thousands of Europeans would soon be under Nazi control.

Meanwhile, Japan, Hitler's Axis partner in the Pacific, was making it obvious that she, too, was preparing for war. A Japanese army spokesman, Major Kunio Akiyama, was widely quoted for a remark he made on the third of March. Japan, he said, had the heart of a dove, but a snake had just placed its egg in the dove's nest. This snake, he explained, was the combined governments of the United States and Britain. And the egg consisted of three moves the Japanese perceived as offensive: the fortification of Singapore, the arrival of Australian troops in Malaya, and the impending fortification of Guam and Samoa. When a news correspondent asked Akiyama what he thought would hatch from the egg, an ominous answer was forthcoming: "Only God knows. But the dove will protest vigorously."

Nearly every day of Estel Browning Myers' young life had been a struggle. The oldest child of Kentucky sharecroppers, his first home was a rustic, three-room cabin in Kentucky with no running water or electricity. In 1923, his father realized a sharecropper's earnings were insufficient to raise a family. So he moved them by horse and wagon to the big city: Louisville. Estel was three years old at the time.

The Myerses' five-room frame house stood two blocks from Churchill Downs racetrack, and Estel eventually became the big brother of four younger siblings. In reality, the family didn't have much, but they never seemed to want for much, either. Their clothing was made from flour sacks, each piece handed down as soon as it was outgrown by its previous owner. Meals were simple and repetitious: biscuits and gravy for breakfast, navy beans and corn bread for lunch, soups and stews for dinner. Entertainment centered on the family's prized possession, a piano. Mother played by ear, church hymns mostly. The Myerses were poor, but so was everybody else they knew, and having nothing for comparison, they lived life without regret.

In 1929, the Great Depression touched everyone, but it grabbed the lower classes by the throat. Businesses closed and factories shut down. Thousands of men and women stood in soup lines and prayed for relief from hunger. Myers' father was let go from his job as a brakeman with the Louisville-Nashville Railroad. There were no prospects for another job in town; he had no choice but to move his family back to the country.

Again they turned to farming. Their cash crop was tobacco, but they also raised truck crops to sell, saving enough to eat for themselves. With chickens, cows, and hogs for slaughter, the Myerses never went to bed hungry. Life rolled along smoothly until, in the fall of 1937, it took an unexpected turn.

Kentucky was flooded by tremendous rains that year, at exactly the moment the year's tobacco crop was to be harvested. The country was still Depression-ravaged, and the Myerses' money from the previous year's sales was nearly all spent. Since the flooding had ruined almost all the tobacco, there would be very little left to harvest. A small harvest meant very little money, a $2.37 profit, to be exact. The next year brought the opposite problem: a life-choking drought. The Myers family never recovered from the back-to-back disasters. The bank sold the animals and the farm, and after all the creditors were taken care of, the family was left with nothing.

This time it was Estel, now nineteen, who went to Louisville in search of a job. The United States Navy offered training, a steady paycheck, and more promise than any of his other options.

Like most young people of his time, Myers was only remotely aware of the political and military maneuvering that had been going on in the world around him, particularly in Asia. They'd been taught in school about the great earthquake that struck Japan in September of 1923 and how it had destroyed Tokyo, Yokohama, and surrounding areas. They'd read about the nearly one hundred forty thousand people who had fallen victim to the quake, and about the aid that had flowed to the distraught population from the U.S. and Europe. And he'd heard rumblings about Japan attacking neighboring countries. But the truth of it was he had been too busy just surviving to pay much attention to what a tiny country half a world away was doing.

Japan, on the other hand, was well aware of what was occurring in the United States and elsewhere. The relief sent for earthquake victims assuaged a building tension between East and West, but only briefly. As worldwide depression spread in the late 1920s, Japanese industry was moribund, and the country had made no preparations for such a catastrophe. To keep herself functioning, Japan needed natural resources beyond what was available on the Home Islands. In addition, an endemic distrust of all things Western was creeping throughout the Japanese government and military. They were of a single mind: Japan had to be strong. Japan had to be ready for whatever may come.

The Chinese state of Manchuria possessed the resources Japan needed. It was readily accessible through Korea, which was already a part of the Japanese Empire. Manchuria was in Japanese hands by 1931, and a pattern of aggression and isolation began. In retaliation for the loss of Manchuria, China began a boycott of all Japanese goods in 1932. In turn, Japan moved into Shanghai, inciting riots before withdrawing.

In March of 1933, Japan left the League of Nations. And in 1937, their relationship having festered for decades, China and Japan went to war. Japan did not wish to be drawn into a long conflict, wanting to guard her military resources in the event of an even larger offensive from a more imposing enemy. For her part, China was in no condition to effectively resist the well-trained Japanese armies and was forced to withdraw her troops, although she never surrendered. To celebrate, the victorious Japanese general allowed his troops to slaughter a quarter-million innocent citizens in Nanking. The horrified world had no way of knowing this was only a portent of things to come.

By 1938, in spite of all efforts on the part of the United States to establish at least the probability of world peace, President Franklin Roosevelt recommended to Congress a twenty-percent increase in American naval strength. Congress authorized the increase posthaste.

In turn, the Navy medical department saw an increase in the volume and variety of its work. The usage of medical supplies, both afloat and in hospitals, was studied, and an allowance list of supplies and equipment that would be needed in a national emergency was prepared. In short, plans were made to provide the necessary medical support for the Navy in the event of war.

War did indeed break out in Europe on September 3, 1939, making the escalation of naval medical supplies and personnel a matter of even greater urgency. While the position of the United States was not yet clearly established, it was apparent that the war would affect the country to some degree. When the war started in Europe, the U.S. Navy had 4,267 hospital corpsmen. Estel Myers was one of them.

After five months of training and finishing in the top third of his class, Myers took the corpsman's pledge.

"I solemnly pledge myself before God and these witnesses to practice safely all of my duties as a member of the hospital corps.

"I hold the care of the sick and the injured to be a privilege and a sacred trust and will assist the medical officer with loyalty and honesty. I will not knowingly permit harm to come to any patient.

"I will not partake or administer any unauthorized medication. I will hold all personal matters pertaining to the private lives of the patients in strict confidence. I dedicate my heart, mind, and strength to the work before me. I shall do all within my power to show in myself an example of all that is good and honorable throughout my naval career, so help me God."

A naval corpsman was trained to perform a wide range of services. He was a first aid man, a nurse, and a sanitarian. He assisted physicians and surgeons and assisted in the administration of the station's medical organization. And when no medical officer was available for supervision, he acted in the place of the medical officer.

Myers felt more than adequately prepared for his new career in the hospital corps. And so it was that on April 3, 1941, Hospital Apprentice First Class Estel Myers departed the U.S. Naval Station, Treasure Island, California. The skiff taking him across Oakland Bay headed for Pier 7. Once there, he would board the USS *Henderson,* and the next chapter of his life would begin.

"Welcome to the Hilton Hotel, gentlemen, and I use the term 'gentlemen' loosely." Six hundred men had boarded the *Henderson* with Myers and were now divided into groups of one hundred. Each group was assigned to a master at arms, and the one Myers' group followed had the name Hilton stitched on his uniform shirt. Hilton had led them into the ship's berthing quarters and was now giving orders.

"Here's how this works." Hilton pointed to the bunk beds surrounding them, twenty rows of beds stacked five high. "You see those bunks? Each and every one of you gets your very own. No pushing, no shoving. There's a hundred bunks and a hundred of you. It works out real purty," he told them with a sarcastic drawl.

"You see those lockers?" Hilton continued, pointing. "And those? And those? Well, there's one of those for each of you, too. Stow your gear in 'em, except for peacoats. Those'll go in other lockers topside. Pinups and photographs on the inside only. Nothin' on the outside. Pictures make me homesick. When I get homesick, I get agitated, and then it ain't fun around here. We don't want that now, do we?"

Hilton looked around. No one said a word. "You got thirty minutes to get yourselves squared away. Report topside with your peacoats at sixteen hundred hours." Throwing his chest out and turning smartly on his heel, the master at arms strode out.

Myers looked around at the unfamiliar faces. Maybe he'd seen a few before back in Norfolk at Hospital Corps School or at the Naval Hospital in Philadelphia. Or maybe they just looked like faces from home.

Navy policy required that everyone serve a year of shore duty performing their chosen job before being assigned to a ship. Sea duty was what they'd all signed up for, but thus far all they knew was that they'd get their shore duty assignment sometime while aboard this ship. A low hum of voices filled the berthing quarters, and the air was electric with anticipation.

Men were already moving toward the rows of bunks, so Myers did the same. He knew he didn't want a top one. It was hot enough where he was standing—the top bunk would be stifling. But for some reason, a bottom bunk wasn't appealing, either: if for some reason the ship took on water, Myers figured it would be better to be farther above the floor. So he threw his blanket and peacoat on the second bunk up and hauled his seabag over toward the lockers.

"You ever see anything like this?" a voice to his right asked him.

"Nope," Myers answered. "Reminds me of the bakery back home. The bunks look like the ovens, and we're the bread."

"Is that so? Where'd you say home was?" the stranger asked.

"I didn't. But it's Kentucky."

"No kidding! Damn, I always wanted to meet a genuine Kentucky Colonel." A seaman first class stuck out his hand. "Name's Rollo T. Brown. But everybody calls me Browny."

"Hello, Browny. Estel Myers." Myers shook the hand Browny proffered. "Where do you call home?"

"The Windy City."

"No kidding? I always wanted to meet a genuine gangster!"

Browny chuckled. "Doc, the closest I ever got to a gangster was in the movie theater. You don't mind if I call you Doc, do ya? It fits, you being a corpsman and all." Browny pointed to the red cross on Myers' shirt.

"Doc" had a nice ring to it. Myers smiled. "Nope." Their seabags were empty by this time, and Myers continued. "Say, there's a bunk over there next to mine, third row, second one up. Why don't you grab it?"

"Done." Browny walked over to the bunk in question and claimed it with his blanket.

After settling in, the men arrived topside to find the late afternoon air clean and fresh. There was just enough of a breeze to gently ripple the flags on the masts above them. Hilton's men fell in, along with the other five units and their respective masters at arms. Below their feet, the *Henderson*'s bathtub-shaped hull bobbed gently as the ship's commander stood on a small deck above to address them.

"Men, your country thanks you for the service you're about to give. If we do indeed see action, chances are the man standing next to you won't be coming home. It's unfortunate, but that's the way war is. Keep your eyes open and your heads up. Good luck."

Myers had always been self-assured, never one to worry about things beyond his control. Paying attention to what was in front of you had always worked for him in the past, and he saw no reason to change now. He looked sideways at each of the men next to him. There was no question in his mind that *he* would survive any action he saw. But it was a damn shame those other guys weren't going to make it. At 1700 hours, the *Henderson* weighed anchor. Two hours later, the six hundred men saw the last slice of American soil disappear, along with the evening sun, below the horizon.

Chow that first night wasn't the best, but Myers had had worse. The main course was pork chops, a little dry but otherwise edible. Served with the chops were canned corn and a big helping of navy beans in some kind of thick liquid. When the beans and the pork chops touched, the liquid took on a meat flavor, making it almost like gravy. Dessert was canned peaches and cookies. It wasn't exactly like his mother's cooking, but the meal was filling if not entirely satisfying.

After chow, games of pinochle and acey-deucey sprang up wherever there was enough room for a handful of men to gather. The men talked about sweethearts left behind, and Myers shared stories about the girl he planned to make his wife when he returned from duty.

Lights-out was ordered at 2100 hours, and by 2400 hours the ship had put about a hundred miles behind her. At about that point the Pacific Ocean is affected by a variety of currents, all of which combine to make for sizable waves even in relatively calm conditions. The waves caused any ship to pitch and roll considerably but the *Henderson* reacted really badly. She had been built to carry cargo, the idea being that when full to capacity, her rounded hull could sink lower in the water. But carrying men instead of cargo made her far too light, and she bobbed up and down in the water like a bottle.

This was nothing out of the ordinary to the ship's crew. But it was startling to the men in their bunks, most of whom were novice sailors. At one point or another that first night, nearly all of them stumbled from the berthing quarters to the head, where they lost their evening chow. By morning the urinals, concave stainless steel troughs, were full to the brim, and each time the ship rolled the urinals' contents sloshed over the side.

The few men who had been able to control themselves during the night found the slop at reveille causing some of them to succumb as well. Myers had managed not to get sick, and although Browny had been ill, he'd at least made it to the head. The fellow on the other side of Myers did not fare as well. He had gotten sick as soon as the waves started, and by morning he was feeling so poorly he wasn't even making an effort to get out of his bunk. Instead, he lay there like a human geyser.

Breakfast was served at 0700 hours. About half the men went, including Myers and Browny. The latter was not at all enthusiastic about food.

"What are we having?"

"Looks like hot prunes, some kind of dry cereal, and milk," Myers answered.

The two men wove through the tables until they found places and sat down, looking morosely at the food in front of them. Before they had taken a bite, a man across the table made a funny gurgling sound and bent over. The sounds of his retching beneath the table set Browny off again. By this time, Myers was no longer able to control himself, either. As he ran out of the mess to heave over the ship's railing, he seriously wondered if joining the Navy hadn't been a mistake.

Several of the ship's crew were heard to suggest that if the men ate bread, their stomachs would settle. This suggestion spread, and after a lousy day or two, most of the men found their sea legs.

The crossing seemed to make time crawl; the only activity that generated interest was eating. On days when a man was not on work detail and didn't have to report somewhere, his main job became standing in the slow-moving chow lines. He finished breakfast and washed out his dishes, then got back in line to wait for lunch. He'd repeat the procedure to wait for dinner.

The *Henderson* was scheduled to make a stop in Hawaii for refueling and to offload some of the troops. The men's orders were to be given out prior to that, and the most logical time was in the morning right after muster. It took three days and three musters to make assignments to all six hundred men. Browny's orders were to report to Pearl Harbor Ship Yard, 14th Naval District, Honolulu, Hawaii. Myers would stay on the *Henderson* until she arrived in Shanghai, China. The Navy had joined forces with the 4th Marines to protect American interests in the region, and Myers was assigned to hospital duty there.

"Ya know what the funny thing is?" Myers and Browny were lying in their bunks the day before they were scheduled to arrive at Pearl Harbor. Browny took a deep drag on a smoke and continued. "The funny thing is that I joined the Navy 'cause there weren't any other jobs in Chicago. Those poor suckers back home will be sweeping sidewalks and shoveling snow for a buck a day while I'm basking in sunshine surrounded by hula girls."

Myers chuckled. "You lucky dog. You probably won't even see a Jap."

"Yeah, but I wouldn't mind the chance to take a shot at one or two. And you, you'll be living it up in the Paris of the Orient. I heard about Shanghai and all the cheap bars and whorehouses. And even if the Navy does see some action in China, our Uncle Sam is so much tougher than those little bastards, we'll overrun 'em. There won't be any guys hurt bad. You're gonna spend your days treating hangnails and hangovers. Say, Doc, how much liberty you got in Honolulu before you have to shove off?"

"I dunno. Hilton said we'd get at least one day."

"Well, since we don't know when we'll get our next liberties, what d'ya say we really paint the town red. We'll hit all the hot spots, drink ourselves into a stupor, and wake up with beautiful women lying next to us."

"The drinking sounds swell," Myers answered. "But I'm afraid you'll have Hawaii's beautiful women all to yourself. When I get home, I plan on marrying that girl I left behind. I promised I'd be faithful, and I mean to keep that promise."

Browny gave him a playful punch in his shoulder. "Myers, you are such a sap."

*   *   *

Myers had a foggy recollection of the Hawaiian Islands being mentioned in school, but he'd learned a lot more after he'd joined the Navy. In fact, he'd learned about all the groups of speck-like islands in the Pacific: the Philippines, the Marshalls, the Solomons, and the Marianas. Guadalcanal and Iwo Jima. So many places with names no one in his hometown had ever heard of. He wasn't sure what to expect, and nothing would have prepared him for what he saw.

Honolulu looked like a movie set to a man who, prior to joining the Navy, had never even been out of Kentucky. No matter which direction he looked, palm trees swayed seductively, and caramel-skinned people in colorful clothing smiled happily. The soft breeze carried with it a sweet odor, a combination of the sea and the blossoms dancing in every garden. Estel Myers didn't have a terribly concrete image of heaven, but he was relatively certain Hawaii might be close.

But Hawaii was much more than a beautiful setting. Pearl Harbor, which lay to the west of Honolulu, was home base for the United States Pacific Fleet. When all the warships were in port, they numbered over ninety. In addition, nearly four hundred aircraft were located at the three airfields nearest the harbor.

Browny had reported to his new commanding officer as soon as they had disembarked. He stowed his gear and was told that the first twenty-four hours in Hawaii were his own. He collected Myers from a bar around the corner from the Navy Yard, and together they began to explore the city.

"I can't believe this place is part of the United States. How come I never heard about it? I would have come over here even without the help of the United States Navy!" Browny was throwing back his third drink in a bar filled with American servicemen and pretty women adorned with flowers.

"Sure looks like you're in the gravy here." Estel was working on his third drink, too.

"Doc, can you imagine what it would have been like if we'd decided to join the Army and then the U.S. declared war on Germany?

We'd be up to our asses in mud and snow most of the year. Even if there is a war over here, how bad can it be? This is paradise!"

The *Henderson* was scheduled to continue her journey to China the next day, leaving at 0800 hours. Myers was back aboard the ship in plenty of time, although without having had much sleep. A man of his word, he'd left the pretty girls for Browny, spending his remaining hours in Hawaii talking with an old man he'd met in a bar. Together, they scoffed at the rumors that the Japanese assumed it was their divine right to rule all of the Pacific. How ridiculously bold of them! The likelihood of that ever happening was so minute, both men assured each other, that there was a greater chance of lightning striking the ships in Pearl Harbor.

CHAPTER TWO

★

Pearl of the Orient

Myers and his elderly acquaintance might have considered a threat from Japan a lark, but the United States' Office of Naval Intelligence did not. As early as the 1920s, they began to seriously study the ramifications of a possible transpacific war against Japan. U.S. Marine Corps Major Earl H. Ellis voiced his thoughts on the subject.

". . . It will be necessary for us to project our fleet and landing forces across the Pacific and wage war in Japanese waters," Ellis said. "It is not enough that the troops be skilled infantrymen or artillery men of high morale; they must be skilled water-men and jungle-men who know it can be done—Marines with Marine training."

Following Major Ellis' wise advice, the 4th Marines sailed from their San Diego home base to Shanghai, China, in February 1927. And as the Marines had no medical corps, a contingent of Navy medical personnel was stationed with them. The Marines' stated objective was to protect American business interests, missionaries, and diplomatic personnel in Shanghai's International Settlement, a collection of foreign enclaves. Each country represented in the International Settlement was immune from Chinese law and protected by its own troops and gunboats. Initially the protection was to be from any internal Chinese strife, but the developing tensions between Japan and China began to pose an even greater threat to the foreigners.

An American military presence in China was not a new concept:

a small fleet of shallow-draft, twin-screw gunboats had cruised the waterways since the turn of the century. China was a vast nation, made unstable by warlords, revolutions, and civil wars. Her largest city, Shanghai, had been the site of many anti-imperialist struggles. Its coastal location at the mouth of the Yangtze River made it an economic and strategic jewel, a treasure well worth fighting over.

About half of the boundary of the International Settlement rested on natural barriers—Soochow Creek on the northwest and the Whangpoo River on the southeast. On the west, the defense perimeter was pushed out beyond the political boundary to the tracks of the Shanghai-Hangchow-Ningpo Railroad, the embankment of which made a natural defensive position. These barriers were useful to the Marines and the military of other foreign powers when Japanese military entered the city in 1932 and then again in 1937.

By 1940, the joint Marine-Navy objective was firmly established. According to a Congressional directive, the Marines' role, if necessary, was "to seize, establish, and defend, until relieved by Army forces, advanced naval bases; and to conduct such limited auxiliary land operations as are essential to the prosecution of the naval campaign."

In 1941, one hundred and fifty thousand of Shanghai's four million inhabitants were foreigners. Fifteen hundred of those were American military, including Estel Myers. And the *Henderson*'s late April arrival came none too soon for him. After leaving Browny in Honolulu, Myers was anxious to get to his own assignment and more than a little curious about the city itself. Some of the men aboard ship had been there; others had just heard stories. Sin City, they called it. The world's pleasure capital—an exotic sanctuary with much to teach a young man from Kentucky.

"Blood Alley, that's where the action is." At 0700 hours on a Friday, the day after Marine payday, Myers and another hospital assistant by the name of Frank Stover were taking inventory at the Naval Hospital in the International Settlement. Stover continued, "They say there are more than five women for every man. And all of 'em yours for the taking. Those gals love Yankee dollars."

Myers was more practical. "Yeah, and how many seagoing bell-hops are gonna come running in here to see the pecker-checker after a night on the town? I hear the girls on Blood Alley are just about the lowest class you can buy."

"That's no way to talk about the Marines and what they do with their girlfriends," Stover told him. "Besides, some of those girls are probably clean."

"Yeah, Stover, and I'm an admiral in the Navy," Myers said. "There can't be—" He was cut off mid-sentence when three MPs clattered in, all shouting at the same time.

"Get ready, you guys!"

"Where's the doctor? Get a bunch of doctors!"

"Huge fight broke out at the Majestic!"

Myers put in calls for hospital reinforcements and sent a runner for the doctors, who were still in their morning meeting. Stover set up extra cots in the hallway so they could start triage as soon as the casualties arrived. And arrive they did, groaning and bleeding pro-fusely, in a fleet of ambulances.

"What happened?" Myers bent over an unconscious Marine with an ugly gash on his forehead and a broken nose. The Marine's buddy hovered nearby, holding a towel to his oozing mouth with one hand and two of his teeth in the other.

"It wasn't our fault, Doc. We didn't start it. It was those damn wops—think they're all Romeo. We'd been havin' fun since midnight at the Majestic. Got paid yesterday, so we was drinking and dancing, not botherin' anybody. Some wop soldier came in, didn't spend a red cent, just waltzed over to a honey and whispered somethin' in her ear. He takes her out to a rickshaw, see. A corporal I know—well, he'd been dancing with her, sorta makin' plans, ya know?"

"Yeah, I saw it," another man chimed in from the next cot. "It just ain't right, stealing somebody else's girl. So a bunch of us thought we should have a little talk with the greaseball before he left in his rickshaw. He got real mad 'cause we was interfering, and before you knew it, everybody was going at it."

The man holding his teeth picked up the story again. "We had 'em licked, too, 'cept word got back to their barracks and reinforcements showed up in trucks with knives and clubs and bayonets and everything but the kitchen sink."

"Is that when your buddy here got clocked?" Myers asked.

"Well, it was either then or when our MPs arrived. They started clubbing people, too, to break up the fight. Then the Italian MPs showed up and things started to calm down."

"Poor Old Man Wong. Did you see him, Roberts?" the man on the cot asked. "Old Man Wong owns the place," he explained to Myers. "He was mad as a wet hen, runnin' around, cussin' us all out. His joint's a mess. There was even one girl ended up getting tossed into the bass drum."

Myers moved on to other men. Those who could talk coherently related similar stories. Once the last stitch had been sewed, the men were ordered to remain in the hospital, even those who were otherwise healthy enough to have gone back to their barracks. It was rumored the C.O. wanted to have a word with them, which turned out to be quite an understatement.

"Whew! Those guys are gettin' it," Stover told Myers. He had just joined Myers in the dispensary to restock the shelves. "The C.O.'s really blowing his top. Says some of 'em are even headed for solitary in the brig."

Myers winced. "That's rough."

"You been there?"

"Yeah." Myers shook his head in disgust. "It was a screwy stunt I pulled the night I graduated from Hospital Corps School. I got plastered so bad that when time for my shift came around, I was still drunk. I didn't think anybody'd notice, so I reported for duty. But the head doctor noticed. I got ten days in solitary on bread and water. I don't plan on ever bein' stuck in the brig again."

Stover let out a long whistle. "And here I thought you were such a good boy, Myers. I might have to change my opinion of you."

"You beat your gums too much, Stover. We got thirty minutes to get this stuff restocked before our four hours are done and the next shift comes in. How about we head over to that little café in the French Concession, Pop's Place, for some chow. We don't have to be back here until fifteen hundred hours."

"You're on. Last one done buys."

A Christian evangelist once observed, "If God lets Shanghai endure, He owes an apology to Sodom and Gomorrah." For Myers, Stover, and the rest of the American military personnel, there weren't enough hours in the day to soak up all the transgressions this city had to offer. Bar girls, affectionately known as B-girls, were paid a commission by the establishments for every man in a uniform they enticed to drink. After purring, "Dahlink, buy me one drink, please," the drinking sometimes led to a lengthier relationship, lasting two or three hours. The price? Usually just one thin dime.

Since Shanghai lies at the same latitude as New Orleans, the same kind of Turkish bath heat envelops the city during the summer. Many servicemen found frequent clothing changes to be a necessity if they wanted to remain at their best for whatever opportunity came along. Fortunately, laundry was easily affordable, too. At one point, an enterprising laundryman passed out flyers on the pier in the International Settlement, hoping to work his way into doing an entire ship's washing. The flyers went beyond describing just the services; they also assured discretion.

Dear Sir,

Would you please give me authorization for can get pickup your ship's laundry at quay. I will perform surly and speedy as showed in price list and serve free of charge (no pay) for Captain's. Exact officer's and other officer's and Chief's would be served at half price. Relating to your ship's secret we would be blind, no ear and shut the mouth.

Some servicemen solved the laundry problem by simply buying more clothing. A tailor-made suit could be had for $5, and for a dollar more, some shops offered a hat to match. The hats were made using a machine capable of identifying every contour of the head, thus ensuring a perfect fit.

Most transactions were conducted using local currency, known as the Chinese Mex. The exchange rate was sixteen Chinese Mex to one American dollar. A movie was four Chinese Mex and a quart of duty-free imported liquor went for six more. This was relatively wholesome entertainment at a very reasonable price.

In 1941, U.S. servicemen made between $21 and $30 a month, depending on their rank. The breadth of the temptations and the incredibly low prices encouraged some GIs to spend more than they otherwise might have. It wasn't unusual for some men to draw only pocket change on payday, having borrowed heavily against their pay throughout the month.

Despite an eat, drink, and be merry attitude, the American military was not oblivious to Shanghai's ugly side. It was a city of extremes, from grinding poverty to indecent wealth. In the squalid quarter, a gang called the Green Gang ruled opium dens, and houses of prostitution operated openly. The Green Gang fought with others for power and supremacy. It was a common belief that Shanghai had more gangsters than Chicago ever did in Capone's heyday.

Crime and the exploitation of Chinese citizens were rampant. Bodies floated in the city's canals and the Yangtze. The poor and homeless lived in the streets and routinely froze to death during the winter. Some of the more fortunate poor who had shelter depended on every family member to pull his weight. Boys, therefore, were viewed as having value; they could be put to work as soon as they could walk and contribute to the household income. Girls, on the other hand, were seen as burdens and often killed shortly after birth. Their tiny bodies were thrown in the gutters, to be picked up and hauled away in carts making rounds through the city. The only salvation for girls was if their family believed they could sell them to wealthy foreigners as guaranteed virgins; $5 for a five-year-old was the usual going rate.

All of this caused tremendous emotional conflict for servicemen like Myers and Stover, far from home and family. At times, their existence in Shanghai was a surreal dream, where all their wishes could be fulfilled. Other times, the strange land filled with exotic people made them feel as though they weren't just on the other side of the earth from home but on another planet entirely.

It was near lunchtime several weeks after the incident at the Majestic that Myers and Stover arrived at one of Shanghai's busiest intersections. Johnny Sikh, whose job was traffic control at the intersection, saw them coming. The Indian stood proudly, directing rickshaws and rice wagons, his colorful turban bobbing in rhythm with his rapid arm movements.

"U.S. Marines, U.S. sailors! Coming through. Everybody stop." Johnny blew hard on his whistle and made a dramatic show out of stopping traffic for the men to cross.

"Hey, Marines, hey, pals! I stop traffic for you. You need main dish? Johnny Sikh knows where the best girls are. You need cheap booze? I know a guy on Foochow Road. You bring me some too, okay?"

Stover patted the happy Indian on the back as he and Myers passed him. "Not today. Me and my pal are just looking for some lunch."

"Okay, but you come see Johnny Sikh if you need anything. Hey, don't take any wooden nickels, Joe!"

Myers and Stover headed for a little joint that was famous for its fried rice. The food was good, hot, and guaranteed to be made from chicken and not a neighborhood stray. Stover had bought a pack of Al Chings, a popular brand of Chinese cigarettes. Once they ordered, the two men lit up and began discussing what they thought might happen next in the giant chess game of which they were a part.

It was the thirteenth of September and the war in Europe was at a fevered pitch. The fact that Great Britain, New Zealand, Australia, and Canada had declared war on Germany two years earlier only seemed to fuel the Führer's fire. In his possession were Austria, Czechoslovakia, Poland, Holland, Belgium, Luxembourg, most of

Scandinavia, and now France. He had rained blitzkriegs over Britain and was advancing on Moscow. Meanwhile, Italy, one of Germany's partners in the Tripartite Pact, had conquered Albania and Ethiopia. The third partner in their pact was Japan.

Myers and Stover discussed the possibility of a troop buildup in Europe that might include them.

"I don't think we'll be sent to Fritzville." Stover had a definite opinion about this. "Not unless we declare war on them."

"You're probably right," Myers agreed. "And since the Brits left Shanghai, we're about all that's keeping the Japs from taking over the entire International Settlement. And those Nips gotta be upset over us freezing their assets in the States. Now they got no gas, they got no oil, and no money. They got nothin'. Can't run an army that way."

"And I don't think they got it in their stomachs to try anything," Stover added. "If they wanted a fight, they would have done something by now."

The fried rice arrived and their conversation moved across several subjects, including the girls back home and those they'd met in Shanghai. After having been in Shanghai for five months, the city's mysterious attraction had worn off. Peculiar Chinese customs were now beginning to wear on them. The tradition that most bothered Stover involved the Huang Pu River, which ran through the heart of the city.

"Place stinks. And you know why? There's some ancient custom that says they gotta be buried where they were born. So bodies sit on the docks in boxes all day long waiting to get picked up and taken upriver to wherever their hometowns are. You know, this whole place is starting to give me the creeps. I wouldn't mind leaving it behind."

The wheels of change for the two men were already in motion. Stover received orders two days later to report to a hospital facility in Olongapo, on Subic Bay in the Philippines. The day after that, Myers found out he was to be attached to the Canacao Naval Hospital in the Philippines. The two men shipped out a day later, September 17, 1941, on the *Henderson,* the same ship Myers had taken from the States.

The trip from Shanghai to Luzon, the largest of the seven thousand islands that make up the Philippine archipelago, took seventeen days. The ship stopped first in Olongapo to off-load supplies and men, including Stover. The *Henderson* continued southward, sailing into Manila Bay, past a peninsula named Bataan and an island named Corregidor. She arrived at the Cavite Naval Yard, one of two prongs that jutted out into the southern end of the bay. Some of the men would remain there to work on the ships. The rest of them were trucked to the other prong of land, Sangley Point. Here, they would go to work at the communications towers, the air station, the fuel tanks, or, as in the case of Myers, Canacao Naval Hospital.

CHAPTER THREE

★

Monsoons and Medicine

Hospital Assistant Leonard Tarpy had been stationed in the Philippines for six months, since April of 1941, and he knew his way around pretty well. He knew where the best eateries were—*karinderias,* the Filipinos called them. He knew he liked *sinigang* soup and *halo halo,* a sweet dessert with fruit and custard. He knew just how much body English was needed to throw a strike at the bowling alley up at Fort Stotsenberg. And he knew that an afternoon siesta was a great way to nurse a persistent headache caused from too much bamboo gin the night before. All in all, Tarpy's tour of duty in the Philippines had been pleasant. But that didn't mean he wouldn't be glad to board the ship that would take him stateside in two months.

Tarpy was the first person Myers met when he reported to the Canacao Naval Hospital on Sangley Point. Like Myers, Tarpy was compactly built: five foot eight or nine, lean at about a hundred and sixty-five pounds or so. But that was where the similarities ended. Myers' hair was dark and looked wavy even with a military cut. Tarpy's was blond and straight, like straw. Myers' speech was rich with a Kentucky drawl. Tarpy's Wisconsin roots were evident in his accent.

"So you been up in Shanghai, eh? How was it? I mean, I've heard stories. Booze, women, anything a guy could want for practically peanuts."

"That 'bout says it all," Myers told him.

"Where you billeted?" Tarpy asked.

"Hospital barracks. Same as you, I expect."

"Yup. Anybody explain to you how we spend our days yet?"

Myers shook his head, so Tarpy continued.

"Well, reveille is at oh five hundred. We drill some and then re-port here around oh eight hundred. Most of the work is routine—scrapes and bruises, an occasional broken bone. We get some malaria cases, but that's about as exciting as it gets. At twelve hundred hours the next shift reports and we have the rest of the day to ourselves. I know a couple girls—Filapinas—so I usually look them up after my siesta."

"Sounds like a country club. What do you do at night?"

"Probably nothing as wild as you're used to in Shanghai. There's usually a cockfight somewhere. *Sabong,* they call it here. It's the national sport. I go to Duff's just about every night—that's a cabaret downtown owned by a Marine and his Filipino wife. The Rainbow Hotel and Garden's pretty nice, too. They bill themselves as the only place in town with real entertainment."

So far, it sounded pretty good to Myers.

"There's a smoker held about once a month. Sometimes they're stag and sometimes girls are invited."

"Smoker?" Myers knew all about cigarettes and smoking; after all, one of the crops they'd raised on the farm was tobacco. But how that related to whether or not women were involved was a mystery.

"Yeah," Tarpy answered him. "It's a bunch of boxing matches be-tween the ships. If you pay attention to the scuttlebutt about the guys fighting and you place your bets right, it's a great way to pick up a couple bucks. And there's always a good picture showing at the re-ceiving station here at the hospital, or over at the Marine barracks. I think right now something with Abbott and Costello is playing at one of them."

Tarpy tipped back in his chair and folded his arms across his chest. "Yep, most of the time life's pretty good around here."

Myers had to agree that it did indeed sound like the good life.

And the grounds of Canacao hospital couldn't have been more beautiful. Set on Canacao Bay, the thirty-six-acre grounds were filled with stately shade trees, flowering shrubs, and colorful plants. Running along the sea wall adjacent to the bay, lamps resembling Japanese stone temple lanterns provided lighting at night.

Tarpy told Myers that the buildings were fireproof and earthquake-proof. The wards were broad, airy, and cool as they were amply shaded and ventilated. Besides the administration offices, there were treatment rooms for different specialties, laboratories, clinics, and x-ray and dental offices. The third floor of the main building was devoted entirely to surgery, with a modern elevator conveying patients to the floor.

"The hospital's equipped to handle about three hundred patients. We got ten doctors and two dentists and, counting you and me, there's about a hundred corpsmen. Guess that's about it."

Not bad duty at all, Myers thought.

As had been the case when Myers arrived in Hawaii and China, he had very little advance knowledge about the Philippine Islands. The seven thousand islands cover an area slightly larger than the state of Arizona, with the majority of the population on the eleven largest islands. The capital city, Manila, was five thousand miles from Pearl Harbor in Hawaii and seven thousand from San Francisco. But it was only eighteen hundred miles from Tokyo.

The Philippines have been described as the rainbow's end for weary travelers, a mecca of ocean breezes, luscious fruits, and glorious sunsets. The countryside was rich with pastoral beauty and peasant charm, while Manila was a blend of cosmopolitan metropolis and country life rooted in centuries past. Manila boasted an air-cooled, luxury resort, the Manila Hotel, and the Santo Tomas University, an institution of higher learning older than Harvard. These landmarks lived alongside the Intramuros, or Walled City, one of the most graceful and extensive samples of medieval architecture in the Far East.

The Pasig River ran through the heart of Manila, where it wasn't unusual to see liners and freighters cruising next to local *cascos, bangkas,* and other fishing boats. Poor Filipino women beat clothing on rocks at the dirty river's edge. Running along the oceanfront, mansion-lined, tree-shaded Dewey Avenue could easily be mistaken for a similar street on Miami's or Chicago's Gold Coasts. There was, however, one difference: Dewey Avenue, just like all the other streets in Manila, was shared between motorcars and horse-drawn *carromata* carts.

Until the United States occupied the Philippines, Manila's coastal area was a low-tide mud flat. Beginning in the early 1900s, the Army Corps of Engineers created land where none had been. Jutting out from the new land, they built Pier 7, which became the most noticeable landmark on the Manila Bay waterfront. Cruise ships from ports of call around the world arrived daily at the pier, delivering wealthy passengers eager to soak up everything the alluring tropical city had to offer. Manila was clearly the Far East's most American-like city.

The United States had maintained military forces on the Philippines since 1898, when Commodore George Dewey ended Spanish domination of the islands by sinking the Spanish fleet in Manila Bay. When the Washington Naval Treaty was signed in 1922, the Japanese agreed to limit its shipbuilding if the U.S. would agree to stop construction of any new fortifications in its Pacific possessions, which included the Philippines. Therefore, only the islands near the entrance to Manila Bay, most notably Corregidor, were well protected. The same act granted the islands commonwealth status in 1935, with independence scheduled for 1946.

As soon as it received commonwealth status, the National Assembly passed the Philippines National Defense Act, a plan for self-defense that included a small, ten-thousand-man force, supplemented by a four hundred thousand reserve. This reserve was thought to be large enough to discourage any invasion plans by foreign nations.

General Douglas MacArthur summed up the importance of the islands' defense in a 1935 speech: "I believe the future security of the Philippines is of major importance to the interests of the United States in the Far East. . . . Let us be prepared lest we, too, perish."

MacArthur had been advising the commonwealth on defense matters and came out of retirement in 1937 to help them organize their forces. But creating an army and training the reserves was an undertaking of enormous proportions. Due to his minuscule budget, he faced chronic shortages in weapons, transportation, communications, housing, and uniforms. On top of that, the islands' linguistic diversity created serious communication problems within the units as officers, soldiers, and new recruits often did not speak the same language. In addition to the new force, the United States Army also maintained regular units on the islands. About half of the 22,532 regulars included Philippine scouts.

MacArthur was nearly alone in the belief that losing the Philippines would deal a critical blow to the U.S. on many fronts. Finally tiring of the uphill battle, MacArthur retired from the service. But when the Japanese announced their plan for a Greater East Asia Co-Prosperity Sphere in mid-1941, Roosevelt called MacArthur back to active duty.

Some months previously, the U.S. Joint Chiefs of Staff had devised a basic defense for the Philippines, which they presented to MacArthur upon his return. If the islands were attacked, War Plan ORANGE, as it was called, proposed limited defense of Manila Bay and other critical adjacent areas, those already reinforced. Meanwhile, the Army garrison was expected to withdraw to the Bataan Peninsula to the west of Manila and to the tiny island of Corregidor off its shore, which measured only seven thousand yards long by twenty-five hundred yards wide at its widest point. There, they would hold out as long as they could until reinforcements could be dispatched. American naval officials believed that it would take at least two years to build up a sufficient relief force.

The bottom line, the U.S. military concluded, was that in the event of a declaration of war, America should commit the majority of her resources where they would do the most good. A "defeat Germany first" strategy was adopted, because it was assumed that Europe was a more threatened theater. Even if it meant sacrificing the Philippine Islands and the Americans living there.

For his part, MacArthur strongly opposed War Plan ORANGE, suggesting the U.S. instead commit itself to building a powerful force in the Philippines. When Chief of Staff George C. Marshall finally gave his stamp of approval to MacArthur's plan for reinforcing and equipping the Philippine forces, the latter estimated that it could all be in place by April of 1942. Even as early as December 1, 1941, things had begun to improve in the islands, militarily speaking. The fighting force stood at 31,095 men, the most recent arrivals bringing with them 108 M3 tanks.

To their discredit, however, the War Department did not even consider the difficulty in maintaining such a large force in the Pacific. And the logistics of transporting War Plan ORANGE reinforcements were not feasible given the ships' current schedules and limited space. But no one thought to make any changes.

Meanwhile, MacArthur continued to organize his command into four separate forces. The North Luzon Force, the most strategically important, included the Bataan peninsula and all of northern Luzon. This he placed under the leadership of General Jonathan Wainwright. A second force called South Luzon was commanded by Brigadier General George Parker, Jr., and stretched east and south of Manila. The Visayan-Mindanao Force was led by Brigadier General William Sharp and covered the two islands of the same names. The last group, the Reserve Force, was stationed just north of Manila and was under MacArthur's direct command.

Ironically, the Philippines now had the largest concentration of aircraft outside of the continental United States, the only fact making a prolonged defense of the islands even remotely thinkable. One hundred and seven P-40 fighters and thirty-five B-17 Flying Fortress bombers stood ready for action. Yet missing from the equation were maintenance and repair facilities and enough space to spread the aircraft out to protect them from sabotage or attack.

December 1, 1941, felt no more like autumn than barbed wire feels like lamb's wool. Although the monsoon season was drawing to a close, the sticky tropical heat made morning drills highly unpleasant. Later that day, when Myers and Tarpy arrived at the hospital, the patients grumbled about the same thing, saying that if the mosquitoes didn't kill them, the heat surely would.

"I heard through the grapevine that the powers in Washington have ordered everybody in Shanghai to ship out," Tarpy announced one morning as he and Myers were making their rounds, checking on patients.

"Yeah, I heard the same thing," Myers answered him. "You must have been talking to Simpson up at the mess. So what d'ya think that means?"

"I'll tell you what it means," the guy with the broken leg in bed sixteen piped up. "It means that we better get our asses in gear and prepare for an attack. Nothin' works right around here and everything's covered with an inch of mildew. Have you seen the weapons? Enfield and Springfield 1903 rifles, hand-me-downs from the last war, maybe the Civil War. And there's not enough ammunition to hold any kind of decent training. Hell, even the rations are old. I once bit into a D ration full of worms."

"You're nuts!" This came from Charles, a cook who had nearly sliced off his thumb butchering a chicken the night before. "There ain't gonna be a war with Japan. Take a look at your basic Jap. He's scrawny, can't see worth a damn, and too busy bowing all over the place to pull a trigger. If you're scared of somebody like that, you're just plain yellow!"

"Who's yellow?" the man with the broken leg challenged.

"You are, you chicken shit," the cook shot back.

"Why, I oughta—"

"Knock it off, you guys," Myers told them. Neither of them was in any condition to fight the other, let alone the Japs.

"Yeah, well, just the same," the broken leg continued, "those little bastards have something up their sleeve. I've heard talk from guys in the Signal Corps. Something's brewing."

The cook snorted.

The quiet voice of a warrant officer from several beds down spoke up. "Any you guys ever hear of a rear admiral by the name of

Yarnell?" Nobody answered out loud, but all of the men within earshot thought a minute and then shook their heads.

"Well, one Sunday morning about eight or nine years ago, he wanted to test the idea of a surprise attack using aircraft carriers. He sent planes from his ship, the *Saratoga,* and planes from the *Lexington* flying into Pearl Harbor on the Hawaiian island of Oahu, just as neat as you please. Nobody paid any attention. Half the men were still in their bunks. He could have wiped out the entire Pacific Fleet if he'd been an enemy.

"Now, don't you think if I heard that story, some Jap probably heard it, too? We lose the Pacific Fleet and we lose the Philippines. That means you and me and everybody else on these islands are left here hanging out to dry. Don't count the Japs out, gentlemen. The biggest disservice we can do to ourselves is not be prepared."

The words hung in the hospital ward like a heavy cloud. Some of the patients waved the warrant officer off, going back to whatever had occupied their minds previously. Myers fell quiet, thinking about what he'd just heard. A little while later, he called down to the other end of the ward.

"Hey, Tarpy. We got forty-eight comin' to us in a couple days. How about we get out of this heat and head up north to that place you're always talking about? If the Japs are gonna attack soon, I want to get as much sightseeing done as I can."

All around him, the patients in the ward protested the unfairness of the healthy guys getting all the breaks.

About a hundred and fifty miles north of Manila lay the Philippines' summer capital, Baguio. Nestled on a small plateau, a mile high in cloud-capped mountains, it was the kind of place where a fire felt good after sundown even in the summertime. The well-to-do made the trip by plane, train, or used their own motorcars. Most servicemen like Myers and Tarpy made the trip by bus, jostling along with the native Filipinos: families, farmers, and the elderly.

The bus zigzagged its way up into the mountains, past green rice fields, primitive palm-leaf huts, and sugar mills. One might mistake the trip for a journey through the Alps or the mountains of Colorado, except for the fact that the vegetation was punctuated with brilliant bougainvillea vines, while carabao, the local beasts of burden, wallowed in every mud puddle large enough to hold them.

A medley of languages floated through the bus: English, Spanish, and Tagalog, the Philippines' unofficial language. The bus continued past the military academy, a Pacific West Point where the Philippine Scouts trained. Finally, the town of Baguio sprawled before them, with homes and businesses tucked among the fragrant pines. It wasn't hard to understand why even the president of the Philippine Commonwealth had a summer home in this cool oasis.

Unlike the hustle and bustle of Manila, life in Baguio moved at a more leisurely pace. But that wasn't to say it had nothing to offer. Quite the contrary: Baguio had every modern convenience desired by tourists, including good hotels, natural hot springs, golf courses, and many social opportunities.

It was Sunday when Myers and Tarpy made the trip, and that meant market day. Since the town was the gateway to the Mountain Province, the province's native tribes brought in their goods to sell. This included a former headhunting tribe, the Igorots, who had recently become famous for their woodcarving. Locally grown fruits and vegetables were abundant, as were livestock and baked goods.

Several venders were selling the Filipino delicacy *balot*. Myers could see that it was an egg of some sort, but refused Tarpy's enticement to try one until he knew what kind of egg it was. Tarpy finally explained that it was a duck egg. Myers had eaten duck eggs before. Not like this, Tarpy assured him. Just before the duck is ready to hatch, the Filipinos hard-boil the egg, cooking the baby duck inside. The big joke among American servicemen was that one could never be sure which end to begin eating so as to avoid biting into the duck's ass.

The two men spent the evening hours in a little cabaret, downing San Miguel beer. When the bar closed, they found a protected spot underneath a small grove of pine trees and slept off the beers' effect. They awoke the next morning, ate a hearty breakfast, and caught a bus back to Manila. By 0800 hours the next morning, they were back on duty at the hospital.

On December 5, Tarpy got word that he'd been promoted to pharmacist's mate third class. Myers' promotion to the same rank had come through four days earlier. The two men celebrated the next night in Manila at their favorite cabaret, Duff's. They discussed profound issues with great sincerity.

"How come if it's December 6 in Manila, it's only December 5 in Hawaii?" Tarpy asked Myers.

"Because we crossed the International Date Line coming over here," Myers answered him.

"What did it look like? Did you see it?" A trickle of beer ran down Tarpy's chin from his last swig.

"I'm not sure," Myers said thoughtfully. "But I'm pretty sure I saw a sign on a buoy that said 'Welcome to tomorrow!' "

They both broke into guffaws and moved to a new topic: air raids.

"You got any idea what we're supposed to do if the Japs attack?" Myers asked.

"Yeah, I saw something a couple months back," Tarpy answered. "I think we're supposed to stay with whatever patients we're assigned to and then head for shelter under the building."

"How do we get the patients out of the wards?"

"I dunno," Tarpy said with a shrug. "I think we're supposed to carry them on their mattresses and get the ambulatory patients to help."

Myers shook his head. "Doesn't sound like a great plan. And it sure won't work very quick."

Tarpy shrugged again. "I guess it's the best idea they've got."

The following morning, Sunday, December 7, Tarpy awoke with a toothache. He said he didn't think he needed anything more than a warm compress. Myers told him he was crazy and that a bad tooth could really mess a guy up, but Tarpy ignored him and spent the day in pain. The morning sun rose resplendently over the Philippines on December 8. Tarpy was in real misery. He hadn't slept much and his face was swollen to such an extreme that it looked as though he had stuffed a tomato in his cheek. He had been granted sick leave and was still lying in his cot when a petty officer rushed in, grabbed the guy sleeping on the cot next to Tarpy, and shook him roughly.

"What, honey?" the guy slurred. "I didn't do nothin'."

"Wake up, you stupid fool! The Japs have just bombed Pearl Harbor. Get up, grab a weapon. Get ready."

The guy never opened his eyes. "You ain't funny. Leave me be. Lemme sleep." He rolled over and pulled his pillow over his head. The petty officer never heard him, having already run out to assume his battle station.

Tarpy decided that the toothache wasn't going to go away by itself, and after he got up he went to the dentist's office in the next building over. An orderly nervously told him that the doctor was currently on liberty but would be back in two days, on December 10. Then he asked if Tarpy had heard about the Japanese attack in Hawaii. Tarpy told him he had, but that right now the bad tooth was his primary concern. He made an appointment with the orderly to see the dentist at 1100 hours on the tenth. Then he ambled over to the hospital, hoping to get some painkillers and take it easy the rest of the day.

Although preparedness had been lacking thus far, the top brass decided that Canacao Hospital's proximity to the Naval Yard put it in the target area and ordered that immediate arrangements be made for the patients. When Myers had arrived at the hospital at 0800, his orders were to send the ambulatory patients back to duty and prepare to move the rest of them to Sternberg Army Hospital near downtown Manila. Sternberg was the Philippines' only general hospital and, as such, was well equipped. The dependents' ward was vacant; in the remote chance that hostilities might develop, all dependents had been sent stateside months earlier. It was here that Canacao's patients would be sent.

Myers was busy scribbling on charts of the departing patients, half listening to a Manila radio station playing in the ward. Every few minutes a news flash was announced, with broadcaster Don Bell repeating that Pearl Harbor had been bombed. Everyone in the ward was horrified by the very idea. And when Bell's flashes began to include reports of attacks in the Philippines at Clark, Nichols, and Iba airfields, someone yelled, "Turn that moron off!"

Tarpy arrived, and taking one look at him Myers knew he wouldn't be much use regardless of whether or not the Japanese attacked. He told Tarpy he'd cover for him and sent him back to the barracks.

Two of the patients were due for injections before they left, so Myers prepared the syringes. He glanced at his watch: 1100 hours. A new case of malaria had just been admitted so Myers set up his quinine schedule and pinned the notes to the man's pants legs so they wouldn't be lost in transport. The next time he looked at his watch, it was 1145 and the new shift had arrived.

"Hey, Myers, looks like these guys are all ready to go. We'll take it from here. Why don't you go ahead and knock off?" one of the pharmacist's mates offered.

"Thanks, fella." Myers washed up one last time and headed for the mess hall. Despite the threat of war, the weather was glorious, and men sat under canvas awnings outside the mess hall, eating their noon meals. Myers waved at a couple of guys he knew sitting over in a corner under one of the awnings, went inside to fill his tray, and came back out to join them.

"Hey, what d'ya hear about Pearl?" Myers asked as soon as he sat down.

"Nothing definite," one of the men answered. "Nobody seems to know what kind of damage there was. Radio communication's been sporadic."

"Hell, everything we own is in Hawaii," another man injected. "We're all in deep shit if the Japs messed things up bad."

The men continued the discussion, first about what may or may not have happened at Pearl Harbor, and then the sorry state of their own equipment and when the promised new supplies might arrive. They were suddenly aware that everyone else had left the mess area and a great deal of commotion was going on all around them. Men ran, fully loaded with combat gear, shouting as they went. Myers and the men with him jumped up from the table and ran to the road, questioning the first seaman who ran by.

"What's goin' on?"

"The Japs have attacked the airfields," the seaman gasped. "They've hit Clark and Nichols. Damn near wiped out all our air power. They're probably headed for us and the Navy Yard next."

It had been nine hours since the Japanese had reportedly struck Pearl Harbor. The events now unfolding on the Philippines should have been expected, yet the men were still surprised. They fell in with their respective units to await orders. When Myers reported, Tarpy was dressed and armed.

"This must be a real war." Tarpy winced in pain from his tooth. "They've given us extra bullets."

The troops and medical corps were put on standby and held their collective breath. Questions flew around with great abandon, but most of the answers were rumors or guesses. Some wondered why MacArthur and his Air Corps commander, General Lewis Breneton, hadn't taken action sooner. Rumor was that one of them had not communicated sufficiently to the other. The men were divided as to whose fault it might be.

Others tried to calculate when the attack had begun. Somebody said they'd heard about a false alarm of incoming enemy fighters over Clark Field at 1030. Supposedly the aircraft scrambled, orders were confused, and the planes never took off. At 1100 hours, the pilots received orders to get ready to attack. As the planes were being fueled and armed, the Japanese arrived with over fifty high-level bombers with accompanying fighter cover. Because of the confusion and lack of communication, the Japanese were virtually unopposed.

Another guy asked what else had been damaged. A petty officer swore he heard that Fort Stotsenburg, a cavalry post adjacent to Clark Field and about sixty miles north of Manila, had been pounded to dust. Buildings were decimated, and casualties were estimated at two hundred. Another man claimed he'd heard on the radio that at

Nichols Field, American fighter planes had recently been uncrated and were in the process of being made combat ready. Men had been working on them around the clock in the hopes they wouldn't be caught on the ground when the fighting began. But the work wasn't accomplished quickly enough. He said the projection was that the Far East Air Force had already lost half of its planes, on this, the first day of the war.

The big question was where would the damn Japs hit next? All of Sangley Point, the little scrap of land jutting into Manila Bay, waited. This included the town of Cavite, the Cavite Naval Base, the communications towers, the fuel tanks, an air station, and Canacao Naval Hospital. The Japanese attacked Nichols Field again on December 9 but still left Sangley Point untouched.

Myers and Tarpy had been assigned to a battle dressing station in the dispensary building located in the Navy Yard. They were headed there when the Japanese finally arrived to begin their attack of Sangley point. Their high-flying bombers sailed at about twenty-one thousand feet. The anti-aircraft shells fired from the ground burst four thousand feet too low. The bombers kept coming, unopposed. Myers looked around and saw men running toward what looked like the cellar doors outside the farmhouses back home. He and Tarpy followed them, finding themselves in an underground concrete locker.

The attack lasted about an hour. The Japanese bombs knocked half of the naval base into the bay. Since most of the buildings were made of wood, the rest of the base went up in flames. The thick black smoke billowing from these raging fires singed the men's noses and burned their eyes as they scrambled out of the underground locker. Some tried to put out the fires, but they were unfamiliar with the pumps on the fire trucks, and the flames raged on.

Myers and Tarpy, still carrying their medical kits, found an unscathed truck and drove it the short distance to the port area. Dead and wounded were scattered on the ground like pickup sticks. Many men had been caught out on the docks when the planes came in. One seaman told them everyone was so amazed at the sight that they had just stood there staring.

"We saw this perfect 'V' formation coming at us dropping leaflets," the seaman said. "Then somebody shouted, 'Leaflets, hell, those are bombs!' We all started running, but some of the guys just couldn't make it in time." He looked at the charred bodies around him with tears in his eyes.

Myers and Tarpy triaged the wounded as best they could and drove back to Canacao, which had been relatively undamaged. Other teams of corpsmen were doing the same. Soon, about a dozen vehicles raced back and forth between the Navy Yard, the port area, and the hospital.

Although the bombers were gone, the noise was still deafening. These were noises foreign to the men's ears: the roaring conflagration all around them; the earthquake-like concussions as ammunition and gasoline dumps exploded; the inhuman screams of men, frightened and in pain. None of these men had combat experience. None knew what to expect. Many never got the chance to fight back.

CHAPTER FOUR

★

Hearth and Home

Back in the States, on Sunday, December 7, 1941, the football season was winding down and the New York Giants had a game that day, heading toward finishing first in the Eastern Division under head coach Steve Owen. Joe Louis was wowing boxing fans with his "cosmic punch." This was the year Spam became known as "the meat of many uses," and a new Plymouth coupe could be had for $700. Women across the country were cooing over the rugged good looks of Clark Gable, while men's eyes lingered on the likes of Gene Tierney, Lana Turner, and Rita Hayworth.

As the country slowly extricated itself from a depressed economy, a new interest in travel had begun to grow. The railroad ads in the evening newspaper encouraged Americans to make a "Grand Circle" of their country. For $135, an individual could spend an entire week on a train, including meals and a sleeper car, crisscrossing the country from New York City to San Francisco. If the high seas were more to the traveler's liking, a variety of cruise lines were eager to please. One in particular, the Matson Navigation Company, promised pineapples and balmy breezes in their 1941 advertising campaign. It was a lavish expense far beyond what the Myerses could afford, but it painted an enticing picture nonetheless. With the innocence manifested by an entire country, Matson proudly announced, "All roads lead to happiness in Hawaii."

While Estel Myers was serving the country in the Pacific, his twenty-year-old brother, Orville, was finishing basic training in the Army. Their married eighteen-year-old sister, Iola, was taking care of her new baby, while their fifteen-year-old brother, Kenny, was juggling school with his job at a local filling station. Burt, Jr., the youngest of the Myers children, was completely engrossed in basketball, playing on a team that competed year-round.

On December 7, they were all to meet for Sunday dinner at the home of Orville's girlfriend. Kenny finished work at the filling station early that day, and by 12:45, he was on his bike heading toward Louisville's east side.

Kentucky winters are always a mixed bag of weather, as is true for most of the Ohio River Valley. No two days are ever alike, and it was not unusual to see sunshine dissolve into rain and then sleet within a twenty-four-hour time period. This day was no different; though the sun had been shining when Kenny arrived at the filling station in the morning, the day had quickly turned bleak, and a cold rain was soon sputtering down. By the time he had completed his thirty-minute ride, Kenny was cold and wet and looking forward to the warm glow coming from the house that was his destination.

He knocked on the door and waited patiently for it to open. When it did, the dismay every young man feels when he's in the presence of crying women flooded through him. Orville's girlfriend, her eyes puffy and pressing a handkerchief to her nose, stood at the door. Beyond her in the sitting room, a chorus of sobs came from the girl's mother and Iola. The men were grouped around the living room's largest piece of furniture, an RCA radio. Their faces wore grave expressions.

After listening for several minutes, Kenny asked his brother what had happened.

"The Japs just bombed Pearl Harbor in the Hawaiian Islands," Orville told him. "That's part of America, Kenny. The Japs have attacked America and now we gotta defend ourselves."

Upon hearing Orville's statement, the women's crying escalated. Kenny's thoughts ran the gamut, from loathing for this as yet unknown enemy to the realization that his brother Estel would be very near the fighting and possibly in danger.

In the weeks prior to December 7, ongoing negotiations had been conducted in Washington, D.C., between Japanese and American officials. The Japanese ambassador and his staff were insistent that their government was trying in good faith to soothe tensions between their country and the United States. They defended their acts of aggression in Asia with great voracity and asked repeatedly for the U.S. to lift the freeze on their assets. Secretary of State Cordell Hull was not moved in the least, but continued to receive the foreign officials conveying their missives from Tokyo.

At the same time, the American military was monitoring Japanese radio transmissions, employing top-notch cryptologists to break most of the codes used. By the end of November, it was widely known that use of the terms "East Wind Rain" was a reference to the United States. "North Wind Cloudy" referred to Russia, and Britain was known to the Japanese as "West Wind Clear." These code names were particularly important in helping to determine what Pacific aggressions the Japanese might take next.

The codes weren't foolproof, however. On December 5, a radio operator received a transmission that included "North Wind Cloudy," which he deciphered as a reference to a possible invasion of Russia. This didn't fit with the current intelligence reports stating that Russia was not a probable target in the near future. A day later it was finally concluded that the words were not the coded part of the transmission but simply a part of the daily Japanese weather forecast.

Without exception, top American military officials placed the Pacific Fleet, based in Pearl Harbor, at the forefront of any successful counterthrust against the Japanese. But the possibility of an attack did not seem feasible to them. It was a well-documented fact that none of the Japanese long-range bombers would be able to reach Hawaii from their bases and return safely to home airfields.

A greater possibility was sabotage against American ships and aircraft. To guard against such sneak attacks, Pearl Harbor continued to be completely lit up from dusk to dawn like a giant bull's-eye, right up until the last night of peace. In addition, hundreds of aircraft were ordered from their dispersal areas to a central location at which they could be more easily guarded. The Army Air Corps was a well-trained force, which, given a thirty-minute notice, would easily be able to disperse the aircraft again.

December 7 was a beautiful Sunday morning in Hawaii. Seamen were taking it easy, sauntering on docks or sleeping in, completely oblivious to a dozen missteps, miscues, and dropped balls that would change the course of their lives. Non-military individuals, too, were unaware of what was literally just over the horizon. In fact, when the first Japanese aircraft appeared in the mist over Diamond Head, tourists in the area congratulated themselves for being present to witness American aircraft flying such remarkably realistic practice runs.

Japanese Admiral Nagumo had committed the Japanese 6th Fleet to the attack. Riding the waves two hundred miles to the north of Oahu, over 460 Imperial aircraft were about to be employed in his two-wave attack. Thus far in military aviation's brief history, a single attack had never involved more than one carrier and a handful of aircraft.

The first attack began at 0740. American ships were berthed or at anchor around Ford Island almost exactly as Japanese intelligence had predicted. A few ships were missing, but along Battleship Row, eight out of the nine ships were present, constituting the very backbone of the American fleet. The harbor also contained two heavy cruisers, six light cruisers, twenty-nine destroyers, five submarines, a gunboat, nine minelayers, and ten minesweepers. In addition, several dozen auxiliary ships, like tenders, oilers, tugs, ammunition and supply ships, lay at anchor, making a total of ninety-four warships. The only targets missing from the anchorage were the U.S. aircraft carriers.

The first wave of the Japanese attack included forty torpedo bombers, forty-nine high-level bombers, fifty-one dive-bombers, and forty-three fighters, and lasted just thirty minutes. By the time it was over, all of the American battleships were seriously damaged and engulfed in raging flames. American airpower took an equal beating. Aircraft hit by Japanese firepower exploded and burned as helplessly as the fleet they were supposed to be protecting.

The second attack force arrived an hour after the first, with fifty-four high-level bombers, seventy-eight dive-bombers, and thirty-five fighters, its purpose being to mop up anything left from the first wave. It lasted sixty-five minutes. The Americans had recovered slightly between the two waves and were able to get off some anti-aircraft fire. Poor visibility also hampered the Japanese in the later attack. Of the twenty-nine aircraft the Japanese lost in the whole attack, twenty of them were downed in the second wave.

At 1000 hours it was all over. The attackers formed up and headed back for their carriers. The entire scenario was nearly a mirror image of what Rear Admiral Yarnell had executed as a test nine years earlier when he successfully simulated an air attack on the harbor.

No other war in history had started with such a resounding victory for one side on the very first day of hostilities. Amidst the fires and carnage in the harbor, 18 of the warships were sunk or suffered major damage. Surrounded by smoke and explosions at the airfields, 188 of the 394 aircraft were destroyed and another 159 were damaged. The most terrible loss came in American lives: 2,403 were killed, missing, or mortally wounded. Another 1,178 were wounded. In this one attack, the United States Navy lost almost three times as many men as it had lost in the Spanish-American War and World War I combined.

The Myers family huddled around their radio all afternoon as reports flooded the airwaves with more information about the unthinkable attack. First one ship was reported hit on Battleship Row, then four, then all of them. Casualty figures followed: a hundred, a thousand, three thousand men dead or wounded. An announcer on the scene reported that the aircraft destruction was indescribable. The planes had all been caught on the ground, neatly parked wingtip to wingtip. The impossible had happened, the announcer said. The United States of America had been attacked and badly crippled.

The Myers family came together around the radio the next day as well. From coast to coast, Americans listened to President Franklin Roosevelt's unsettling report of the Japanese military campaign. It was a radio announcement of tremendous complexity, which spread across the International Date Line and seven time zones:

Yesterday, December 7, 1941, a date which will live in infamy, the United States of America was suddenly and deliberately attacked by naval and air forces of the empire of Japan.

Yesterday, the Japanese government also launched an attack against Malaya. Last night, Japanese forces attacked Hong Kong. Last night, Japanese forces attacked Guam. Last night, Japanese forces attacked the Philippine Islands. Last night, the Japanese attacked Wake Island. And this morning, the Japanese attacked Midway Island.

Japan has therefore undertaken a surprise offensive extending throughout the Pacific area. The facts of yesterday and today speak for themselves. But always will our whole nation remember the character of the onslaught against us. No matter how long it may take us to overcome this premeditated invasion, the American people in their righteous might, will win through to absolute victory.

President Roosevelt then asked Congress to declare war on the Empire of Japan. Congress immediately complied. As the next few days passed, the President made more speeches heard on radios in homes and places of business, impressing upon the nation the importance of every man, woman, and child having a part in the fight. Never before in the existence of the medium of radio had it been such a lifeline. It was used to move and inspire, to educate and inform an electrified nation and prepare them for the long struggle ahead.

As the Christmas season approached, a second Myers son went overseas. Scarcely a week after the bombing of Pearl Harbor, Orville was assigned to the U.S. Rangers and would eventually be sent to the battlefields of North Africa. In an effort to achieve normalcy for the family, Mrs. Myers baked her traditional molasses cookies and made her famous peanut butter and chocolate fudge. The family Christmas tree was decorated as usual with strings of popcorn and homemade ornaments, and the stockings were hung from the mantel.

But in 1941, the family's living room had a new decoration: a small red and white flag hung near the door, emblazoned with blue stars, one for each of the Myers boys serving in the armed forces. Only through the will of God would the stars remain blue. Gold stars were issued for the servicemen who would not be coming home. Although she pretended to be adjusting the Christmas tree's popcorn strings, Lena Mae Myers frequented the living room, weeping softly for her sons so far from hearth and home.

CHAPTER FIVE

★

The Japanese Tidal Wave

Prior to December 8, Myers hadn't yet formed a solid opinion of the Japanese. But others in the military clearly had, as Ernest Hemingway profoundly wrote as the world around him careened toward war.

"All through the Pacific and the Far East in 1941 I heard about the general incapacity and the worthlessness of 'those Little Monkeys,'" Hemingway said. "Everywhere I heard what we would do to [them] when the day of the great pushover came. One cruiser division and a couple of carriers would destroy Tokyo; another ditto Yokohama. No one ever specified what the 'Little Monkeys' would be doing while all this was going on. I imagine they were supposed to be consulting oculists trying to remedy those famous defects in vision which kept them from being able to fly properly."

This sarcastic theory did not prove true. In reality, the Japanese had been preparing assiduously for what became the most resounding series of defeats ever suffered by the American military. It was glaringly clear to even the most inexperienced military observer that Japan's goals were to dominate the Southwest Pacific, overpower the resource-rich Dutch East Indies, and create a defensive perimeter around Southeast Asia. To do so, Imperial forces had to eliminate American naval power in the central Pacific and British naval power in the Far East.

Capture of the Philippine Islands was vital in order for Japan to achieve her goals. The job of securing the islands had been given to Lieutenant General Masaharu Homma. A career military man, Homma was fifty-four years old when he launched the attack on the Philippines. He had spent much of his career on foreign soil, first as an observer with the British forces in France during WW I. In 1925, he became the resident Japanese officer in India, and five years after that he was made a military attaché to London. As the war with China escalated, Homma returned to Asia to command the Japanese forces before receiving his orders for the Philippines.

Homma had at his disposal sixty-five thousand troops, the entire 14th Army. This included the 16th, 48th, and 61st Divisions and the 65th Individual Brigade, two tank battalions, two regiments and one battalion of medium artillery, three engineer regiments, five anti-aircraft battalions, and a large number of service units. Air support would come from Formosa (now known as Taiwan) in the form of Lieutenant General Hideyoshi Obata's 5th Air Group. The nearly 400 planes included 144 bombers and 110 long-range Zero fighters, 54 light bombers, 17 heavy bombers, and 72 fighters. On the seas, Vice Admiral Ibo Takahashi, who commanded the 3rd Fleet, made available to Homma the carrier *Ryujo,* five heavy cruisers, five light cruisers, and twenty-five destroyers.

Homma's attack was scheduled to the last detail. On the first day, army and navy aircraft would establish air superiority by destroying American aircraft and air installations. Advance air bases would be established on Luzon, Bataan Island, north of Luzon, and other neighboring islands. Then the press toward Manila would begin. Military strategists assumed that the fall of the capital would mean the destruction of the vast majority of U.S. and Philippine forces.

Imperial Japanese Headquarters had given Homma all the necessary tools. They also gave him an exact timetable to accomplish his objective: Luzon was to be conquered in fifty days. After that, half of his forces would be deployed to operations occurring elsewhere.

On behalf of the Allies, General MacArthur had far less to work with. There were thirty-one thousand troops available from the

Army and another fifteen thousand from the Air Corps. Most of the scant number of planes located in the Philippines were at Clark and Nichols Fields. Some of them were ancient. Seventy-five brand-new B-17 Flying Fortresses were due to arrive by spring, but as of December only thirty-seven had been delivered. Naval power was also minimal. Admiral Thomas Hart, commander of the United States Asiatic Fleet, had two cruisers, seventeen subs, and thirteen destroyers left over from the previous war, along with six motor torpedo boats. The Allied military forces would have an enormous task ahead of them to survive the deadly Japanese tidal wave.

Amid the thunderous chaos of the attack on the Philippines, bombs fell and bullets spewed from the Japanese aircraft. At the outset of the attack, the American soldiers had been simultaneously excited and nervous. They were green and undertrained. Many of them had never fired their rifles. After ten minutes, they became veterans in their own minds, interested only in killing before they could be killed.

When one man's ammunition ran out, Myers saw him take off his boot and throw it at a low-flying fighter. Another man could be heard yelling over the cacophony: "Get those bastards out of the air!" And several others were so awed by the sight of the Japanese planes in the air overhead, they insisted on exposing themselves to the firepower just to take pictures. Myers decided that evidently the devil takes care of his own because not one of the amateur photographers was hit.

He and Tarpy made trip after trip to Canacao in their commandeered truck, loaded with as many patients as they could manage. Once at Canacao, the patients were further triaged and taken by ambulance to Sternberg Hospital in Manila ten miles away.

Carnage punctuated the scenery around the young corpsmen. Charred human forms lay in every direction, sometimes in a collection of two or three, entangled beneath the skeleton of what had once been a truck. It appeared as though these men had sought cover beneath it, but when a bomb blast exploded the truck, the men were instantly incinerated.

Death was everywhere, and often the dead appeared to be the lucky ones. A man missing an arm refused to lie still long enough for Myers to apply a tourniquet. He insisted on going off in search of his missing limb. Other men, their bodies laid open from shrapnel as if by a giant can opener, were for the most part beyond help. They screamed out in pain, whimpered for their mothers, and watched their lives flow out of their bodies into red puddles beside them.

Some men had been hit by flying debris that was so precisely implanted in their bodies, it looked as if it belonged there. One man had been impaled on a piece of metal two inches wide and several feet long. It had passed completely through his body and into the body of the man standing behind him. The first had died instantly, but the second was still alive, although too terrified to extract himself from the corpse for fear he might do more harm to his own body.

Myers stood looking from one direction to another, not sure which way to go next. A thought floated into his head: this gruesome bloodbath created by the Japanese attack was beginning to resemble slaughtering day back on the farm. Just as he had watched his father quartering a hog, he could see at least four different severed human body parts right from where he was standing, the blood-sodden ground spongy beneath his feet.

Tarpy had just left with a truckload of patients when a Filipino soldier walked up quietly and stood beside Myers as he knelt over a man taking his last breaths.

"Excuse me. Doctor?" the soldier asked in a soft voice. Like most Filipinos, he was small in stature and reserved, clutching his hands in front of his chest.

"No, no, I'm not a doctor. Do you need a doctor?"

"I think so," the man replied. He moved one arm from his chest. The other arm remained on his chest, but his hand dropped limply, suspended only by a thin string of tendons at the wrist.

Myers was surprised at the sight of the man's hand dangling like a fish at the end of a line. But he was long past being sickened at the sight of such injuries. By his calculations, it had been three hours since the Japanese first attacked. During that short time he'd checked hundreds of bodies. He'd seen men missing legs, men whose heads had been split open like ripe melons, soldiers whose ragged corpses no longer even looked human.

The Filipino was bleeding badly, and it was obvious to Myers that his mangled hand could never be reattached. The man was clearly in shock and would probably die if they waited for Tarpy to return.

Myers talked the man into lying down and dug through his medical bag.

"Are you in pain?" he asked him.

The patient looked at him blankly. Myers decided on giving him morphine to relax him for what was coming next.

"The hand has to come off, buddy," Myers told him. "I'm really sorry, but there's just no way to salvage it and I don't think we have enough time to wait for my pal to get back with a truck."

The man continued to stare into Myers' eyes, not saying a word, but nodding his head in understanding.

"So first I'm gonna stop the bleeding with a tourniquet."

Myers continued speaking while he made a few twists on the tourniquet, then he wiped away the sweat running into his eyes. "Now, I've never done anything like this, but I don't think it'll be too hard. Just relax." Myers looked around and picked up a piece of wood lying nearby. "Bite down on this."

The man did as he was told. Myers pulled a scalpel out of his bag, set his jaw, and quickly cut through the tissue still attaching the hand to the arm. The whole process took less than a minute. Myers stared down at the severed hand he held in his own. *Why, it wasn't any harder than pulling my kid brother's tooth,* he thought.

"Myers! Hey, Myers!" Tarpy was running toward him, wild-eyed. "Run for cover! Here they come again!"

The roar of Japanese Zeros grew louder as Myers and Tarpy grabbed the one-handed patient and dragged him into a nearby foxhole with them.

The nightmarish routine continued nonstop. Dead men, wounded men, Japanese bombers, diving into craters. It seemed to be a never-ending circle of horrifying events. Long after the sun had set, the still-burning fires illuminated the Navy Yard like the light of day. Myers and Tarpy continued throughout the night, transporting the wounded to Canacao and returning to the Navy Yard for more.

As the wounded were evacuated from the target areas and then re-evacuated to Sternberg Hospital in downtown Manila, it became obvious almost immediately to the chief medical officers that although it was a large facility, Sternberg was not going to be able to handle all of the casualties. Added space was needed and there was no time for a major construction project.

Several of the officers and their staff members began scouting around Manila in search of large buildings that could be converted into hospitals. Eight such locations were found. Collectively they were known as the Manila Hospital Center; individually they were called "annexes of Sternberg." They included the popular nightclub the Jai Alai Club; Estado Major, an old Army barracks; the Spanish Club and Girls' Dormitory, used together as a single hospital unit; the Philippine Women's University; Santa Escolastica, a school; Fort William McKinley; and the Holy Ghost College. The Army and Navy pooled the medical teams to staff these facilities.

On the morning of December 11, final steps were taken to completely evacuate Canacao Hospital. All remaining patients were moved to whichever annex was handling their particular need, as determined by the diagnosis tag each wore. Following that, the medical staff was in a sense told to loot their own hospital. Myers and Tarpy were ordered to collect all movable equipment and supplies and relocate them to a staging area where they could be loaded onto trucks and taken into Manila for distribution to the annexes.

Each time the Japanese returned on yet another bombing run, the scavengers ran for cover. But one group of five corpsmen from Canacao that Myers had gotten to know weren't quick enough. From where he crouched in a trench, he watched as Japanese airmen swooped down and let loose their destruction. The corpsmen were blown to eternity.

While they waited for the enemy fighters to finish their strafing, a couple of the men in the trench with Myers swapped stories.

"One guy told me about something that happened up at Clark Field. He said an anti-aircraft gun knocked down one of our own planes. The pilot was rescued, but he was pretty burned up."

"Yeah, well, get this," a second shouted over the gunfire. "I heard a piece of shrapnel stamped 'U.S.A.' fell onto one of our boats."

"You mean we're bombing our own Navy?" the first man asked.

"Naw, the guy that told me said we've been selling scrap metal to the Japs for years. They're turning it into shrapnel and sending it back to us in dividends!"

The storytelling would continue until the fighters had left and the party could resume their hunt for usable equipment.

When they got back to Canacao with their loot, the men were given their new assignments. Myers was assigned to Estado Major, the old Army barracks, while Tarpy went to Santa Escolastica.

Estado Major was just a few blocks from Sternberg, on the adjacent Arroceres Street. The two-story frame buildings were old and dilapidated, and perilously close to the Quezon Bridge, which, judging from the amount of bombing it took, was considered a primary military objective by the Japanese. The medical officers had determined that the convalescent, ambulatory patients would be housed here, along with overflow convalescents from Sternberg and most of the patients from Fort William McKinley. The military had managed to set up five hundred beds in this makeshift hospital, but time did not allow extensive renovations to occur, and they neglected to designate adequate space for a mess hall. This was not as big a problem as it might have seemed; with the constant air raids, not having a place to eat seemed a trivial problem.

Myers set to work immediately, changing dressings and checking splints. One seaman who had been hit at Cavite was in particularly good spirits, considering the whole country was under attack.

"Doc, I'm so happy I could just shit," he confided to Myers.

"That so?"

"Yep, two nights ago I signed a hell of a big chit at a club downtown. Seventy-five bucks worth. I saw the Japs blow up the damn club, and my chit along with it. My friends and I got crocked free of charge!"

"Hey, Doc!" another patient called. "Got a smoke?"

Myers reached into his pocket and pulled out a cigarette for the guy before noticing both of the patient's hands were bandaged.

"Got caught with my hands in the cookie jar," the soldier joked. "Mind holdin' it for me?"

"Sure thing," Myers told him. "Time for a break anyway."

Myers lit two Lucky Strikes, put one in the soldier's mouth, and inhaled deeply on the other. The soldier spoke again, squinting through the smoke.

"I hear we got a little problem up in northern Luzon."

"How's that?"

"Well, just before I grabbed a hot anti-aircraft gun, I was receiving a message from up there. Seems the Japs have already landed at the towns of Vigan and Aparri. What d'ya suppose their next move'll be?"

"Hard to say," Myers answered him. "But I heard some good news a little bit ago. We scored hits on a Konga-class battleship. Pretty heavy damage."

The soldier nodded and squinted some more. A doctor rushed up and cut the conversation short.

"Corpsman, they've hit Nichols again. More casualties. Grab a couple guys and head over there. Take whatever vehicle you can find."

Myers stubbed out his cigarette and ran off in search of other corpsmen. It wasn't until he was outside that he remembered he hadn't extinguished his patient's cigarette. The guy was just going to have to fend for himself.

Nichols Field was enveloped in choking smoke. Myers and the other corpsmen stopped their truck, grabbed their medical bags, and scattered in different directions. The stench was overwhelming. The dead bodies created by the first bombing runs weren't keeping well in steaming tropical heat. Burial crews had been trying to take care of them, but in many cases the maggots had beaten them to it. Some of the bodies, bloated and various shades of yellow and purple, looked animated as the white worms wiggled in and out of ears, eyes, and mouths. Of everything he'd seen thus far, these sights were surely the hardest for Myers.

Since the population of the area had already been decimated by previous bombing runs and evacuations, the corpsmen found few survivors as they worked their way around the airfield and its remaining buildings. Myers knelt beside one man, bandaging a head wound, when he became aware of a sound that stood out boldly in all of the ugliness surrounding him. Music, a beautiful tropical-sounding melody, was coming through a broken window in the shack against which the injured man was now slumped. Myers raised up and looked through the window. There was a desk, a chair, several shelves stacked with papers, and in the corner, a small table with a radio, still playing. The irony was difficult to comprehend. Buildings and runways had been destroyed, men had been mowed down, and yet this shack and its delicate contents had seemingly been untouched.

From the distance, Myers heard the steady drone of plane engines and realized the Japs were on their way back. He grabbed his patient by the shoulders and dragged him away from the building and into a slit trench a hundred feet away. As if one Japanese pilot had been able to read Myers' mind, he flew a slow, lazy "8" over the shack, guns blazing. The wood popped and shattered, and finally something within the building gave a cough and the whole thing went up in flames.

Myers and the other corpsmen returned to Estado Major with their load of patients and then returned, making several more trips. By 1800 hours, all the casualties had been admitted to the hospital. The men took a quick break for some food and continued working until they dropped with exhaustion.

"Corpsman." Myers felt his shoulder being shaken. He opened his eyes and looked into the face of a doctor wearing a blood-spattered surgical gown. "We need experienced personnel over at Santa Escolastica. Besides, we're getting the hell shaken out of us from all the bombing the Japs are doing over the bridge. We're probably gonna be closing down soon."

Myers stood up, and the doctor put his hand on the corpsman's shoulder. "The guys around here said you worked the last two days as if the devil himself was on your tail. I hate to lose you, son, but they need you over there."

After Myers choked down a hard, tasteless biscuit with a gulp of lukewarm coffee, he was on his way to his third assignment in as many days. As harrying as all this transferring made the medical staff, the patients were even more disoriented. They, too, had been moved from place to place, depending on where the bombing was and the severity of their particular injury.

Myers thought about looking up Tarpy when he arrived at his new location, but he had no more than walked through the door when he was met by a doctor whose surgical gown was dyed scarlet with blood.

"Good, you're here. We're trying to set up this hospital and take care of patients at the same time. We're backed up everywhere. These patients were triaged once, but that was awhile ago and their conditions may have changed. Take a look and regroup them if you need to."

The doctor scurried by and Myers was thrust back into wading through the wounded. The nurses working at the hospital sped by in one direction with sterilized instruments on their way to surgery, and hurried in the other direction with gore-drenched sheets and towels. All the while, the intermittent blast of air-raid sirens shrieked.

Myers worked at a feverish pace taking care of patients, running supplies where they were needed, and assisting wherever he could. All personnel were placed on twenty-four-hour duty status, and many of the medical officers arranged to sleep in the hospital to facilitate care for the sick and wounded. Although efforts were made to schedule rest periods for them, when the influx of patients was particularly heavy, they were occupied as long as two or three days without rest. They all shared the burden without complaint.

Many of the incoming patients had been injured during scavenging missions at the Navy Yard, similar to the group Myers had witnessed being cut down by Japanese Zeros. Although the majority of the equipment and supplies had been hit, the Navy was still hopeful that it could salvage parts to repair other damaged equipment. The men, often intent upon what they were doing and having grown accustomed to the planes flying overhead, would be caught unprotected by the unceasing wave of Japanese bombs. Some would arrive at the hospital with bullet holes peppering their entire bodies. Some arrived with limbs or other body parts crisply charred from the explosions and fires that followed bombing runs. Myers recognized many of the men from happier pre-war times—all-night drinking and dancing at the Luzon Café and Night Club, poker games that went on for days, reminiscing about girls back home.

The atmosphere was unnerving even to the most war-hardened: machine guns chattered throughout the day, followed by ack-ack fire and enemy bombers dropping their ordnance on the city. The bombs' concussions sent debris flying through windows, while cigarettes and water glasses vibrated off bedside tables. Although disorganization and confusion ran rampant, the patients were amazingly well taken care of. Myers and the rest of the medical staff believed to their very core that any deaths that occurred during this chaos were not due to inadequate treatment.

"New orders, Myers." Another corpsman known simply as Tex was pushing a cart laden with instruments down the hospital hall, spreading the word as he went. "The colonel's gettin' permission to send the really bad cases out on a ship to Australia. We gotta get them and the supplies ready to go." Myers only heard half of this news; his eyes were riveted on this man's hair. It was thick and black, and looked as if he'd just been dropped out of a spring twister.

Two or three more corpsmen joined them in the hall. Tex shoved a shock of the hair off his forehead and continued.

"They're just waitin' on the damn Japs to give their approval for safe passage. Sons of bitches—how cruel can they be, not lettin' these poor boys get some rest so they can come back and whip their asses!"

As the days and nights ran into one another, Myers caught bits and pieces of the military strategy being played out on the island around him. By neutralizing U.S. air and naval power in the Philippines in the first forty-eight hours of the war, the Japanese had gained a position they had never anticipated. They had destroyed eighteen of the thirty-five Flying Fortresses at Clark Field, as well as fifty-six fighters and twenty-five other planes, while only losing seven of their own aircraft in the process. As there was no safe place to land, the remnants of the American bomber force withdrew to Australia, leaving only a handful of fighters.

Defense of the Philippines now relied solely on its ground forces, which at the time had no lines of supply or escape. MacArthur had chosen to use the tactics laid out in War Plan ORANGE as a last resort, and instead divided all of his available resources between the four separate forces responsible for defending the islands. This caused the combined American and Filipino troops to be spread thinly.

Prior to the onset of hostilities, the largest concentration of American aircraft outside the continental U.S. was in the Philippines. But after Japanese forces landed at Legaspi, in southern Luzon, on December 11, the Americans wisely decided to withdraw the few bombers that remained. The Asiatic Fleet, under the command of Admiral Thomas Hart, also departed, taking with her four destroyers, thirteen submarines, six gunboats, assorted support craft, and some PT boats in Manila.

General Homma did not intend to make his major troop landing until he could provide air support for his infantrymen. Therefore, he planned half a dozen preliminary landings, mostly on the coast of northern Luzon in order to capture airstrips. Wisely guessing this might be Homma's plan, MacArthur had chosen to preserve his military strength for one main counterattack. Thus some of Homma's early landings went entirely unopposed.

On December 19, the Japanese secured the island of Mindanao in the southern part of the archipelago. December 22 dawned cold and rainy, with a heavy surf. After two weeks of diversionary tactics, a large Japanese invasion force landed at Lingayen Gulf on the western shores of Luzon. The main attack of the Philippines had begun. General Homma, with a contingent of eighty ships and forty-three thousand troops, waded ashore through both a raging typhoon and the resistance of the United States–trained Philippine reservists. Homma landed tanks and artillery later that day and began advancing south toward Manila despite the valiant resistance of Major General Wainwright's Philippine Scouts.

MacArthur's dark mood mirrored the weather: his personally designed defense plan had failed. He notified his commanders that War Plan ORANGE was now in effect, reactivating the old war plan that called for the defense of only the Bataan Peninsula and the island fortress of Corregidor. The same day, all hospital expansion occurring in Manila ceased. Still, the Americans believed that the Japanese would be prevented from taking the islands.

The Japanese landing forces at Lingayen joined with those from Vigan in the north on December 24, sewing up the northern and western part of Luzon. On the east, landing parties at Lamon Bay joined with those farther south in Legaspi, overtaking the southern and eastern parts of Luzon. Following the initial Japanese bombings and landings, their forces overtook the Philippine Islands with greater speed than even the savviest military analyst could have predicted. Luzon, an island slightly larger than the state of Kentucky, was already well on its way to becoming the main prize of the Japanese efforts as they began their push toward Manila.

Allied troop withdrawal to the Bataan Peninsula also started on December 24. Hoping to avoid further casualties and destruction, MacArthur moved his headquarters to "the Rock," the island fortress of Corregidor at the mouth of Manila Bay. Additionally, in an official communiqué, he declared Manila an "open city," as had been laid out in the Hague Convention of 1907:

> In order to spare the metropolitan area from ravages of attack, either by air or ground, Manila is hereby declared an open city without the characteristics of military objective. In order that no excuse may be given for possible mistake, the American

high commissioner, the Commonwealth government, and all combatant military installations will be withdrawn from its environs as rapidly as possible. The municipal government will continue to function with its police powers, reinforced by constabulary troops, so that the normal protection of life and property may be preserved. Citizens are requested to maintain obedience to constituted authorities and continue the normal processes of business.

Manila's newspapers and radio stations published news of the open city proclamation throughout the day. MacArthur's hope was that the city's six hundred twenty-five thousand citizens would be spared further attacks from the Japanese. The unspoken consequence of the proclamation was that the city would also be more likely to be occupied at some time in the near future. Nonetheless, a creative citizen hung a huge banner across the front of City Hall that read "Open City—No Shooting." As far as Pharmacist's Mate Myers was concerned, it did little good.

"Just listen to that." Myers and Tex were having a smoke outside the hospital. They had sought shelter from the rain under an overhang at the front of the building.

"Ain't that a beautiful sound?" Tex asked, waving his finger like a conductor's baton in time to the "Star Spangled Banner," which along with the Philippine national anthem, was being played over the loudspeaker outside City Hall each morning and evening.

"Sure is," Myers acknowledged. "Why the Japs bombed so many other buildings, but haven't dropped an egg on us or City Hall yet is a mystery to me."

Tex was still listening to the last strains of the familiar tune fading away. "Ya know, I played football at SMU before I enlisted. It always amazed me. There you'd be on the field, surrounded by all these tough guys swearing to kill one another, and they'd strike up the National Anthem. By the time the band finished, more than a few guys would wipe their eyes."

"I never played for a college or anything," Myers said, "but I really like football. Maybe if we get some time in the next couple days, we can put a game together with some of the guys."

A truck roared up toward the door where the two men stood. Its windshield was broken out and bullet holes riddled the hood and doors. A couple of men from the 200th Coastal Artillery jumped out and ran back to the truck bed, shouting for help.

"We found these guys half dead in this truck," one of the soldiers explained as Myers and Tex ran up. "They musta got hit driving. That one guy looks pretty bad off."

The two men were slumped against each other, both unconscious. Judging from the amount of blood everywhere, Myers wondered whether either of them was still alive. He felt the first man's wrist and then his neck.

"I got a pulse."

"I don't," Tex said softly, looking down at the second man. Two nurses carrying a stretcher had appeared. "Mark him killed in action," Tex told them.

Myers and Tex loaded the survivor onto the stretcher and took off at a trot across the driveway and into the hospital. As they ran into the surgical area they saw a doctor scrubbing up for the next patient.

"Got a table waiting, fellas," the doctor told them. "The next case can be bumped back for this poor guy. Take him on in, then scrub up—I'll need some extra help."

The wounded man's shirt was cut away, revealing a chest punched with holes and lacerated with jagged tears, evidence that he'd been hit with shrapnel.

"Get the plasma hooked up to try to get him out of shock," the doctor told Myers. "And, you, corpsman," he said to Tex, "you know how to administer ether?"

Tex said that he did.

"Okay, you get that started. Nurse! I need a new instrument tray."

They began the surgery, with the doctor determining which of the wounds appeared to need attention first. "This one went deep," he said, probing with his finger in the man's chest. When the doctor removed his finger, blood shot from the hole and sprayed them all.

"Got a major bleeder!" the doctor yelled. "How's the ether doing? We gotta open him up."

Tex looked down at the soldier's ashen face. "Okay. Go ahead."

The doctor began his incision and worked his way through the layers of tissue until he had exposed the heart. "Oh, God. His aorta looks like it was sliced open with a letter opener." He turned to Myers. "Son, you gotta put your finger here until I can get this vessel oversewn. If he keeps bleeding from it, he won't last another five minutes."

He directed Myers to hold the two sections of the aorta together with his fingers, trying to keep the huge vessel from spurting and maintain its blood flow at the same time. Another doctor, a corpsman, and two more nurses arrived to assist. The whole group worked briskly and silently.

One of the doctors broke the silence, asking Myers, "Your fingers okay?"

"Sure thing. Just do what you gotta do," Myers told him.

They all heard the music at the same time a few minutes later. The jubilant sound of "O Come All Ye Faithful" being sung by a choir floated out of City Hall's loudspeaker and into the operatory. Tex picked up the tune. One of the nurses began to sing. Myers could almost see his mother sitting at the family piano, playing.

Christmas and home seemed remote from the war they were living. Yet they all began to repeat the words, either silently or out loud: "O come, all ye faithful, joyful and triumphant."

Triumphant, as in pushing the Japs back to hell where they belonged, Myers thought.

The doctor monitoring the patient's blood pressure brought them back to the moment. "There must be a bleeder someplace else. His pressure's dropping fast."

Myers stood his ground, holding together the man's aorta as the surgical team worked around him. Sixty seconds later, the doctor with the blood pressure gauge shook his head.

66   *Judith L. Pearson*

"Pressure's gone."

The surgeon looked at the barely quivering heart lying in the man's open chest.

"Dammit! We lost him."

In the silence that followed, the men and women in the operatory heard the choir reach the end of the hymn: "O come let us adore Him, Christ the Lord."

Chapter Six

★

Bahala Na

While the war Myers was witnessing around him had escalated during the first two weeks of December, it virtually cartwheeled to a climax during the final week of the month. On December 22, the first cadre of Medical Corps officers, nurses, and enlisted men left by truck convoy for Bataan. On December 25, the majority of the remaining military personnel was transferred by boat to Bataan to establish hospitals there.

During the first three weeks of the war, the various hospital staffs maintained records on the approximately two thousand military and civilian patients who were admitted to the Manila Hospital Center. When a patient was transferred to a different annex, Myers and the other corpsmen saw to it that his records accompanied him. When the withdrawal to Bataan was ordered, all patient records were sent by boat to Corregidor, the theory being that the headquarters there was impenetrable. The records never made it, however; midway there, the ship was sunk by Japanese dive-bombers and all the records were lost.

While MacArthur's open city declaration was intended to deter enemy bombings of Manila, the Japanese evidently decided it provided an excellent opportunity to show off their strength. Intermittent bombing continued, particularly along the Pasig River, where native fishing boats still bobbed serenely at the river's edge.

Neither did the enemy show any concern for the Christian holiday of Christmas. They doubled their bombing runs on that day, planes roaring overhead, hitting, among other targets, the old Santo Domingo Church. Mass was in progress, and many of the worshipers were killed.

By the day after Christmas, the entire Canacao Hospital staff and their remaining one hundred and fifty patients had been ordered to Santa Escolastica in central Manila. Myers and Tarpy's reunion with men and women they hadn't seen since the start of the war was brief, given the workload. But it had an extremely positive effect on them all. Despite the panic and terror of Manila's citizenry, despite witnessing death and carnage nearly every waking moment, and despite a rapidly diminishing store of supplies, morale among the medical corps was indescribably high. Cooperation and teamwork sustained their efforts.

At the onset of hostilities, before they had all been reassigned to the annexes, District Commandant Admiral Rockwell had issued his last instructions to the Canacao group: "Maintain a hospital in the naval tradition in the Manila area." And by God, that's what they intended to do.

On December 28, the chief medical officers decided that Sternberg Hospital, a wooden building sitting dangerously close to Japanese targets on the river, was unsafe. The few patients there, mostly from Cavite, were also transferred to Santa Escolastica. Some would be further evacuated. But the doctors determined that others just couldn't be moved any farther. At that point, all hospital staff members were then given a choice—they could either relocate to field hospitals on Bataan or Corregidor, or remain in the city with the most critical patients and await the arrival of the Japanese.

Myers, Tarpy, and Tex had decided to stay in Manila with the patients. A week had passed since any of them had had a real shower or a full night's sleep on a bona fide bed. They slept on gurneys and cots when available, the floor when not. Bathing meant splashing themselves with water from buckets or sinks. They had discovered early on in the war that the heat and humidity, coupled with the strenuous workload, made their uniform shirts feel like wool body bags. Without access to laundry facilities, spending their days bare-chested made the most sense.

Some of the army nurses who remained in Manila were transferred to Corregidor on December 29. The final evacuation to Australia of nurses and patients who could be moved was accomplished on December 31 under the cover of night.

All the while, parts of Manila were blazing infernos, roaring flames mocking the city's strict blackout orders. The gas and oil storage areas at Pandacan had been burning since the initial bombing runs. In the port area, buildings and ships caught fire from one another like firecrackers on a string. No effort was made to put the fires out, the theory being that the fewer buildings the Japanese found in usable condition, the better.

The doctors who volunteered to remain at the hospital were now the ranking officers. They traveled from ward to ward, instructing patients and corpsmen alike how to behave when the enemy arrived.

"If you have weapons of any sort—guns, knives, grenades—turn them all in now, boys," a weary captain ordered. In response, an impressive collection appeared on the floor of the main ward.

"Keep your mouths shut, no wisecracks, speak only when spoken to," the captain continued. "These Nips aren't fooling around. If you do, it could have tragic consequences."

Patients and medical personnel alike sat apprehensively in wait for the Japanese to arrive. All wondered if they might toss the Americans out of the hospital to make room for their own wounded. Or might the enemy take the easy road and kill them all?

"All I can say is *bahala na*," Tarpy announced.

"What the hell is that supposed to mean?" Tex growled at him.

"The Filipinos say it. It's Tagalog and it means whatever happens is gonna happen and there's nothing we can do about it anyway. So we might as well just quit worrying."

Myers spoke up. "He's got a point. There's not much we can do about it right now. How long can the war last, a week? A couple at the most? You know help's on the way; Roosevelt isn't just gonna leave us here."

"Just the same," Tex continued, "I got a bad feelin' about this. I never been good at takin' orders."

"You're in the Navy, you idiot," Tarpy challenged him. "You been takin' orders since you enlisted."

"Yeah, but I *want* to do what the Navy tells me. I'm damn sure I ain't gonna want to do what the Japs tell me."

The men fell silent and waited. They heard explosions at nearly the same time they felt the concussions. Someone, probably the Army, was blowing up what was left of the oil storage and supply dumps. Myers looked out the windows in the direction of the sounds and saw huge pillars of flames shooting toward the sky. At the stroke of midnight, as a new year was born, Manila was dying. And the future was anybody's guess.

The Bataan Peninsula is twenty-five miles long, twenty miles wide at its base, and shaped like a big thumb jutting southward into Manila Bay. American military strategists considered it the perfect place from which to wage a defensive battle. An added plus was that the peninsula was covered with rugged mountains and heavy jungles, and criss-crossed with small streams and deep gullies.

The defense of Bataan was fairly straightforward: using two forces facing the opposing coastline and using the peninsula's Mount Natib, a promontory 4,222 feet high, as the dividing line, they could create two lines of resistance. War Plan ORANGE concluded with the assumption that the two lines, together with those forces on Corregidor and the American air power in the Philippines, would be able to stave off any enemy advances until the Pacific Fleet could fight its way over to reinforce them. Never in their wildest dreams did the strategists fathom that, so early on in the war, American air power would be reduced to burning rubble or that the Pacific Fleet would be a ghostly shell of its former strength.

General Wainwright was charged with holding back the main Japanese assault while keeping the road to Bataan open for the hasty withdrawal of American and Filipino troops. But in their haste, they were forced, in many cases, to leave most of their food, medical supplies, ammunition, and equipment behind. Suddenly, a drastic consequence of MacArthur's preferred plan of dividing his forces to defend the entire island chain became all too evident. Supplies that had been dispersed from their original depots in Bataan and Corregidor to support the four defense forces set shortly after Japan's initial attack were now being abandoned. The retreating troops were short on still-functioning trucks, short on roads, and short on time. Everything being left was destroyed. They burned railroad cars and blew up bridges. They put sugar in the gas tanks of abandoned trucks and shot holes in the engines of tanks.

The assumption made by War Plan ORANGE was that the forty-three thousand troops in Bataan would be resisting for at least six months, and the area was provisioned accordingly. In actuality, on January 1, 1942, there were eighty thousand troops and twenty-six thousand civilians, and enough food to last them just thirty days. All personnel in Bataan were immediately placed on half rations. In an area where a healthy, active man requires thirty-five hundred to four thousand calories a day, the hardworking defenders were rationed to two thousand. At one depot alone, they had had to leave behind enough rice to feed all the soldiers and civilians on the peninsula for five months. Now, the search for food quickly became as urgent a problem as resisting the enemy's assaults. As the battles raged on, the rations were cut and then cut again.

The island of Corregidor was the Allies' other Philippine stronghold. Aptly nicknamed "the Rock," the tadpole-shaped, volcanic rock outcropping lay two miles from Bataan at the mouth of Manila Bay. Food supplies on Corregidor were more plentiful than on Bataan but by no means abundant. When General MacArthur relocated the headquarters of the United States Army Forces in the Far East, otherwise known as the USAFFE, to the island, the number of personnel increased from the anticipated seven thousand to ten thousand. These individuals, too, were immediately put on half rations.

Corregidor had several disadvantages. First, the fortification was built during the days when wars were fought from battleships. Therefore, all of Corregidor's batteries faced seaward, making them useless against air attacks or ground assaults from across the channel on Bataan. Secondly, Corregidor sat much lower than the surrounding shorelines. This gave the enemy ideal opportunities to observe and fire upon the Allies while being protected from return fire.

Corregidor's only advantage as a defensive position was that the island was honeycombed with a series of tunnels, safely located under a rocky shell. The main thoroughfare, Malinta Tunnel, ran straight through the island with lateral tunnels on both sides. The subterranean web had multiple floors, running water, and electricity, and provided space for offices, supplies, hospitals, and berthing quarters for most of the men and women. The remaining troops were located at the island's various defense positions, assigned to fend off enemy attacks.

While the Japanese were leveling the rest of Luzon, they hadn't touched Corregidor. The USAFFE believed that was due to the threat of the anti-aircraft batteries covering the Rock. In reality, the only reason was that the Japanese just hadn't gotten around to it yet. Then, on December 29, they sent in fifty-four bombers to unleash hell upon the underground fortifications.

The top floors of some of the tunnels sustained damage. The number of people, combined with the tunnels' small size, the dust-clogged air, and the fear experienced by everyone but the unconscious, caused near panic, even among the most seasoned veterans. Additionally, part of the Philippine Army, whose numbers had looked impressive on paper, literally took to the hills. Most of them were just boys with no training. Flying bullets were more than they had bargained for.

Before the start of hostilities, Japan had intended to complete the occupation of the Philippines before taking on the next offensive in the Dutch East Indies. The ease with which they had made their initial landings prompted them to move up their timetable. At the beginning of January, the Japanese Imperial Headquarters reassigned an entire division of the 14th Army, some of Homma's best troops, along with air support, to the East Indies. Tokyo replaced these with a brigade of recalled reservists.

But the revival of War Plan ORANGE threw Homma off his

tight schedule. In addition, the reassignment of the 14th Army division left the Japanese outnumbered three to one on Bataan. Suddenly, this eradicated any chance the Japanese may have had to bring the campaign on Luzon to a speedy conclusion.

Protesting the position he had been put in, Homma contacted Imperial Japanese Headquarters, writing:

> The operations in the Bataan Peninsula and the Corregidor Fortress are not merely a local operation of the Great East Asia War. . . . As the Anti-Axis powers propagandize about this battle as being a uniquely hopeful battle and the first step toward eventual victory, the rest of the world has concentrated upon the progress of the battle tactics on this small peninsula. Hence, the victories of these operations do not only mean the suppression of the Philippines, but will also have a bearing upon the English and Americans and their attitude toward continuing the war.

Homma couldn't have been more accurate. The brief respite given to the Allied defenders while the Japanese repositioned their troops was the chance needed to dig in and prepare to take a stand. Not since the defense of the Alamo did such an uphill battle carry within its waging the source of so much national pride and dedication.

Also during the Japanese repositioning, PT boats were able to make trips back and forth across Marivales Bay between the southern tip of Bataan and Corregidor. The boats ferried a variety of personnel and a few supplies. Still anchored in the bay was the submarine tender, the USS *Canopus,* which the Japanese hit during their first bombing run of Corregidor.

Although damaged, the ship's machine shops, valuable for repairing other equipment, were operational. The trick was to encourage the Japanese not to bomb her again. To accomplish this, the captain decided to make the *Canopus* look as though she'd been completely incapacitated. He pumped water into her tanks to give her a list, and released the booms so they could flap in the breeze. During daylight hours, the crew dispersed and the ship appeared abandoned. As soon as night fell, the men returned and worked until dawn, mending the diminishing supply of weapons of war.

Throughout Santa Escolastica, the men and women waited. Patients barely moved in their cots. Corpsmen and nurses leaned against walls or sat on the floor. Some stood watch at positions near open windows to spread word of the enemy's arrival the very moment they were spotted.

As had been the case every day since the Canacao Naval Hospital had first opened its doors, the medical officer of the day kept an official journal outlining the day's activities, which was then approved by the medical officer in command. It was the opinion of the commander that even if the physical hospital no longer existed, as long as some or all of the staff was together, a journal should still be kept. On Thursday, January 1, 1942, Myers happened to see what the officer of the day had written for the day's events.

"Looks like we're gettin' shots today," he commented to the officer, reading, " 'Cholera and dysentery immunization on staff medical officers, nurses, and hospital corpsmen.' "

"Yep," the officer answered him. "Can't be too careful. We don't want to catch anything serious when those Nips arrive."

On Friday, January 2, the hospital had 163 patients. The hospital commander conducted an inventory of the personal effects belonging to the patients and staff.

"I ain't givin' 'em this ring," Tex announced. "It belonged to my mother. She gave it to me when she died, and I'm givin' it to my wife when I find one."

"Well, not that any woman in her right mind would want to marry you," Myers told him, grinning, "but if you want to keep the ring, you better hide it."

"Where? Like in a mattress or somethin'?"

"You honestly think we're gonna ride out the war here at this hospital and then collect our belongings and go home?" another corpsman piped up. "You heard about what the Japs did to the Chinese?

They'll probably kill us as soon as they take what they want. Myers, you were in China. You tell him."

"Yeah, it was pretty bad in China. But hell, the Chinese aren't the same as Americans. They don't know how to fight. We do! The Japs aren't gonna kill us." Quietly, he said to the corpsman, "Shut up, you stupid fool. You wanna scare everybody else just 'cause you are?"

Myers turned and looked at Tex for a minute. "Okay, here's what you do. Take a piece of surgical tape and tape the ring in your crack just above your asshole."

Tex frowned. "And then what?"

"The rest is up to you." Myers shrugged. "But it's one place the Japs may not look." He turned and walked down toward the end of the ward to check on a couple of patients.

"Hey, Doc?" one of them called to Myers. "I found this Bible in a building at Nichols Field. The writing in the front says it belonged to some guy named James Breckenridge from Iowa. He got it from his Sunday School teacher in 1934. I thought maybe when I got back home, I'd write to the address in it and return it to him. You think the Japs'll let me keep it?"

"I just don't know, seaman," Myers answered. "But I think you stand a better chance if you don't try to hide it. They don't believe in God anyway, so unless they think it has some value, maybe they won't take it away."

The man was satisfied and the waiting continued.

That afternoon a War Department communiqué was released, stating:

"Advanced elements of Japanese troops entered Manila at 3:00 P.M. American and Philippine troops north and northwest of Manila are continuing to resist stubbornly attacks which are being pressed with increasing intensity."

Hearing this news on a hospital radio shook Myers unexpectedly. He wasn't afraid, exactly; it was more a sense of foreboding. Listening to the chatter around him, he realized he wasn't alone in his feelings. This disquietude was made worse when, at 1905 hours, a fire broke out in the galley incinerator pit.

Someone had stowed live ammunition there, and the exploding shells sounded as though Homma himself was coming through the hospital, shooting everyone in sight. Panic spread but was quickly mitigated when the source of the racket was discovered and the fire was extinguished by the yard watch. Nervously, the hospital's inhabitants bedded down for the night.

At 0445 hours, the morning of January 3, a racket again burst through the steamy darkness. Myers awoke and listened, thinking it was more ammunition. He even smiled at the thought that it would be quite a boisterous start to his twenty-second birthday. But the noise had been made by the butt of a rifle pounding on the front gate of the compound and the word spread quickly among the hospital staff. The Japanese had arrived.

The yard watch opened the gate to find a single Japanese soldier. The soldier made no effort to enter and said nothing. Awakening the watch seemed to be his only purpose as he quietly strode away. Any further sleep on the part of the hospital staff would have been impossible, and to a man, not one of them even tried. Reveille was sounded as usual at 0600 hours, the buildings and grounds were inspected as happened every day, and at 0645 hours, the front gate was opened. About a half hour later, another Japanese soldier arrived. This one carried a rifle with a fixed bayonet. Myers heard that he searched the front gate sentry and examined the man's personal effects. The soldier returned the items and he, too, went away.

Apprehension hung in the humid morning air, making it difficult to concentrate on the duties of the day. As Myers made ward rounds, he saw out the window another Japanese soldier speaking to the American gate sentry and motioning toward the gate in big swinging movements with his arm. Finally the sentry seemed to understand and closed the gate, which appeared to satisfy the soldier.

Word was passed that a small contingency of Japanese troops was seen moving up Pennsylvania Avenue toward Santa Escolastica. The doctors had made sure that both red crosses and white flags were visible from all sides of the building. Once the Japanese troops had assembled in the front, the American doctor serving as commanding officer of the hospital went out to meet them, holding his hands high above his head. A brief discussion ensued and the doctor turned around and walked back into the building, followed by a portion of the Japanese contingency with their guns drawn. The moment in time that everyone had nervously contemplated had arrived.

The first thing Myers thought when the Japanese entered the ward where he, Tarpy, and Tex waited was that these much-hated enemies looked more like kids playing soldier in grown-up uniforms. They were short, wiry men with stubby legs and shaved heads. Their pants were baggy, their leggings drooped, and their kits were askew. Contrary to the popular description bantered about throughout the military, not one of them wore glasses. Despite their appearance, Myers knew that these badly wrapped, little brown packages had been taught from birth the glory of dying for the Emperor. They would think nothing of killing, even if it meant they would be killed in the process. Such was the price of glory.

The first group of soldiers who entered carried .25-caliber rifles with bayonets affixed to them. Following them was the American C.O. of the hospital and a group of three Japanese officers who strode in and surveyed the room with a haughty glare. Finally, one of them spoke.

"Doctors?" He waved his hand toward the middle of the ward where Myers, Tarpy, and Tex stood with their hands on their heads.

"Corpsmen," the C.O. answered. The Japanese officer who had spoken English looked confused. "Helpers," the C.O. tried again. The officer nodded his head in understanding and said something to his fellow officers. One of them barked out orders, and the soldiers began looking everywhere, rummaging through everything.

"Keep calm, everybody," the C.O. said. "They've done this in every room. Let them take whatever they want. Just be agreeable."

"No more talk," the officer said sharply. He slapped the C.O. hard across the face.

The Japanese moved systematically through the ward. They yanked open drawers and peered in cabinets, stuffing the medical supplies they found into duffel bags. They pulled cots apart and searched the patients, taking watches, rings, and anything else that appealed to them.

A couple of times, they picked up pictures of wives and girlfriends and made comments in Japanese that caused their comrades to laugh vulgarly. The American to whom the picture belonged might bristle but would restrain himself when the C.O. said calmly, "Steady, man."

Finally, one of the soldiers got to the man clutching his new-found Bible. The soldier grabbed it, looked through it, and called to the English-speaking officer for advice. The officer walked up and thumbed through the book before speaking to the patient.

"There are pictures?"

"No, no pictures. It's a Bible. Stories about our Buddha." The patient pointed toward the ceiling.

The officer grunted and said something to the soldier. After a bow of acknowledgment, the Bible was tossed back to the American patient. Once they had finished pulling things apart, the Japanese contingent left the ward, leaving a stunned silence in their wake.

"That's it?" Tex asked in disbelief. "Jesus Christ, what do we do now?"

No answer came. After so many long days up to their elbows in blood and guts, after so much trepidation at who and what the enemy was, the scene was almost anti-climactic. Myers wiped the beads of sweat off his upper lip, and in an effort to ease the tension he announced, "Well, fellas, today's my birthday. I guess maybe we could use this time to plan a party."

There were a few deep sighs and feeble chuckles. Tarpy looked at Myers and slapped him on the back. "Well, if that don't beat all. Myers, I'll bet you're the first captured American to have a birthday. Maybe we should invite the Emperor and General Homma to your party, too."

"Only if I can have first crack at 'em, me being the honored guest and all."

As his troops officially installed themselves at Santa Escolastica and other facilities in Manila, General Homma had fulfilled the main mission that Imperial Japanese Headquarters had assigned him. He had even halted his troops ten miles outside of the city and ordered them to clean up and rest before officially taking Manila. It was Homma's belief that clean and well rested troops also bore greater self-respect and self-restraint. This proved to be true, as the Japanese had entered the city in an orderly fashion with no looting or wanton destruction.

Tokyo newspapers boasted that the entry of Japanese forces into Manila "not only finally seals the doom of the United States armed forces in Luzon, but in effect places the entire Philippines under Japanese military dominance."

It was true: Homma had taken most of the Philippine Islands away from the Americans. But the victory was incomplete—the Japanese couldn't use Manila's port facilities or Manila Bay. As long as Corregidor stood, with its big guns and accurate gunners, the enemy could not make free use of what was considered the most useful harbor in the western Pacific. The Japanese had to defeat the troops on Bataan and Corregidor in order to put those final pieces of the islands in Japanese possession.

The battle of Bataan continued to rage furiously. The Americans fell back to their second line of defense in mid January and Homma called for MacArthur to surrender. MacArthur ignored him and told Washington he'd reached his final line. There would be no troop withdrawal, he told the President—the Japanese advance would halt there. The general also still believed there was aid coming to the Philippines, a thought that gave him even greater confidence that his troops could hold out.

The beleaguered Americans on Bataan were hammered by the Japanese Army, their endurance stretched beyond human limits by a merciless blasting from the air and ground artilleries. But bombs and bullets were not the only enemy. They were now down to a thousand calories a day. Hunger became the great leveler and food was all the soldiers thought about. They ate dogs, iguanas, and snakes. When those became scarce, the men turned to carabao, mules, and ponies. They even tried monkey, although it was distressing when a head or a hand appeared on one's plate.

By mid February most soldiers suffered symptoms of malnutrition. Their legs felt watery and flashed with pains that would increase and then ebb. Rapid movement brought vertigo and increased heart rates. An hour after they ate breakfast, they suffered from fatigue. By midday, some would double up with intestinal pains. Their reduced stamina invited illnesses that they otherwise might have been able to throw off. Soon, the enemy was everything, everywhere.

Beriberi, the first nutritional disease to appear, was soon followed by pellagra and scurvy. Mosquitoes carried malaria, which everyone had, some more severely than others. Dysentery, picked up from bacteria in the soil and water, caused them to suffer from diarrhea up to twenty times a day. Gas gangrene, another airborne bacterial disease, hit the injured men at an alarming rate. The bacilli thrived in the jungle soil and would infect penetrating wounds before they could be treated. Inability to detect the gangrene allowed the infected wounds to heal with the bacteria trapped inside. It killed the tissue around the wound and, if left unchecked, was a victim's death sentence. Once diagnosed, the treatment of choice was to literally fillet the infected body part. The open incision exposed the bacteria to the air, thereby killing it. Later in the fighting, lack of time for the open-air treatment resulted in hasty amputations, often the only way to save a man's life.

The Japanese were well aware of the suffering occurring in the American camp. Their soldiers were sick, too, although they were continually resupplied with food, medical items, and ammunition. Homma's chief of staff suggested that they simply allow disease and hunger to take their toll on the American and Filipino troops, eventually forcing them to surrender. But Homma wanted a definitive military solution.

As if armed with superhuman fortitude, the Americans and Filipinos fought on. One group intercepted a Japanese suicide squadron and chased them into dense brush. Some Japanese dug into foxholes while others tied themselves up in trees to serve as snipers. The Americans drew within 125 yards, and the captain gave the Japanese one last ultimatum: "Surrender, you bastards, we've got you surrounded!" An answer was shouted back in perfect English: "Nuts to you, Joe!" A short time later, the Americans had eliminated the suicide squadron and returned to their unit unscathed.

Toward the end of March, Bataan began to die. And Corregidor was beginning to feel the effects of a relentless enemy. Out of the small contingency of aircraft usually on the island, only one P-40, beaten up and wired together, remained. President Roosevelt had ordered that MacArthur leave Corregidor for Australia. There he would reorganize the Allies to go on the offensive against the Japanese. The ship carrying MacArthur also carried mail from the defenders of Corregidor. All troops were ordered to write a letter home, but one man protested saying he had no one to write to. His petty officer told him he better write to someone or his captain would let him have it. So the man wrote a note to President Roosevelt. "Dear Mr. President, Please send us another P-40. The one we've got is all worn out."

For fifteen days after that, the Japanese struck with everything they had. The filth, disease, and death the Allied troops withstood rapidly turned young men old. The seventy-eight thousand who remained in the steaming jungles were well on their way to starvation long before they even thought about becoming prisoners of war.

On April 3, Good Friday, Homma attacked the American lines for five consecutive hours with artillery fire and air power. Under MacArthur's orders, General Wainwright, who, in the wake of MacArthur's departure, was now in charge of the troops, ordered counterattacks. A general of lesser rank, General King, however, realized that prolonging the fight would do nothing more than increase the casualty rate. He disobeyed Wainwright's orders and capitulated on April 9. General Homma had secured a victory, but it had cost him three thousand Japanese soldiers' lives, with another five thousand wounded.

Homma demanded that General Wainwright now surrender all of the Philippines, including the last stronghold, Corregidor. Wainwright refused and Homma was furious. He was already in disgrace in Japan because he was well past his predicted victory date of February. The Japanese commander was ultimately returned to Tokyo where he sat out the rest of the war. But not before he exacted some revenge.

His first act was to proclaim that since Wainwright had refused a complete surrender, the Bataan defenders would not be treated as prisoners of war but rather as captives. This differentiation meant that their treatment was brutal at best, and more often ruthless and inhumane. On April 9, with reinforcements newly arrived from Japan, Homma took his second act of revenge. He began a bombardment of Corregidor of staggering proportions.

For over twenty-seven days straight, one hundred pieces of heavy artillery shelled the Rock with an estimated 1.8 million pounds of shells, turning it into a desolate wasteland. The Japanese then began making landings on the northeast end of the island. They faced heavy resistance but were able to establish a beachhead that was soon reinforced with tanks and artillery.

A radio operator hidden somewhere on Corregidor tapped out this final message on May 5:

> . . . Lots of heavy fighting going on. We may have to give up by noon. We don't know yet. They are throwing men and shells at us and I feel sick at my stomach. . . . They bring in the wounded every minute. We will be waiting for you guys to help. . . . The jig is up. Everyone is bawling like a baby. They are piling dead and wounded in our tunnel. I know now how a mouse feels. Caught in a trap waiting for guys to come along and finish it up.

The same night, a pilot arrived who had volunteered to make the last night flight to Corregidor with badly needed medical supplies. He urged Wainwright to leave with him. But the general replied, "I have been with my men from the start and if captured I will share their lot. We have been through so much together that my conscience would not let me leave before the final curtain. . . ."

Twenty-four hours later, on May 6, 1942, General Wainwright radioed Homma asking for terms, hoping to surrender only those forces on Corregidor. Homma refused the partial surrender and General Wainwright called for all troops in the Philippine archipelago to lay down their arms.

*   *   *

While the fight for the Philippines raged on, the Japanese kept Myers and the other Americans at Santa Escolastica in Manila. The American sentries were removed from around the walls of the buildings and replaced with Japanese. All Americans were ordered to remain inside the compound and not loiter near the walls. Piece by piece, the Japanese confiscated radios, automobiles, and eventually every bit of medical equipment the Americans had risked their lives to pluck from the destruction of Canacao. They also took all of the quinine, used for the treatment of malaria.

As the civilian patients became well enough to be released, the Japanese allowed them to return to their homes. Americans were moved to other locations, although no one within the hospital knew where they were taken. And while the enemy was not particularly friendly, neither was he the devil decked out in khaki that they had expected. Some semblance of military life was allowed to continue, including rank advancements, and Myers was made pharmacist's mate second class.

By May 9, the total patient census at Santa Escolastica was twenty, with the staff numbering about thirty. Everyone else had been taken into Japanese custody. At 0945 hours, two Japanese officers and a doctor arrived. They told the Americans that the hospital facility was too good for them and they were ordered to leave quickly.

Myers heard the officers assure the American doctors that they were being moved to a well-equipped facility, but nothing could have been further from the truth. They were marched about a mile and a half to Pasay Elementary School. The school, filthy and undersized for the number of men, quickly became overcrowded. There was little food and even fewer medical supplies. On May 30, the entire Pasay population was again moved—this time to Bilibid Prison in Manila. On that date, of the 475 hospital corps assigned to the Asiatic Station on December 7, 1941, 265 were dead, missing, or on prisoner lists. This was a disheartening statistic in this tempestuous contest of strength and will.

Chapter Seven

★

Bushido

Myers had excelled in Hospital Corps School in Norfolk, Virginia. Several years earlier, he had pored over the Hospital Corps handbook, memorizing treatments that would be vital during time of war.

> . . . Assess wounds quickly and treat the most life-threatening first. . . . Whenever possible, patients should be stabilized with plasma, a blood-volume expander, to prevent or treat shock. . . . If a wounded man is in pain, administer morphine. . . . In the case of a head injury, sulfanilamide crystals should be sprinkled on the wound in lieu of morphine. . . .

Like other corpsmen, Myers learned how to operate x-ray units, could serve as a preventive medicine or lab technician, act as a dental assistant, and perform tasks usually reserved for nurses. Along with studying, he simultaneously served as acting petty officer of his class. So impressed were his superiors that they recommended he be considered petty officer material upon graduation.

Sadly, very little of this knowledge was of any use in the hospital at Old Bilibid Prison during the summer of 1942. There were few supplies, even fewer pharmaceuticals, and thousands of sick and dying men. What remained of the original staff at Canacao Naval Hospital had arrived at Bilibid Prison to find twelve thousand defiled, diseased men in a place designed to hold four thousand. The hospital patients' horror stories about the final days on Corregidor and the Bataan Death March stunned Myers. Caring for them, as well as worrying about his own survival, weighed heavily on his mind.

Old Bilibid Prison stood like a giant concrete box at the corner of Azcarraga Street and Quezon Boulevard in downtown Manila, about two miles from the port area. It had been built by the Spanish a century earlier as a penitentiary but was declared unfit for criminals in 1939, when inmates were transferred to New Bilibid at Muntinglup, south of Manila. The Japanese reopened the old prison after the fall of Manila for use as a POW processing facility. From there, prisoners were dispersed to the penal colonies and work camps in the Philippine provinces. Throughout the war, the population of Bilibid varied, but it was always well over its normal occupancy rate.

The prison compound was square, with 600-foot-long, 15-foot-high side walls topped with 2,300-volt wires. Inside the walls, eleven single-story buildings radiated from a large central building like the spokes of a wheel. The Japanese used only half of these 200-foot-long, 50-foot-wide "spokes" for POW housing and hospital wards. A twelve-foot wall ran through the middle of the compound, dividing it into two sections. The Japanese topped this wall, as well as its perimeter, with high-voltage wire and machine-gun posts, making escape highly unlikely.

At first, part of the prison compound was used to house Filipino civilians while the Americans were kept in the west sector. The POWs' barracks had barred windows, resembling a zoo but allowing for light and air circulation. The buildings had little insulation, though, and the roofs of some of them had been damaged in the bombing of Manila. They were partially repaired with whatever was on hand, such as strips of tin and even cardboard. The makeshift roofs were no match for the torrential downpours of the Philippine rainy season. They leaked constantly, adding to the sewer-like feeling and smell of the place. The concrete floors and walls remained damp, making an ideal breeding ground for disease-carrying mosquitoes and roaches.

In general, sanitary conditions were nonexistent: all of the plumbing, as well as the lighting, had been stripped when the rat-infested hulk of a building was condemned. Straddle trenches, dug to a minimum depth, soon overflowed and were full of maggots. The prisoners' morale quickly disintegrated and an atmosphere of hopelessness hung thick in the air, along with the latrines' stench.

The prison grounds had a variety of ancillary buildings. The main hospital building was in the center of the prison compound, south of the guardhouse. Less critical patients and transients stayed in what had previously been a two-story administration building. When overcrowding made it necessary, some of these men lived in the former prison hospital, which was also used as a dispensary. It was without a roof. An old chapel became an isolation ward. The prison's smallest building was the old execution chamber. The Japanese never used it, although they never let the prisoners forget it was there.

The rules for POWs that had been in place at Pasay were enforced at Bilibid as well. They were typed in English and posted around the prison camp. The rules ranged from irritating to deadly:

Anyone trying to escape will be shot. If he escapes, all other men will be shot. Anyone trying to communicate with persons on the outside will be shot. Men notifying a Japanese sentry of anyone trying to escape will be rewarded!

All Japanese sentries and soldiers will be saluted at all times except when men are working. Officers and Room-masters will be saluted at all times.

Sick men will notify their Room-master of their ailments. He will turn in a list to the officer each night with the name, room number, prison number, and ailment of each man concerned. . . . Men feigning sickness will be severely punished by the Japanese authorities.

Violations of the above orders will be punished according to the seriousness of the offence committed.

It was the bowing and scraping to these repulsive enemies that most infuriated Myers. All POWs, regardless of rank, were expected to salute or bow to all Japanese soldiers. American generals and colonels, men whom Myers admired for their strength and leadership, had to salute Japanese privates or face brutal and sometimes fatal consequences. Additionally, POWs in all the camps were divided by rank. Thus, with the exception of patients in the hospital, the officers were separated from their units. It was a derivation of the "divide and conquer" theory. The Japanese hoped it would cause confusion among the men and make escape or insurrection less likely.

Perhaps the greatest insult to Myers and the other medical personnel was the absolute disregard for any of the agreements the civilized world had made among themselves with regard to the rules of warfare. Under the Geneva Convention of 1929, the signatories agreed that should chaplains and medical personnel fall into the hands of the enemy, "they shall not be treated as prisoners of war." In addition, the convention established guidelines to insure the humane treatment of prisoners of war. But the Japanese were not signatories to this or any other agreement regarding warfare and had no intention of adhering to any such conventions.

The Japanese did, however, have tremendous pride in their navy—*kaigun,* they called it. They felt somewhat magnanimous toward other navies as well, even those of an enemy. Thus, when Myers and the rest of the naval staff from Canacao arrived at Bilibid, they were placed in charge of the prison hospital. The task before them was enormous. Initially, there were one hundred and sixty-two patients in the hospital. By June 7, the number had risen to two hundred and one. By the end of June, seven hundred and sixty patients were hospitalized.

The first order of business for the doctors and pharmacist's mates was to improve the sanitary conditions inside the buildings as well as in the camp in general. The monsoon season was at its peak, and the waste from the dysentery cases that filled the latrines soon ran over and mixed with the mud in the main compound. The Canacao staff dug new troughs and crude but workable urinals and latrines that even had a flush system constructed from large gasoline drums. When filled with water and overturned, the contents of the latrine was washed down the trough and into the camp's main drainage system.

Not every problem was solved as simply, though. The Japanese had furnished the camp barracks with three or four hundred wooden bunks covered with straw mattresses. These mattresses were heavily used in the hospital and the medical staff could never clean them off sufficiently between patients. They soon became filthy and crawled with vermin.

Medical supplies were practically nonexistent, and the staff had only been able to bring a few things with them. There was plenty of surgical equipment, but very little plasma, and only questionable methods of sterilization. The chief medical officers determined that only men in the direst need received surgery. Of the pharmaceuticals, quinine was in the greatest demand, used in the treatment of malaria. The Japanese provided an amount that would save the seriously ill, most of which had been confiscated from the Americans in the first place, but there was never enough for prophylactic use. Even the medical staff became victims of malaria, and Myers soon fell ill along with the others.

The hunger, filth, and illness struck Myers deeply. Even at his family's lowest point when they lost their farm, he had never witnessed the kind of hopelessness he encountered during those early days in Bilibid. One fact stood out with blazing clarity: the Japanese culture and history were so completely foreign to that of their Western prisoners that all of the enemy's actions were beyond comprehension.

A case in point arose from the ancient Japanese warriors of the eleventh and twelfth centuries. Known as the *bushi,* their doctrine espoused preparedness in all things, including one's own death. Willingness to die for one's lord was required.

When the American generals surrendered to the Japanese in order to save the lives of soldiers who surely would have been massacred had the fighting in the Philippines continued, the enemy was dumbfounded and then disgusted by what they perceived as an act of cowardice. The *bushi* believed that men who surrendered were men disgraced, unworthy of soldierly treatment. This philosophy became a code called *bushido* and was witnessed firsthand by the Allies immediately when Bataan capitulated.

Simultaneous with the capitulation, a new chief of staff arrived to serve under General Homma as he finished mopping up the Philippines. Colonel Masanobu Tsuji epitomized the American caricature of the Japanese: he was small of stature, bald, and bespectacled. He had an unwavering belief in his own immortality and claimed a direct line to Japan's minister of war, Tojo. Prior to his arrival in the Philippines, he had successfully led campaigns aiding in the capture of Malaya and Singapore. He had absolutely no tolerance for Japan's newly acquired prisoners of war in Bataan.

Tsuji believed that all prisoners should be executed, the Americans because they were colonialists and the Filipinos because they had betrayed their fellow Asians. Evidently convinced by this logic, a division staff officer phoned a Colonel Imai, who was involved in rounding up the Bataan prisoners, telling him: "Kill all prisoners and those offering to surrender." At the time, Imai was holding more than a thousand Filipino and American prisoners and demanded that the order be put in writing.

A similar order was received by a garrison commander in Bataan, a Major General Torao Ikuta. Another staff officer called Ikuta and told him that his own division was already executing prisoners. Ikuta also asked for a written order. There were other officers, however, who carried out Tsuji's oral instructions with no request for a written directive.

Similar ideals were reinforced by the *Japan Times & Advertiser* newspaper on April 28, 1942. It wrote of the white soldiers:

"They surrender after sacrificing all the lives they can, except their own . . . they cannot be treated as ordinary prisoners of war. They have broken the commandments of God, and their defeat is their punishment. To show them mercy is to prolong the war. . . . An eye for an eye, a tooth for a tooth. Hesitation is uncalled for, and the wrongdoers must be wiped out."

*   *   *

"My God, this is awful!" Myers' voice broke in frustration at the sight of all the filthy, gaunt men prostrate on the bare concrete floors. "The flies are walking in and out of these guys' mouths and across their eyeballs. They're just lying there, so weak they can't even swat 'em away."

Tarpy wiped off his hands and moved toward another patient. "The guy over there in the corner"—he nodded his head toward the man in question—"he's got a wound so full of gangrene you can smell his flesh rotting from twenty feet away."

"Hey, Doc," a feeble voice to Myers' left called. "Can you help my buddy here? He won't eat or drink anything. I been tryin' to help him, but I plumb ran outta juice, too."

Myers looked down at the man speaking and then at his friend on the floor next to him. The soldier who had spoken had huge sores on his lips, caked with blood. They looked like raisins to Myers.

"Sure thing, I got some water right here." Myers shooed at the flies and knelt down between the two men. "Where you guys been, anyway?"

"Bataan. We held out as long as we could. Damn Japs just kept comin'. We were on quarter rations; half the guys were real bad off with malaria and jungle rot of some kind. We kept waitin' for help, but it never came. General MacArthur went to Australia, General Wainwright went to Corregidor to replace him, and General King was in command in Bataan. He had to surrender before they massacred us all."

"How'd you get here?" Myers looked closely into the semiconscious soldier's eyes while his buddy continued.

"We marched. Stumbled, really. Japs lined us up and started us off before the ink was dry on the surrender papers. Anybody tried to rest got hit with a rifle butt if the Jap that hit 'em was in a good mood. If he wasn't, the soldier got shot or bayoneted. They were killin' us off left and right."

"Holy God!" Myers whispered. "How long did it take you to get here?"

"I dunno, about a week, I guess. They wouldn't let us stop. Nothing to eat or drink. I had some Australian potted meat called Camp Pie. Ate it before we took off. Tin can said it was mutton, but I think it was everything but horns and hooves. That's the last food I had the entire week, except for the grass and leaves I ate along the way."

A major who was strong enough to walk had been making the rounds, talking to his men. He stopped in front of Myers and the two patients on the floor. After listening for a few minutes, he picked up the story.

"Homma never figured on capturing so many. I heard he was expecting twenty-five thousand or so. And he expected we'd have our own rations and medical supplies. Shit, we left most of that behind while we were runnin' for our lives. Wasn't any twenty-five thousand soldiers, there was seventy-six thousand of us combined with the Filipinos. Japs didn't have any extra food or water. They told us not only were we worthless for surrendering, but dumb asses for trying to fight a war without any supplies."

The first man spoke again. "But that wasn't the worst of it, Major. What was worse was the way they treated us. They got a big laugh out of our suffering. It was like a game to them. Some of the guys were so weak to begin with they were zombies from the start. My buddy and me"—he motioned to the man Myers was examining—"we tried to help another fella who didn't look like he was gonna make it. Japs hit us both with rifles and kept screaming, 'Speedo, speedo!' The guy finally fell down and the Japs were all over him, stickin' him with their bayonets like they were checking a pork chop to see if it was done and laughin' their fool heads off."

As Myers talked to more of the nearly dead patients around him, more of the story began to unfold. They'd heard that Homma had planned to march the men nineteen miles at most. They'd stop in a town called Balanga, halfway up the peninsula, at a field hospital and from there be issued Japanese army field rations. Homma had arranged for two hundred trucks to take the men another thirty-three miles to San Fernando, where they'd have another field hospital. After that the prisoners would be carried by freight train the thirty miles to Capas, near Clark Field, and marched the final eight miles to a prison camp called O'Donnell. That was before Homma realized he'd captured so many demoralized, starving, and disease-ridden men.

The first staging area for the march, which the prisoners described as the Death March, was Balanga. Men poured into the town for days after the surrender and were herded into groups like cattle. The Japanese destroyed every semblance of command among the prisoners, just as they had done to the troops arriving at Bilibid. There was no shelter, no food, and no water.

"Men dropped over like dried twigs and the Japs didn't even care," one man told Myers. "I decided I just was not gonna die. I wanna get back to the States. But some of them other guys," he said shaking his head, "they said they figured this was only the beginning of bad times ahead. They just gave up the ghost right then and there."

Once the Death March got underway, the men packed the road to San Fernando, staggering step by step for the next ten days. Some groups were forced to make that entire march in a single nonstop ordeal, except for an occasional ten- or fifteen-minute halt. Other groups made overnight stops along the way.

"I seen a group of Jap guards come into the pens where they had us divided up," said one man with an enormous bayonet slash in his leg. "They'd herd out a group, drive 'em down to the beach of the river nearby, and make 'em stand in the burning sun six, maybe eight hours. Then they'd herd 'em up again and get 'em started on the march. It just made no sense what they was doin' and nobody could stop 'em."

A man with a broken leg told Myers, "Japs kept stopping us along the way and taking anything they wanted from us. They took watches and rings, anything that caught their eye. Some they let keep their mess gear, others didn't even have any to start with. No canteens, either."

One Marine sergeant told about seeing a soldier's body run over so many times by the trucks carrying Japanese guards that it was completely flattened into the dusty road. Another Marine had seen a

Japanese soldier cut off an American's ear with his sword. "The Jap stuffed the ear into the American's mouth and told the guy to eat it. Can you imagine that? Being made to eat your own ear? The guy started gagging and the Jap lost patience with him. He stabbed him a bunch of times with his sword and moved on."

"I started counting dead Americans I passed by the side of the road," an Army corporal said. "I lost count after I got to seventy-two. I don't know for sure, but I'll bet we lost a couple thousand men on that march."

Men were beaten for walking too slowly, for falling, and for being unable to get up. Sometimes they were beaten for no reason at all. Those who'd been wounded in the fighting prior to the surrender were ordered to march along with the uninjured ones. And if they were too weak to move, they were left behind to be executed by a Japanese cleanup squad.

By the time the march arrived at the halfway point to San Fernando, the men were desperate for food and water. If they tried to drink from muddy carabao wallows along the road or pull bark off a tree to eat it, the nearby guards mowed them down with rifle fire. Other guards didn't seem to mind if the men around them ate as long as they kept moving. In those groups it was a common sight to see men chewing on stalks of sugar cane torn from a field as they passed. In that way they were able to get both food and something to drink from the cane's juice.

Myers heard stories about men being kicked in the head and face by heavy Japanese boots, many to the point of death, and having their hands tied so tightly behind them that their circulation was cut off at their wrists. Men were stabbed with bayonets or shot, not fatally, but just enough to cause excruciating pain and misery. And all the while the Japanese guards jabbered commands in a language that was entirely foreign to their prisoners and therefore impossible to obey.

An Army corporal finished the story. "When we finally reached San Fernando, they took us to the town's train station and packed us into narrow-gauge boxcars. It was so hot and we were so dehydrated that any of the guys who'd had dysentery weren't even shittin'.

Nothin' in, nothin' out. Some of the guys in the back of the cars couldn't get any air at all and started to pass out."

Myers shook his head. The stories he'd heard were so horrible, he simply couldn't digest them. "Almighty God, what makes men do something like that to other men?" he asked no one in particular.

"These ain't other men, son," an older sergeant told him. "They're animals. The ones who could speak English screamed things at us like, 'Go you to hell!' and 'Yanks insult Nippon many times. Now we get even!' We didn't even know what they were talking about."

The sergeant wasn't far off base. Myers knew that many Japanese guards in general, especially prison camp guards, had come from the dregs of their society. Some had previously been prisoners themselves. Some were mentally unstable and couldn't pass the entrance requirements for any other type of work in the military. And some were half Chinese, called Taiwans. They were treated as inferiors by the "pure bloods" so they vented their shame and anger on the POWs. None of them wanted to be there. But the Japanese military chain of command was busy winning control of the Pacific and had neither the time nor the inclination to monitor the guards' behavior.

Myers had made the rounds in his little sector of the Bilibid hospital and was back near the man with the sores on his lips.

"So, Doc, what do you think about my buddy?" the first man asked. "Anything you can do for him?"

Myers knelt down next to the semi-conscious man again and shook his head. "He's in a pretty bad way and we don't have any medical supplies to speak of. He's burning up. I'd bet the farm he's got malaria. His fingers are shriveled; that means he's really dehydrated. Malnourished, too." Myers couldn't begin to fathom how most of these men were even still alive.

He looked around the room and said, "I'll see if I can find some quinine for the malaria, and we'll give him plenty of water. At least he's cleaned up some."

Tears welled up in the first man's eyes. "Thanks, Doc. I don't want him to die. I don't wanna die, either. We worked so hard to get here."

For the first time since he'd left his younger brothers and sister back in Kentucky, Myers remembered what it felt like to have some-one look up to you and count on you. He'd prodded his siblings through rough spots on many occasions. That might be what the young soldier in front of him needed.

"Now listen," Myers told him firmly, "nobody's gonna die. The way to keep you and your buddy alive is to just plan on living through it. You guys have made it this far; don't give up now. Besides, we're not gonna be here long. I'll bet the Yanks and tanks are already on their way."

The major had finished making his rounds and was standing be-side Myers again. Myers turned to him. "Guy over there told me they put you guys on a train. You come all the way to Manila in those box-cars?"

"Nope. They unloaded us at Camp O'Donnell. We stayed in that hellhole for a week until Corregidor surrendered. Then they brought us here."

Tex came by and handed some dampened rags to Myers, who asked him where the quinine supply might be. Tex told him that the corpsmen from Corregidor had brought some medical supplies with them. Myers went searching for the Corregidor contingent and didn't have far to go. This group seemed a little bit less physically abused than the group from Bataan, but no less haggard looking. A corpsman stood in the middle of another group of patients relating his story.

"So I arrive at Corregidor in this boat that's been runnin' supplies back and forth to Bataan. We dock, and there sits a black piano. There's a couple seamen standing around, arguing with a soldier. The soldier wants to put the piano on the boat headed for Australia. Says it's the general's piano and it's goin' to Australia with the general. I says to myself, 'Great—we're gettin' our asses kicked by the Japs and the general's takin' a pleasure cruise to Australia *with* his piano.'"

"I hate to break up the party," Myers interrupted. "Did you guys bring any quinine in with you from Corregidor?"

The corpsman pointed to a chief pharmacist's mate in the corner and continued regaling his patients with his stories. Myers headed toward the man the corpsman had indicated and got some quinine from him. He also found some ointment for the lip sores. He had no idea what time it was or even what day it was. He hoped his prediction about reinforcements coming to liberate them wasn't far from the truth.

"You aren't gonna believe what I just heard." Myers was laughing for the first time in a long time. It was August 1942 and he'd been at Bilibid for three months.

"One of the guys over there speaks a little Japanese. He said he overheard a Nip guard talking to another one about a letter he'd gotten from home. The guard's relatives were complaining. They were losing face because they couldn't brag about anyone in their family being killed in the war. The letter told the guard he'd better regain the family's honor by finding himself some fighting and die, or there'd be hell to pay when he got home."

"Damn, that gets me right here." Tex pointed to his heart. "What say we give the little fella a hand, boys."

"Wouldn't I like to," Tarpy muttered through gritted teeth. "You know, boys, I think it's gonna take our troops a couple of years to get back here. That's an awful long time. And I don't mind telling you guys, I'm scared."

"I'm scared, too, Tarpy," Myers said soberly. "The last orders we had were to carry on our hospital duties. I guess if we keep doing that, the time'll pass quicker."

Myers, Tex, and Tarpy were part of the main cadre of POW staff at Bilibid. Their chief medical officer told the corpsmen that when a fighting man is captured, he's through working for a while. But for a hospital corpsman, the work becomes even more taxing. Inconceivably, despite the workload and the oppressive fear that dwelt in all of them, they kept one another going, never relaxing the structure that is an integral part of a United States naval hospital.

For months, the prisoners and patients continued to flow in and out. They arrived from the province work camps near death, plagued with injuries, disease, and malnutrition. It was Myers' job, and that of the other medical personnel, to patch them up as best they could with their minimal medical supplies and an ever-diminishing food supply. Bilibid was nothing more than a human scrap yard, where the unusable remains of men were put back together into somewhat usable men who were returned to work details.

The Japanese insisted a daily schedule be followed without exception. Reveille was at 0600 with the morning muster—*bangou*, the Japanese called it—and ten minutes worth of exercise beginning at 0630. The men were given thirty minutes for breakfast at 0700, and at 0730 the work details formed for the day. Since Myers' work was in the hospital, he never left the camp. Other men based at Bilibid who weren't hospital patients worked on scavenging supplies for the Japanese among the rubble of Manila or working on the grounds of Bilibid. The medical staff created shifts that ran simultaneously to the other work details, plus they had a contingent of doctors and corpsmen on duty through the night as well. Lunch was taken at 1200 hours, and work resumed at 1300 hours and lasted until 1630. Dinner was at 1800 hours, and everyone was required to be back in the barracks at 2000 hours. No talking was allowed after 2100 hours and bed checks were taken. At sunrise, the whole process began again.

Men flowed in and out of Bilibid every week. One group, having recently arrived from the prison camp called Cabanatuan, talked about an experiment their medical staff had tried that seemed to meet with some success. A dose of yeast was given to those patients who suffered from vitamin B deficiencies. The corpsmen propagated the yeast using whatever bits of food they could find that contained sugar.

This gave Tex the idea to collect all the additional sugar foods he could find in the barracks and turn them into hooch.

"All we gotta do is add a little water and let it ferment," he told the men as he made the rounds, collecting the ingredients. "My daddy an' his daddy—shoot, my whole *family's* been doin' this for generations. Any man who donates gets a share of the finished product. The rest of 'em get a swig only for life-saving medicinal purposes."

Tex found a couple of unused demijohns. The large, short-necked bottles had previously held alcohol or other liquid supplies, and he now stuffed them full of the fruit-sugar-water mixture. A few weeks later, he pronounced it ready for consumption. It was the first drinking liquor the men had tasted in ages and it tasted pretty good. The episode also escalated Tex's image in the eyes of his fellow prisoners. Innovation was a highly admired trait amid so much deprivation.

For the most part, though, Myers' days flowed one into another, caring for men who, once they were well and moved back to their respective prison camps, he'd likely never see again. One day Myers was helping a patient who had suffered a raging, malaria-induced fever. While the man ate his meager morning ration of rice gruel, they swapped stories.

"Where were you when the war broke out?" Myers asked him.

"Olongapo."

"I had a friend at Olongapo. Name of Stover. He was a pharmacist's mate, too. Ever hear of him?"

"You know, Doc, I'd only been there a few days when the Japs attacked. I didn't know very many guys. It was a real pretty little mountain village before they bombed the hell out of it. If your friend was anywhere near the bay area, he wouldn't have had better than a fifty-fifty chance of making it."

"Another seaman I met comin' over from the States was one of the guys ordered to report to Pearl Harbor. I've wondered if he made it out okay, too."

"That's the crummy thing about war," the patient said feebly. "You meet people, and then you never see them again. You start workin' on something, and then you get sent someplace else. You never get a chance to see things through to the end; you never get a chance to see how things turn out."

The men who passed through Bilibid talked about the deterrents to escape used in the other camps. Men were arranged in groups of ten, which became known as execution squads. Each man was responsible to the others; if one escaped, the other nine would be executed in reprisal. Often when group executions did take place, the men were forced to dig their own graves and kneel over them, whereupon their heads were cut off with the razor-sharp samurai swords. The heads would tumble into the hole, soon followed by their bodies.

The stories of Japanese brutality never ceased to amaze the medical staff. One man described having his hands tied behind his back and his eyes blindfolded. The guards, *tai-sas,* the Japanese called them, burned him with cigarettes and branding irons. All the while the camp commander and the other *tai-sas* watched and laughed.

But the incessant squalor and lack of food seemed to be killing more men than anything else. An air corps pilot newly arrived from Cabanatuan told Myers that in one day alone, he knew of sixty men who had died.

"The fellas on the burial detail were so weak," the pilot told him, "that they weren't able to dig the graves very deep. As soon as the rainy season started, those shallow graves turned into mud holes and the corpses rose to the top. Like a big jumble of arms and legs and skulls, some of 'em partially decomposed."

Another place Myers heard about was called Tayabas, a town eighty miles or so southeast of Manila. The Japanese were forcing the POWs to build a road through the swampy jungle outside of town. Most men volunteered for work details outside of their camps, hoping that the treatment might be improved.

"We had to live in a river bottom. It rained constantly," a cadaverous soldier who'd been on the Tayabas detail told Myers one day. "We knew the river water was polluted because the Japs watered their horses upstream from us. But we had nothing else to drink or cool off with. The place was thick with mosquitoes and flies. We had no medical supplies and nothing to keep the rain off us. Guys had pneumonia and malaria and dysentery. You name it. The Japs sent about two hundred fifty of us down there. Me and a hundred and fifty other guys made it out alive."

In the first months, it was hard to fill the little free time the men were given. But one day during August of 1942, a volleyball appeared in camp. When the Japanese made no move to confiscate it, someone brought out a basketball, and another guy produced a baseball. As each ball appeared, teams were formed, courts and infields were crafted, and the games began.

Myers had been athletic all his life. His natural ability made him one of the guys everyone wanted in a game. Occasionally, the prison guards would come to watch. That was when the prisoners had the most fun. The Japanese had no comprehension of any of the rules of the games, and weren't sufficiently proficient in English slang to understand the hooting and hollering along with ball playing. The prisoners took full advantage of these opportunities to shout crude insults, seemingly at one another. The insults' real targets, however, were the guards themselves. It seemed this was one of the few chances the POWs had to vent their rage and loathing for the enemy.

Another great deception that occurred at Bilibid was the product of a prisoner who was a former ham radio operator. He crafted a radio inside a box beneath the seat of a short stool. The creation was a painstaking operation, as each part of the radio was pilfered from under the Japs' noses. The power source was flashlight batteries, taken out of lights given to the American officers who were forced to make nightly bed checks. The Japanese were forever trying to understand why the batteries wore out so quickly, which was the line the officers gave them.

The radio operator listened to the news surreptitiously on San Francisco station KGEI almost every night. When a new draft of POWs would arrive from another camp, he'd mention some news items to a few of them. They'd spread the word to others, and everyone, including the guards who might have understood bits and pieces, thought the new men had brought the stories in with them. That was how Myers and the others heard about some of the battles that were turning the tide of the war.

CHAPTER EIGHT

★

Protein for Nicotine

By August 1942, the Americans interned at Bilibid Prison had pretty well pieced together the story of the destruction wrought on Pearl Harbor by the Japanese. Between the POWs who had received direct radio information that day and those who had brought supplies to the Philippines from Australia prior to the capitulation, the story they had was that America had been caught flat-footed and a great deal of the Pacific Fleet was sunk or damaged.

"But ain't it great them Japs didn't get our carriers?" Tex chuckled. "And one of these days, they're gonna catch hell from us."

Myers and the rest were listening to the rehash of December 7 one night before lights out. They nodded in silent agreement.

"My grandmother used to say 'revenge is a dish best eaten cold,'" one of the men nearby said softly.

"What's that supposed to mean?" Tarpy asked him.

"It means, stupid, that sometimes you gotta wait to get back at somebody. But if you get 'em good, it was worth the wait," the man replied.

Another voice spoke up in the darkening barracks. "I heard we got revenge."

Replies of "The hell you say!" and "You're nuts!" rumbled around.

"Yeah, and we heard a month or so ago that the Japanese had

shelled the Washington and Oregon coasts," Tex said. "You gonna tell me you believe that, too?"

"Hey, don't get mad at me, buddy," the voice replied. "I'm just the messenger. But I heard it on pretty good authority. And from a couple guys pretty high up, too. There wouldn't be any reason for 'em to lie."

This was met with a considerable number of opinions as well, none of them very positive. But a few men, including Myers, encouraged the man to spill what he knew.

"What I heard about happened at Midway Island. It's fifteen hundred miles from Pearl and twenty-four hundred miles from Tokyo. So it's midway between the two.

"It don't take no genius to figure out that Midway's important to both sides. We've got a beefed-up base there to defend against another attack on Hawaii or someplace else in the United States. The Japs saw it as a stepping stone for pullin' off just that kind of attack."

At about the same time that Myers and the others had arrived at Bilibid, Japanese reconnaissance had determined that the American fleet was so crippled from the surprise attack of December 7, that it would be a very long time before most of their ships would be seaworthy. The Japanese submarines sent to scout the repair operations in Hawaii confirmed the fact that there were no carriers, nor anything else of significance being prepared to re-enter the war. They concluded that the time had come to take Midway. What the Japanese didn't know was that the subs' reports had come too late. The U.S. carrier task forces were already at sea.

American intelligence had discovered that the Japanese were planning an attack somewhere. There were several possibilities, and Midway seemed likely, but all the American cryptanalysts in Pearl Harbor could discern for certain from decoded Japanese radio traffic was that the location had been given the code name "AF." So the Americans deliberately set a trap, sending a message they knew would be intercepted by the Japanese. The message related a water shortage on Midway. Japanese radio responded by reporting on the same water shortage, substituting the code name AF for Midway. That was the confirmation American Admiral Chester Nimitz was looking for. He got a bonus when the cryptanalysts were also able to come up with an approximate timetable for the attack.

Nimitz and his staff guessed at the size of the fleet the Japanese would use. Judging from the importance of Midway, they surmised the enemy would commit just about everything he had. Nimitz had fewer ships than the Japanese in every category except for the most important category of warfare: aircraft. The Japanese had four carriers with a total of 272 aircraft, while Nimitz had three carriers with 233 planes and another 115 aircraft on Midway Island itself.

The Japanese planned a diversionary battle off the Aleutian Islands, the object being to draw the Americans away from Midway. But Nimitz was aware of this diversion and wasn't fooled into sending his entire fleet elsewhere. When an American seaplane happened to spot the enormous fleet twenty-six hundred miles west of Midway, the Japanese thought it was just bad luck. But that wasn't the case at all; Nimitz had ordered that sweeping searches be made and he deployed his two task forces under Admirals Spruance and Fletcher to meet the Japanese armada.

The morning of June 4, 1942, a thick fog hid the Japanese strike force approaching the island. At 0430, Japanese search planes were ordered out for final intelligence. The catapult on one of the carriers was malfunctioning and her planes went out thirty minutes later. The consequence of this delay was that the American carriers were within the area that those planes were supposed to survey. Once the battle began, it raged for three days, and the two fleets never got within a day's sailing distance of one another. Nearly the entire clash was fought by aircraft. Through planning, courage, error, and pure chance, the Americans prevailed. The Japanese suffered an enormous defeat and lost four carriers and a heavy cruiser.

When the voice in the darkness paused, Myers asked him, "You're not pullin' our legs, are you, pal?"

"Nope," came the answer.

"Damn, then maybe they're on their way to get us right now," Myers said.

The thought buoyed him and some of the other POWs. But there were those who had begun to give up. More disease had hit the camp, including the highly contagious dengue fever. Besides backache and headache, dengue also causes mental depression and a loss of appetite. Men who gave up and wouldn't eat were then more susceptible to other diseases, if the dengue didn't get them first.

Every day the hospital corps seemed to be getting a new lesson in epidemiology. Many of the diseases were brought on from nutritional deficiencies. Thiamin deficiency caused "wet" beriberi, from which men's legs would balloon before the swelling would move to other body parts, potentially damaging vital organs. Then came "dry" beriberi, which caused their legs to ache and nerve endings, particularly in the feet, to give them shocking jolts each time they touched anything. Lack of niacin also caused pellagra, a disease that began as a skin rash and a blackened tongue, then progressed to include diarrhea and dementia, and often even death. The men lacked vitamin A, too, which caused night blindness, corneal scarring, and in extreme cases, complete blindness. The absence of riboflavin brought about dry, cracked skin and light sensitivity in the eyes.

The hardest part of all this for Myers and the rest of the medical staff was that they were absolutely powerless to do anything to help these wretched men. They had no drugs to treat disease, and they weren't certain whether the Japanese had any, either. But they were certain that the Japanese had more food than the prisoners were being given. Most of these diseases were related to nutrition, and with just a little more food many of the men Myers pronounced dead could have been saved.

Their diet consisted of a cup of putrid, boiled rice for breakfast, while another cup of rice and a bowl of mucus-like rice soup, called *lugao,* was doled out for lunch and again for dinner. The rice stunk; it was moldy and combined with stones and the floor sweepings from warehouses. The stones played havoc with the men's teeth. The rice was rolled out to them from the central galley in fifteen-gallon gasoline tins.

Occasionally, a few greens were thrown in with a meal, and only rarely were spoiled carabao meat or fish added. The Japanese never cleaned the fish; they fried them up whole. Initially, the POWs tried to pick out the bones, but when hunger overcame them they ate the entire fish.

Myers, Tex, and Tarpy contracted all the diseases at one time or another. So did the rest of the medical staff. When one fell sick, the others picked up the slack in the workload until the man who was ill could return to his duties. The extra work usually exhausted the others so much that one of them would fall ill next, and the never-ending circle continued.

The inhumanity continued as well and Myers witnessed most of it. One day, Tarpy was ordered to go over sick reports with one of the Japanese guards. According to Imperial standards, a man was only sick if he was unable to work or in danger of dying. The Japanese accused the Americans of deliberately playing sick so they could get out of their work details.

The meeting was held in the hospital ward where Myers and several others of the medical staff were working. It started out with Tarpy bowing to the guard as was required before he was invited to sit down on a cot. The guard sat down next to him. Tarpy began to go through the reports when suddenly the guard pointed at a line and jumped up. Tarpy jumped up, too, as regulations demanded and stood at rigid attention. The guard hauled back and slapped Tarpy across one cheek and then the other. Then without a word he sat down, and Tarpy followed. The report reading continued for a few minutes and the scenario was repeated. The guard jumped up, Tarpy jumped up, the guard slapped both his cheeks, and they both sat down again.

Myers could see the hatred in Tarpy's eyes, but he gave the man credit. Tarpy never made a move against the guard. To do so would have meant possible death. The hospital staff dealt with the aftermath of punishments to their fellow POWs every day. Tarpy wisely restrained himself so as not to be added to the list.

One of the few elements of normal life the Japanese allowed the prisoners was the ability to hold regular religious services. They were conducted at several different times on Sundays so that those on work detail would be able to attend after they had finished for the day. The

Army and Navy chaplains took turns officiating, reading sermons that had to be written in advance and passed by Japanese censors.

At the end of August 1942 a new commandant arrived at the camp, a lieutenant by the name of Dr. Nogi. With him came the promise of better things, but for many men he hadn't come soon enough. Up until this point the Japanese guards exhibited schizophrenic behavior toward their prisoners. Most of the time they were monsters, exercising horrors unknown to soldiers captured in other parts of the world. The variety and extent of the Japanese brutality was something no soldier could have been prepared for. Prisoners were clubbed at the slightest infraction of rules. Sometimes large groups, regardless of their innocence, were hauled out to the prison yard at night and lined up for a mass beating. The men suffered shattered teeth, broken bones, lacerations, and humiliation.

Myers and others were forced to witness what they called the "water cure." A man who was thought to deserve punishment was stretched out on the ground with a rubber tube shoved down his throat. A cask of water was emptied into the tube until the man's abdomen became distended and water seeped out of his pores. At that point, a guard jumped up and down on the man's bare stomach until he was dead.

Eyes were gouged out and men were hung by their thumbs or their heels. And then there was the "hot plate." The prisoner was stripped and made to stand on a metal plate that had been wet down. The guards took turns pricking the man's flesh with live electrical wires.

There were a few Japanese who were almost humane, actually expressing feelings for the Americans' position. Myers overheard a doctor suggesting to a Japanese officer that the prison hospital needed better medical equipment. The Japanese officer replied, "You are unfortunate. You are the prisoners of a country whose living standards are much lower than yours. You will often consider yourselves mistreated, while we will think of you as being treated well."

Oftentimes, the ill treatment of the prisoners by the guards was due to a lack of communication. It became the duty of the corpsmen, including Myers, to report to the prison's front gate whenever a truckload of provisions arrived. One day, the corpsmen were late. The guards who had had to wait for them were livid, thinking the Americans had deliberately been slow, and beat them for it. The fault rested with the camp interpreter, a Japanese soldier named Herri. He was a low-class, rancorous brute, whose English was pitifully limited. He had given the prisoners the wrong information, which often happened. Then, to protect his own hide, he blamed the prisoners for being lazy.

So it was with good reason that the POWs hoped the new camp commandant might mean changes for the better. One night soon after Nogi's arrival, the men were sitting in their barracks, sweat pouring off their half-naked bodies. Manila had been built in a marsh. Along the city's outer edges, where Bilibid stood, the marsh and its humidity were more in evidence. Every time rain fell, as it had the day before, most of the prison flooded, with two to three feet of water remaining for days afterward.

"I don't know which is better"—Tex said, as he swatted a mosquito on his forearm—"having enough clothes so that you got the luxury of takin' 'em off when you're hot, or not havin' any so you don't have to bother takin' 'em off."

"Listen, sourpuss, we're gonna do some *quanning* tomorrow night," Myers told him. "That oughta cheer you up some."

Quan was the Japanese word for stew. The POWs took grammatical liberties and concluded that *quanning* would be the word used for making the stew. That led to the holding of *quan* parties, which occurred when several groups shared their *quans* with one another. Desperate for something to look forward to, some kind of diversion from the incredible monotony of their lives, the *quan* parties became as important to them as their first stolen kiss had been at a Saturday matinee.

"I swear, Myers, you're the happiest son of a bitch I ever met. I could hit you in the head with a rifle butt and you'd be glad 'cause I didn't hit you with a bullet instead."

"Hey, somebody's gotta keep a smile on your ugly mugs!" Myers defended himself.

The men launched into a discussion of what each had to add to the *quan*. Early on in their imprisonment, a "store" had begun operating inside the camp. The prisoners could buy items like beans, garlic, or bananas to add to their *quans*. The POWs sold their remaining personal items—those that the Japanese hadn't taken when they were captured—to get a little cash and then bought what they could afford. The Japanese weren't happy about the store; they felt they lost face by not giving the prisoners enough to eat. So the prisoners explained that the store was actually operating to provide supplemental nourishment to the sick, and that made the captors feel better about it.

Demand soon outgrew the supply. Prices rose and most prisoners were unable to afford much of anything and the store quietly died. After that, the men tried cooking and eating any vegetation they could find, including *kang-kong,* calla lilies. Although it was generally recognized that they contained no food value, like so many trivial things, they made life a little different.

The men's conversations next turned to another favorite topic, memories of home.

"You know, I was a pretty good cook back home," Myers told his buddies. "When my mother would go off to tend to Mammy Klinglesmith, that was my grandmother's name, she'd leave me in charge of making the family meals."

"Yeah, so what do you know how to make?" Tex asked him.

"Well, I know one thing I don't know how to make well and that's rice. I can't believe we actually ate the stuff of our own free will, but that was a long time ago. Anyway, I'd seen my mother make it and figured I could do it, too. We were havin' pork chops for dinner and I thought some rice would go good with it. I filled a kettle with water and put it on the stove. Then I took the sack of rice and poured some in.

"Well, that rice looked pretty puny in the bottom of the kettle and I didn't think I had enough. So I added some more, and then I added just a little bit more. I figured if there was any left from dinner, we could have it for breakfast. Well, that water started boilin', and the rice started to swell up. It rose up to the top of that kettle like a volcano and started spillin' everywhere."

The men were smiling now. "What did you do?" Tarpy asked him.

"Well, I got another pot and then another. My brother Kenny came into the kitchen just then, so I had him fetch anything he could find to put this rice in."

Their group had gotten larger, and now all the men were laughing at the mental image of this Myers being swallowed up by an avalanche of rice.

"We had rice comin' out our ears. I didn't dare throw any of it away. Daddy would have skinned me alive for wasting food. So we ate rice for every meal for a week. Every time I heated it up, it swelled some more. We couldn't even get the dog to eat it. Guess I shoulda known there was gonna be rice in my future."

More laughs and chuckles from the group around Myers. "Hey, Myers!" one of the Army privates piped up. "You think our rice would swell up if we heated it up?"

"Son," an Army doctor in the group spoke up. "This rice wouldn't swell up if Betty Grable herself walked by."

This was followed by hoots and shouts from the other men.

"Rita Hayworth!"

"Lana Turner!"

"Sorry, boys," the doctor told them. "Your sex drive takes a back seat when you're not getting enough to eat. I doubt one of us could get it up, even if we wanted to."

Tex nodded. "Ya know, Doc, the funny thing is I'd rather think about food than sex these days. My mama's specialty is chicken fried steak. She'd take a great big old slab 'a T-bone, flour it up, and fry it in this big ol' iron skillet, then she'd whip up some potatoes and pour sausage gravy all over everything on your plate."

"My mother makes the world's best biscuits and gravy," Myers told his pals. "And once Christmas comes, she'll start making her peanut butter fudge. It melts away in your mouth."

"Every time I eat some of that mashed up *camote* I pretend it's my mama's mashed potatoes," Tex commented.

"What are those?" one of the prisoners who had recently arrived from another camp asked.

"*Camotes*? Why, they're kinda like yams. We got a garden out back outside the execution chamber."

The new man looked surprised.

"Japs don't use the execution chamber," Myers told him. "Anywhere in the camp works just as well."

Tex continued. "Anyway, we grow *mongo* beans, little pea-sized beans, and okra and a little corn. Used to have some ducks, too. Japs ate some of 'em, but the rest just up and died."

The men thought about this for a while.

"Hey, who's got a smoke?" Myers asked. One of the men produced a Philippine cigarette made from *picadura*, which was locally grown, loose tobacco. Often the men got handouts through holes in the prison wall from the Filipinos on the outside. Sometimes they'd get cigarettes, other times some coffee or a tin of meat. The prisoners had to be extremely careful; if the guards caught them communicating with the outside, a severe beating was sure to follow. But the risk seemed worth it. These items had tremendous bargaining power, depending upon the camp's market situation at any given time. Even after the camp store shut down, trading went on between the prisoners, and sometimes the guards even got in on the act.

Men had to be careful, though. It was one thing to trade an occasional helping of rice for a cigarette, but some men traded it routinely. Soon, trading "protein for nicotine" made them too weak to smoke or eat. Their next stop after that was the Zero Ward, the part of the hospital where men were taken to die.

Another commodity the POWs used for trading with the guards were medical drugs. The Imperial Army took its own prostitutes on their campaigns for a little relaxation after a tough day at war. They did not, however, take along enough sulfa, the treatment of choice for VD. It was common knowledge among the prison hospital corps that nearly one hundred percent of the Bilibid guards had some form of venereal disease.

Dr. Nogi issued strict instructions that none of his guards were to use the Americans' medical supplies. But the enticement of treatment in exchange for cigarettes, coffee, or meat was too great for either side to resist, and the guards even fought one another for the privilege of stealing food to trade for drugs. This arrangement worked pretty well for the POWs until all the sulfa was gone.

So an enterprising ring of prisoners began creating fake sulfa tablets using some plaster of paris, sugar, and a little water. They combined the mixture in a carabao horn and poured it into molds made from .30-caliber shells, which were the appropriate size. They even stamped their tablets with a "W," for Winthrop Chemical Company, a drug firm familiar to the Japanese. One hundred and fifty tablets traded for nearly a bushel of *mongo* beans, providing the POWs with badly needed protein. An unknown number of men were saved because of the sale of the fake sulfa pills.

In the spring of 1943, a day arrived that Myers and his pals had been looking forward to. It was *yasumu,* the one day a week that the guards didn't force everyone to work. A day of liberty was a small blessing in their pitifully sorry lives, but this one was special. This *yasumu* was also Tarpy's birthday, and they'd planned a special breakfast for themselves in honor of the occasion.

The *bangou* bell rang as it did every morning and the men fell out. *Bangou* was a check by numbers. At all times each man wore a three-by-five-inch wooden placard bearing his prisoner number painted in red. Since numbers are the same in Japanese and English, it made *bangou* easier to facilitate. And the Japanese loved to call a *bangou,* going through the exercise several times a day for no obvious reason that the prisoners could see.

Although the sun was not yet up when the bell rang on this particular day, the Japanese took so long with their inspection of the prisoners that it had risen by the time they'd finished. Steam rose from the damp ground as soon as the sun hit it. Finally the men were dismissed to enjoy their tiny bit of liberty.

The bill of fare for Tarpy's celebration included pancakes, syrup, and coffee. Of course, achieving this feast required a little resource-fulness and a lot of imagination. The pancake flour was made from rolling a bottle over uncooked rice and pulverizing it. One of them had a culture of yeast growing in a bucket, and they added a little to the flour along with some water. They had arranged to use the grid-dle in the camp galley and while Myers cooked, Tarpy heated up water to melt their precious stash of sugar for syrup.

Meanwhile, Tex was in charge of procuring the coffee. He had saved up enough money to buy coffee from a hospital patient who had made it his cottage industry. The patient bought the grounds from the guards and made five-gallon drums of coffee every day, usu-ally early in the morning before sunrise. He then sold it to the other POWs for whatever he could get, always pricing it so that he could make a small profit plus renew his raw materials. The entrepreneur also merchandized tobacco, and he kept both commodities in iden-tical tins saved from Red Cross boxes.

By the time Tex returned with their coffee, Myers and Tarpy had finished their cooking, and the three sat down to their feast. They all bit into the pancakes and congratulated themselves on the flavor. Be-ing gray-beige in color and paper-thin, they weren't much to look at. They then moved on to the coffee, taking small sips so that it would last as long as possible. Tarpy noticed the flavor immediately.

"Hey, what is this stuff? Whatta ya trying to do to a guy?"

Within seconds, Myers' and Tex's taste buds had caught up.

"Jesus, Mary, and Joseph! This stuff tastes like shit!" Tex sput-tered, examining the brown liquid and the small bits of something that had now floated to the surface.

"My God!" Myers choked. "This is awful!"

"Well, if that mooch thinks he's gonna get away with this, he's got another think comin'!" Tex jumped up off the floor and headed toward the hospital barracks.

The entrepreneurial patient was right where Tex left him.

"Taste this and tell me what you're tryin' to pull, you son of a bitch!" Tex commanded.

The astonished patient took a timid sip and spat it out on the floor. He reached under his bed and pulled out his supplies, checking first one of the Red Cross tins and then the other. He looked up, dismayed.

"Keep your shirt on, pal. I'll give you your money back. But I'm out two ways, see? It was dark when I made the coffee. I grabbed the wrong tin and wasted perfectly good tobacco because I thought it was coffee. Now I gotta give everybody their money back for the coffee and I don't have any tobacco to sell, either!"

Tarpy's birthday celebration continued throughout the day until another *bangou* was called. This time the prisoners were ordered to listen to a visiting colonel who was going to deliver what the guards called "an education speech." The colonel, it turned out, was a propaganda officer with an absurd-looking handlebar mustache. He unrolled a large painting, a panorama of the Japanese destruction of Pearl Harbor. The painting was punctuated with a great number of orange explosions, black smoke, and red flames.

After the colonel gave the men a toothy smile, he spoke in English. "You haf no more a Navy. It is utterly destroyed. What do you think of your future now? There is not the slightest hope of anything but total defeat now for your armed forces."

The colonel's comments were met with silence. After forcing the POWs to stand in the yard for ten minutes of humiliation while the guards chattered in Japanese and laughed, pointing at the Americans, the men were allowed to resume their *yasumu.*

"Okay, you guys," Myers told Tex and Tarpy. "Now it's our turn."

They walked over to where a particularly unpleasant guard they had nicknamed Bullet Head stood. This guard's moniker came from his misshapen cranium.

"So how's the war going, Bullet Head?" Myers asked him.

"War's going," Bullet Head answered. "You see picture. Nippon winning. All American Navy gone boom, boom."

Now came the fun part for the prisoners. The part where they ridiculed the guard's obvious lack of command of English.

"Is that so?" Myers said thoughtfully. "You mean to tell me the USS *Hornet* is gone?"

"*Hai,* boom, boom."

"And the USS *Enterprise?*"

"*Hai,* boom, boom."

"How about the USS Dumb Shit?"

"All boom, boom."

Myers walked away, his shoulders slumping in mock dejection. Meanwhile, everyone who'd witnessed the act worked hard at suppressing their laughter.

Now it was Tarpy's turn. He chose the hated interpreter, Herri.

"You ever hear of Mickey Mouse?" he asked the unsuspecting Japanese.

Herri furrowed his brow and shook his head. Tarpy continued.

"Oh, Mickey Mouse is an *ichiban* American movie star. Number one. I was just tellin' my pals that you look a lot like him."

"I look like *ichiban* American movie star?"

"You sure do. In fact, is it okay if we call you Mickey Mouse?"

Herri considered this. "*Ichiban* Mickey Mouse," he announced, proud of his new status. "*Hai!*"

Yasumu was also the day for taking care of things there never seemed to be enough time for during the other days. Tarpy's birthday or not, the men had washing and repairs to do. The uniforms they wore were no more than tattered rags. As the elbows and knees of their shirts and pants wore out, shorts and sleeveless shirts were made. Any surplus fabric was either used to make patches or unwoven at the frayed spots to make thread. Needles were fairly common in the hospital, but occasionally they had to rely on a sharp thorn to do the mending.

Those whose clothing had worn out entirely had two choices. They could wear Japanese-issue G-strings, resembling those worn by sumo wrestlers, or they could wait for hand-me-downs from the dead. Since clothing was at such a premium, the POWs were buried naked and their clothing was reissued to the living from the Zero Ward.

Shoes posed yet another problem. Whatever the men had been wearing at the time of their capture were the shoes they wore every day after that. When the shoes could no longer be repaired at the camp cobbler shop, the POWs graduated to *clacks,* homemade sandals. The sandals were wooden platforms with strips of old tires nailed on the bottom for traction and strips of leather from their retired shoes nailed across the top.

Most of the men had been accustomed to a simple wardrobe on the outside, before captivity. When they had enlisted, the country had been in the throes of the Depression and many things, including excess clothing, were considered unnecessary luxuries. Still, the list of what they missed from their American lives continued to grow.

Chapter Nine

★

Praise the Lord and Pass the Ammunition

Myers thought about his family every day he was in Bilibid Prison. Until he joined the Navy, he'd never been farther from home than a couple of hours' drive. Even after he enlisted, he felt connected to them, got letters from them, and wrote when he had a chance.

But as a POW he not only felt disconnected from freedom, but also from those he loved. He was sure his mother would be worried about him since she hadn't heard from him, and he made himself a promise that he would never let her know the details of this living hell. He figured the Navy had probably let her know he was a POW, but since neither he nor his fellow prisoners had received anything from the United States since they'd been captured, he wondered exactly how much his family knew. It bothered him immensely that he was probably causing them concern.

For their part, his parents, Lena Mae and Bertram Sr., knew from Estel's prewar letters that he had been relocated to the Philippines after his stint in Shanghai. When news of the initial Japanese attack on the islands reached them, they hoped that since their son was a part of the hospital corps, he would be transferred to an area away from the fighting to take care of fellow soldiers. When all the letters Lena Mae had written to Estel after the hostilities began in December were returned as undeliverable, she wrote to the 12th Naval District in San Francisco.

A response to her request for information arrived from the Navy Department on June 20, 1942. It was two weeks after the American victory at the Battle of Midway and the day before Father's Day.

My dear Mr. and Mrs. Myers,

This Bureau regrets that definite report cannot at this time be made regarding the welfare of your son, Estel Browning Myers, but feels you are entitled to the available facts.

On last report, he was serving in the Manila Bay Area and since the capitulation of the last defense in that area, no word has been received by the Department concerning the personnel. It is presumed that they became prisoners, and as soon as possible will be interviewed by the International Red Cross and report made to this Bureau.

This Bureau appreciates your anxiety and hopes that your patience will extend to the time when definite assurance can be furnished. Until such definite assurance, he will be carried on the rolls as "missing."

Sincerely yours,
Rear Admiral Randall Jacobs
The Chief of Naval Personnel

This was extraordinarily difficult news to receive. Pure torture existed in the word "missing" for those who received such a letter. They did not know the whereabouts or condition of a loved one. It made their day-to-day lives arduous and their futures uncertain. The classification carried financial consequences, as well. Until a serviceman could be determined as deceased, family members were not eligible for back pay, insurance, or pensions.

When the Myers family received their letter, it gave a new meaning to the war efforts occurring around them. President Roosevelt had told Americans early on in the war that the efforts of every man, woman, and child would be needed in order to win the conflict that had now spread across the entire globe. Consequently, not one aspect of American society went untouched by patriotism and the war effort.

American automakers' assembly lines had come to a dead stop back in January of 1942; car and truck production was suspended and the factories were reconfigured. When the assembly lines began again, they turned out machines of war. Production requirements were astronomical: four thousand tanks and forty-five hundred planes had to be produced every month. Navy ships had to be assembled in seventeen days, once the parts were manufactured. Factories producing anti-aircraft guns were on track to turn out twenty thousand by the end of the year.

President Roosevelt had told the nation, "Let no man say it cannot be done. It must be done and we have undertaken to do it." Following that speech, he personally visited the production facilities around the country to encourage the workers. In Detroit, he toured the newly created Chrysler Tank Arsenal. In the suburb of Willow Run, Henry and Edsel Ford escorted him down their half-mile assembly line. In Milwaukee, Roosevelt watched steam turbines and propeller shafts being created at the Allis-Chalmers factory. In Seattle, he was taken to the Boeing aircraft plant and in Portland, to Henry Kaiser's shipyards.

Everywhere FDR went that year, workers cheered him for his leadership. But the cheers that greeted his words were not only from hardened male factory workers. There was a distinctive feminine note to these cheers. Nearly one third of the American workforce in 1942 were women, nineteen million of them in all. They had filled jobs in the tank, aircraft, and armament factories in the absence of the country's men.

The women were told that welding was not so very different from crocheting, and Winnie the Welder was born. Some of them learned to drive rivets at the astronomical rate of 275 in a twenty-seven-minute period, and Rosie the Riveter came into being. They were asked to do the job "he" left behind. They worked nine hours a day, six days a week, humming what had become their theme song: "Praise the Lord and pass the ammunition. Can't afford to sit around a-wishin'. Praise the Lord and pass the ammunition, and we'll all stay free."

The women's exodus to the factories caused a fashion revolution, as they became mass consumers of pants and overalls. To many, particularly those in the Bible Belt like the Myers family, wearing slacks was something only hussies had done previously. But frilly dresses didn't play well in the factory. Major department stores like Filene's in Boston, Hudson's in Detroit, and Marshall Field's in Chicago opened "slacks bars." Together they reported that sales in women's trousers were ten times greater in 1942 than they had been the year before.

Clothing changed everywhere in the country. Women who continued to wear dresses made them with half as much fabric, so that the excess could be used for the war effort. The National Association of Hosiery had announced in January that it would no longer be using silk, so women began buying their Victory Hose made from rayon. Those who couldn't afford hose painted their legs with makeup and drew lines up the back with eyebrow pencils to imitate seams. Neither Lena Mae Myers nor her daughter, Iola, wore hose on a daily basis, making do with bobby socks instead. When purchasing hosiery became rationed, they donated their stamps to the Red Cross, who passed them on to the WACs, WAVs, nurses, and others who needed hose.

Things changed in American kitchens as well. Lena Mae could only purchase coffee, sugar, beef, cheese, butter, and canned goods using ration stamps. Government home economists told citizens to eat more chicken, rabbit, and fish, meats that were not rationed. "Can all you can," American housewives heard, and they were also encouraged to raise Victory gardens, so more processed foods could be shipped to the fighting forces. None of these concepts was new to the Myers family. Eating small game bagged by Bert and the boys had been a frequent occurrence back on the farm. And Lena Mae always canned vegetables from their garden.

While the sacrifices being made by the families were noble, none touched the prisoners of war directly. No Red Cross packages arrived, and no supplements of food and medical supplies ever made its way into Bilibid Prison during 1942. Every meal of every day was the same for Myers and the other POWs: some form of rice prepared in the camp's unscreened, fly-infested kitchen. Bilibid's long, open latrine was less than fifty feet from the kitchen. The latrine ran into the cesspool next to it, home to millions of maggots.

Given those facts, Myers' decision to begin eating cockroaches fell right in line. He was well aware that these vermin carried filth and germs, but he figured he was already being exposed to so many diseases from his fellow prisoners in the hospital that the roaches couldn't make it any worse. Myers had an extra tin can among his possessions that he used as his trap. Saving a bit of rice from each meal, he baited his trap and lured the roaches in. He covered the roaches with water to prevent their escape, and when the next mealtime rolled around he'd boil them and add them to his ration of rice. Myers explained to his pals that although adding roaches to his diet was beneath anything he ever thought possible, he thought it might somehow delay his starvation and suggested they try adding roaches to their rice as well.

Those who did benefit from the sacrifices being made by Americans at home were the military men and women charged with recapturing the one million square miles the Empire of Japan was claiming in mid 1942. The area, nearly one seventh of the world's surface, was three times larger than the combined areas of the United States and Europe.

Retaking this area required an enormous military strategy, which the Allies code-named "Operation Cartwheel." The operation would marshal two main thrusts. The first would use the central Pacific forces and push westward to recapture the Gilbert, Marshall, Marianas, and Caroline Islands. The second thrust would use the southern and southwestern Pacific forces. Their battles would be waged in a westerly direction, beginning on Guadalcanal, the southernmost islands in the Solomon chain.

Military intelligence had discovered that the Japanese were constructing an air base on Guadalcanal. If completed, Imperial planes would have a clear shot at demolishing the important supply line which came from the United States through Australia and on to the Allied forces in the Pacific Theater. Although the unexpected defeat at Midway had cost the Japanese their carrier force, they were determined to maintain a network of bases throughout the Pacific, beginning with Guadalcanal.

The two leaders chosen for this major amphibious assault couldn't have been more different. For the Army, the Supreme Commander of Allied Forces in the southwest Pacific was General MacArthur. He was arrogant, flamboyant, and loved the attention of the press, which often portrayed him wearing his cap at its customary jaunty angle, dark glasses, and corncob pipe. MacArthur also knew more about the Pacific Theater than anyone else in the services. He was an inspiring leader with one of the most distinguished military careers in history.

The naval leader for Operation Cartwheel was the Commander in Chief of the Pacific, Admiral Nimitz. Unlike MacArthur, Nimitz was a mild-mannered gentleman from Texas with a modest nature. But he had also spent his adult life in the military and was known for his piercing blue-eyed stare and military prowess.

From offshore, Guadalcanal looked like a travel brochure photo with white beaches and swaying palm trees. The paradise soon turned to fury. On August 7, 1942, exactly eight months from the day the bombs fell on Pearl Harbor, the Allied armada appeared off the coast of Guadalcanal. After a three-hour bombardment, the Marines went ashore virtually unopposed. But the calm was deceptive.

Two days later, the Japanese struck back fiercely from their fortress, Rabaul, on New Britain Island. The Japanese sank one Australian and three American cruisers. Then, inexplicably, at the point when they could have levied harsh consequences on the Allies, the enemy commander called off the attack. This astonished the Allies and gave them a foothold. They wasted no time in beginning their force buildup on the island. During the next two months, the Japanese hammered the Marines on Guadalcanal as well as the convoys bringing them supplies from Australia. In mid October, an Imperial task force that included four carriers positioned itself north of Guadalcanal. On the night of October 26, 1942, the Battle of the

Santa Cruz Islands began, which cost Japan two destroyers, two carriers, and two battleships. The Americans lost the carrier *Hornet.*

The night of November 13 was the beginning of the Naval Battle
of Guadalcanal. This battle roared for twenty-four hours, at which
point the Japanese mustered their remaining ships in an effort to establish a beachhead. They were met by an American flotilla, which
sank another Imperial battleship and damaged two more cruisers. By
dawn of November 15, it was clear that the Japanese naval effort had
failed.

The Japanese were not done with Guadalcanal yet, though. From
bases established in caves across the island, they waged a land campaign that continued through 1942. It was the first time that U.S.
Marines came face-to-face with jungle terrain. They slashed their
way through vine-choked underbrush and the foul slime of decomposing vegetation, forever threatened by Japanese snipers lashed to
trees overhead. By February 9, 1943, there wasn't a single living enemy left on Guadalcanal. The cost to the Japanese was immense:
twenty thousand troops, eight hundred sixty aircraft and fifteen warships. Plus they had suffered their first defeat of the war on land. At
the same time, it was the Allies' first successful offensive.

During a nightly newscast, radio announcer Eric Sevareid referred
to the victors as "those who are living more miserably than ever before in their lives, fighting for those who are living better than ever
before in their lives."

The Myers family might not have immediately agreed that they
were living better than ever before. As the final days of fighting
wound down on Guadalcanal, Kenny Myers, age seventeen, convinced his parents he should quit school and enlist in the Navy. With
their second eldest son, Orville, stationed somewhere in North Africa
and Estel's whereabouts still unknown, Ken's entry into the war put
a third blue star on the small banner given to families of servicemen.

It was unusual, but not unheard of, for a family to have multiple
sons serving the country, and this included the first family: the Roo-
sevelts had four sons wearing uniforms. The sacrifices, however, were
paying off. The Allies had reached far up into the southwest Pacific

archipelagoes and severed one hundred thirty-five thousand Japanese from all prospect of ever being rescued, feats that had seemed unimaginable less than two years earlier in the aftermath of Pearl Harbor.

By the summer of 1943, the island hopping in the Pacific was in full force. In June, amphibious landings were taking place in New Guinea, the other offensive prong of Operation Cartwheel. In October, the Japanese increased their fortification of Rabaul on New Britain in an effort to stop the Allies from taking the island. One of the operation's directives, however, was that if an island wasn't integral in the grand scheme, the Allied forces would simply go around it. Such was the case with New Britain.

The next islands to be reclaimed by the Allies were the Gilberts. One of the islands in the chain, Tarawa, was an atoll of islets and coral reefs. The enemy had built a network of hundreds of pillboxes, reinforced with concrete, steel beams, and coconut palm logs. Three thousand crack Imperial Marines were holed up in the pillboxes, which Tokyo claimed would prevent the island from being taken by assault.

On the first day, the Americans bombed and shelled the atoll in order to establish a beachhead. When the U.S. Marines stormed ashore, it was through a tempest of Japanese firepower. Landing crafts became grounded on reefs as far out as five hundred yards. From there the Marines had to wade ashore, often finding little safe cover. Some companies lost half their men on that first day but still managed to gain a single toehold on the beach.

By late in the second day a commander of the 2nd Marine Regiment on Tarawa's beach was able to report to a ship standing offshore: "Our casualties are heavy. Enemy casualties unknown. Situation: we are winning." Despite the Allied victory, the battle for Tarawa was one of the bloodiest fights in the entire Pacific campaign. American losses were staggeringly high: 837 Marines dead and another 2,500 wounded or missing in action. The single compensation was that the lessons learned from the battle for Tarawa saved lives in every other amphibious operation for the rest of the war.

In December of 1943 the stage was set for the final phase of the Operation Cartwheel. The two Allied military forces would continue their westward push until they converged on the Philippine Islands. When MacArthur left Corregidor, he had said, "I shall return." Now he could make good on his promise.

When February 1944 arrived at Bilibid Prison, many of the men were detached, dejected, and dying. Although news of Allied victories throughout the Pacific filtered into the camp via the hidden radio, some of the men couldn't see the point of carrying on their fight for life. They felt as though their comrades and their country had abandoned them.

Others, like Myers, Tex, and Tarpy simply refused to quit living. They routinely set goals of when they expected the Allies to return. Their goals were set up in three-month time blocks, and since a calendar was maintained in the camp hospital, they could mark off the days there. When a three-month block expired without liberation, they set another goal of the same length. They never stopped believing that their country would come back for them.

The imprisonment had taken its toll on all of them. Most of the men had lost nearly a quarter of their weight. When they were struck with one of the debilitating diseases floating around camp, their weight further plummeted at an accelerated rate. Myers calculated that nearly half of all the deaths he'd witnessed during his twenty-six months of imprisonment were caused by men who simply said, "I can't eat any more rice."

It was during February that the POWs in Bilibid were allowed to send communications home for the first time. None of them knew why the Japanese had suddenly become so benevolent, although there were rumors that the International Red Cross might be exerting pressure on them to grant their prisoners more rights. On one side of the postcard provided, a camp pencil pusher typed the address of the recipient. Above that was a line for the prisoner to sign his name. The reverse side had five fill-in-the-blank statements. This not only cut down on the length of time to complete the cards, it also limited their ability to convey what was actually occurring in the camp.

Myers and Tarpy were standing next to each other in line waiting to complete their cards. They looked at the questions on the cards they were handed.

I am interned at. . . .

Myers' answer: "Headquarters of Military Prison Camps of the Philippine Islands."

My health is. . . .

Four choices here: excellent, good, fair, or poor.

"The Japs find out you think you're in 'excellent health' and you're gonna be shipped to some camp to run the entire medical facility," Tarpy told him.

Myers checked excellent anyway, not wanting to alarm his family.

I am. . . .

This one was easy to fill in. The choices were injured, sick in the hospital, under treatment, and not under treatment. Myers had never been injured, and although he suffered from the same diseases as everyone around him, he had refused to be hospitalized or treated except for the time he was out of his mind with a malaria-induced fever.

I am. . . .

"I have to think about this one," Myers told Tarpy. "If I say 'not improving,' 'improving' or 'better,' the family'll think there was something wrong with me. If I say I'm well, it sounds like this is a cakewalk. And that's not the truth, either."

"I don't think it's something you're gonna have to answer for on Judgment Day," Tarpy told him. "We all feel shitty. God knows it and I expect our families do, too."

The last part of the card had space for a more personalized, fifty-word message, although it, too, had to be typewritten. The messages were carefully censored by the prisoners' commanding officer. Any effort to sneak references about their condition or treatment meant severe punishment from the Japanese, both for the writer and the C.O. Consequently, nothing but the most mundane drivel was sent home.

Myers' message read like many of the others. "Dear Mother: I am on regular duty status. Think much of Orville and rest. Send my regards to friends, give my love to all. Explain Norma's card to her. Write to me through Geneva Red Cross. Hope to see you all before long. Love, Estel B. Myers."

One of the hardest things for Myers was wondering what was going through his girl's mind. Norma and he had known each other since they were kids. He had always been sure they'd be married one day, but of course he'd never counted on something like a war interrupting their lives. Up until this point, just like his folks, Norma would have no way of knowing whether he was alive or dead. Myers was afraid that expecting a woman to keep her promise to a dead man was more than he could hope for.

It was a stretch for the POWs to believe that these postcards would ever truly make it home. They had seen an occasional Red Cross box, evidence of valiant efforts to get supplies and mail to them. But the agency's success was highly dependent upon Japanese cooperation. The packages contained things that their army lacked, too. Food and medicine were in short supply everywhere in the Philippines, regardless of whether one was a captive or a captor.

The routine was always the same when a shipment of Red Cross packages arrived. Upon the shipment's arrival, the Japanese MPs at the Manila port area went through them. They removed anything that pertained to American war activities, such as cigarette packs displaying Victory labels. To maintain psychological control, the Japanese wanted the POWs to be kept completely ignorant about the status of the war and who might be winning.

The MPs next took out whatever items they wanted for themselves or thought might bring a good price on the black market. Only then was the shipment sent on to Bilibid. The same process of confiscation was conducted at the prison by the officers and guards, often including brisk games of gambling for the most valuable items like cigarettes. By the time the packages finally reached their intended recipients, they were practically barren. Still, for those who hovered at the brink of death, whatever edibles remained were more valuable than gold and revived them, at least for the time being.

As their requirement for labor in and around Manila continued to rise, the Japanese began demanding that the sick, as well as the corpsmen, go on work detail. The Allied C.O. protested, saying the sick would become sicker and the corpsmen were needed at the hospital and should not be forced to risk injury. He was told by a Japanese officer that there was "an emergency," and the men were taken without further ado. One day, Tarpy was selected to go out on a work detail. When he got back to camp that night, he described his activities with the most animation any of them had mustered for months.

"The Japs had some of the guys digging foxholes. I was with a group who moved barrels of gas and oil down to the docks. I get the feeling they want to be able to get it out of here in a hurry if they need to. Or else they're gonna use it to blow up what's left of the port area. I'll bet the Yanks and tanks are gettin' close. We just gotta keep alive 'til forty-five. And that's only six months away!"

Japanese home life was completely altered by the war. Yet from the beginning, the Emperor's subjects were led to believe that they would ultimately be victorious. They had been told that the war was being waged by two power-mad villains, Churchill and Roosevelt. They were told that Allied fighting men were cannibals, and that they even bombed Japanese hospital ships.

Tokyo and other major cities were evacuated during the summer of 1944 of all residents but essential workers. In addition to taking their furniture and personal belongings, many of the evacuees insisted on taking their prized gardens, including the rocks and trees, to reassemble them when they arrived at their new homes. This slowed down the evacuation process, and eventually the government was forced to step in, ordering that all gardens must be left behind.

In July, the infrastructure of Japan's military was severely shaken. Confessing his many failures, General Hideki Tojo, who had commanded the country's war efforts thus far, resigned, as did his entire Cabinet. Filling Tojo's shoes would be General Kuniaki Koiso, who nicknamed himself the Singing Frog, in reference to his sake-induced singing efforts. Koiso insisted that he would attain Japan's objectives in close collaboration with their Axis cohorts.

Meanwhile, the country's trains had all but stopped running. Tokyo was reported to be "a city of troglodytes: holes everywhere. The hospitals are full of broken limbs, as during the nights zealous patriots dig holes into which other zealous patriots fall at dawn. . . . Bandages are scarce (doctors have the right to own five)."

Corruption was everywhere and the black market flourished. There was a shortage of food, fuel, and clothing. Japanese women were, however, encouraged to continue producing sons for Japan's future armies.

Through all of this, Japanese radio continued to broadcast news of the military's victories. The soldiers, peasants, and workers all expected that they would eventually win the war. They had the essential element, *yamato damashii,* the unquenchable spiritual force. It was this force that they expected would match and eventually overcome the United States' material powers: heavier ships, bigger guns, and faster planes. Indeed, since the bombing of Pearl Harbor, American industrial might had produced an incomparable fleet of ships and planes, much to the astonishment of the Japanese.

During the summer of 1944, the Americans put that fleet to use against the Japanese. The Allied storm rolled on to take Guam, Saipan, and Tinian. By September, the fighting had moved to the tiny island of Peleliu in the Palau Islands. The battle there lasted a month, with the Japanese raising the price of every inch of land taken back by the Allied forces. The Americans lost eight thousand men, the Japanese more than eleven thousand.

After Peleliu had been secured, a lone Japanese sniper continued his assault on the Allies setting up a base on the island. Nicknamed the Gopher by the Marines, he would pop out from the honeycomb of caves called Bloody Nose Ridge, fire on them, and then disappear. During a three-week time period, he shot eighty-seven Marines through the head. Revenge finally occurred when a Marine marksman killed the Gopher, fittingly with a bullet through the temple.

Tokyo correctly assumed that MacArthur had meant what he said about returning to the Philippines. So in October of 1944, the Japanese launched what they called *Sho-Go,* Operation Victory. They felt certain it would be a decisive triumph for them. It had to be, as men and supplies were rapidly running out. The battle would be fought in the Leyte Gulf, whose waters lap against the Philippine island of Leyte only one hundred miles from Manila.

For this significant battle, the Japanese had a new weapon of war: the kamikaze, Japanese for "divine wind." The name was taken from the pages of Japanese history, when a typhoon staved off a Mongol attack by destroying their fleet off of Japan's shores. The people believed that their salvation had come from divine intervention.

It was an honor and privilege to volunteer for the kamikaze flights. All during their military training, Japanese pilots had been taught: "Duty is mightier than a mountain, death is as light as a feather. To die for the Emperor is to live forever." In the same vein, just before leaving on his suicide flight, one young pilot made a last entry in his diary. "Like cherry blossoms/In the spring/Let us fall/Clean and radiant."

For the Battle for Leyte Gulf, which became the largest naval battle of all time, the Japanese pitted 70 warships and 716 planes against the Americans' 166 warships and 1,280 planes, including the gigantic 3rd Fleet. In cruising formation, the fleet covered an area forty miles long and nine miles wide.

On October 20, 1944, the Americans landed four divisions against surprisingly feeble Japanese resistance. When they waded ashore onto Philippine soil on the Leyte beach of Palo, the troops were astonished to hear the Filipinos shouting to them in English and the schoolchildren singing "God Bless America." It was the fulfillment of General MacArthur's departing promise to return to the Philippines. Missing from all radar screens at this point was the Japanese navy. The first ships were spotted by a submarine just after midnight on October 23. Planes from the 3rd Fleet were alerted and flew in to sink one battleship and damage several others before the Imperial fleet sailed away.

A second Japanese naval force was then spotted. In four hours time a battle was waged, and again the Americans were victorious, but they had little time to celebrate. The first fleet was headed at them once again. Again a furious naval battle was waged, and three hours later the Japanese retreated. The Americans had wreaked havoc upon the Japanese navy, sinking twenty-six warships.

Simultaneously with the Battle for Leyte Gulf, the Allies began their attacks on Tokyo. During the month of November alone, one hundred and eleven B-29s dropped 278 tons of bombs. The Imperial capital city, built largely of wood, went up in flames like kindling in the ensuing firestorm. The attacks shook the Japanese but did not defeat them.

The Japanese army was strong, with two hundred fifty thousand soldiers on the island of Luzon and another forty-five thousand reinforcements disembarking on the west coast of Leyte. To have any hope of advancing through the Philippines, the Allies would have to win the land battle for Leyte. The fighting continued all through the month of November. By December, although the Japanese knew they had been bested, they continued firing on the Americans, in hopes of killing as many as possible.

A letter written by an unknown Japanese soldier during the fighting on Leyte had a tone of despair that was startlingly familiar to the radio message sent by an American soldier during the fall of Corregidor. The Imperial warrior wrote:

> I am exhausted. We have no food. The enemy are now within 500 meters of us. Mother, my dear wife and son, I am writing this letter to you by dim candlelight. Our end is near. What will be the future of Japan if this island should fall into enemy hands? Our air force has not arrived. . . . Hundreds of pale soldiers of Japan are awaiting our glorious end and nothing else. This is a repetition of what occurred in the Solomons, New Georgia and other islands. How well are the people of

Japan prepared to fight the decisive battle with the will to win . . . ?

When the last gun barrel cooled on Leyte, the Japanese death toll was 56,263. American losses stood at 2,888. But the fate of the remaining Japanese troops and that of the American POWs held in the Philippines was still to be determined.

CHAPTER TEN

★

Into the Beast

One thousand sixty-nine.

Myers, Tarpy, and the rest of the Canacao staff had been tenants of Bilibid Prison Camp for 1,069 days. There had always been a man assigned to keeping up the camp calendar. If he lost interest or died, someone else took over. That was how, on December 7, 1944, Myers knew exactly how long they had been there.

They had survived the blows, the hunger, and the diseases indigenous to the tropics. They ate the stinking food, occasionally embellished with whatever cats, dogs, iguanas, or insects they could secretly catch. They saluted every enemy soldier regardless of age or rank and obeyed a thousand irritating regulations cunningly contrived to humiliate them. But they would not break, nor would they give what their Japanese captors wanted most—acknowledgment of defeat.

The prisoners were used as much as was humanly possible to effect defenses in and around Manila. Tarpy had gone on just such a work detail, and when he returned, once they were out of earshot of the guards, he related to Myers that he had seen U.S. planes.

"What makes you so sure they were ours?" Myers asked him.

"At first I thought they were ours because of the way they were flying—in perfect formation, weaving in and out. I never saw a Jap plane fly that way. Ten minutes later I was really sure," Tarpy said, nodding.

"How come?"

"A guard asked a guy near me, 'Who those planes?' and the guy told him they were probably Japanese. He gave the eye, like he knew they were American. A little while later another formation appeared. Guard asked the same question, got the same answer. Just a few minutes later we saw a plane with a red circle. Had an American fighter on its tail. The fighter hit 'em and the Jap plane exploded. The guard comes over to the guy near me and was he hot! He starts screaming, 'Oh, you sons of bish! You lie like hell!'"

Fresh from their victory in the Battle for Leyte Gulf, the aircraft from the American carriers continued their attacks on Manila. On one particularly successful day, they were able to damage or destroy over forty enemy ships in Manila Bay.

Since then, Bilibid had become one of Emperor Hirohito's busiest prison camps. The Japanese conducted a panicky spasm of withdrawal; already nine drafts of prisoners had been assembled and loaded onto ships in the harbor to be sent to Japan to augment the labor-hungry Home Islands. Since all able-bodied Japanese men had been made into soldiers, the enemy was in desperate need of slave labor to work in their mines and factories.

The Japanese used Bilibid as the clearinghouse for these drafts, and men were sent there from other camps like Cabanatuan, O'Donnell, and Davao. The task of organizing the prisoners once they disembarked at Bilibid was under the direction of an officer named Momata. Each time new men arrived at the camp, Momata demanded that the prison medical staff assemble groups of the strongest men. Had they not been so exhausted and disease-ridden, the order would have given the POWs a big laugh: they would have been hard-pressed to pick out even one strong man from amongst them.

Since August, Myers had seen thousands of men afflicted with a myriad of diseases, despair evident in their tortured eyes, move through the camp. Some died immediately upon arrival, the move from their previous camp being more than they could physically withstand. Other newcomers were allowed a brief respite in the Bilibid hospital before being shipped out. But most were herded into an area on the prison grounds like worthless chattel. There they would spend a day or two before being herded back out again, evidently on their way to the docks and their awaiting ships.

Trying to save the pitifully broken-down prisoners who were gradually losing the will to live provided an unending dilemma for Myers. He wanted to do his best to keep as many men as possible alive and well. But the more a man improved, the closer he came to being yanked away for chain-gang work or slave labor in Japan.

Myers' strong faith and compassion for his fellow man provided scant comfort, particularly when he was confronted by a patient who asked Myers to help him pray for death and a release from his suffering.

Myers' performance in his onerous duties did not go unnoticed by the senior medical officer at Bilibid. In a letter of commendation written in November of 1944, he described Myers as possessing "loyalty, competency in the discharge of duties and maintenance of excellent morale under adverse conditions of prison life in the hands of the enemy." Still, Myers would have traded all those glowing words for just one hot meal consisting of anything but rice.

The POWs' daily rations had been cut to about a cup of rice and another one of corn. The mortality rate in Bilibid from malnutrition had skyrocketed. The Japanese commandant's office issued orders that malnutrition could no longer be used as a cause of death and ordered that the Americans change eight recently drafted death certificates to reflect something else. Malnutrition, he told the doctors, made it appear as though the Japanese weren't taking sufficient care of the prisoners. That would, in turn, cause the Empire embarrassment and humiliation.

Shortly after, another ridiculous order was issued. The Americans were to make room for the sick and injured Japanese to be moved into the Bilibid hospital. Tex commented that if that were to be the case, they'd need a ten-story building, since the POW patients were already practically lying on top of one another.

Throughout November, Allied aircraft peppered the skies above Manila, their bombs and bullets thundering down on enemy ships, planes, and troops. The POWs could see camouflaging and foxhole-digging going on outside the prison walls. And the Japanese held what seemed like non-stop air-raid drills for those living in the city.

There were no foxholes in Bilibid, however. Just a dilapidated, unfinished building dubbed the Big House into which the prisoners were herded for the air raids. It was ludicrous to think that the feeble walls and partial roof would somehow protect the men from any falling ordnance.

In early December the Japanese authorities at Bilibid issued another proclamation. It was announced that the Allies' "stupid resistance to the will of the Emperor could be tolerated no longer." Therefore, every prisoner in camp who could walk on his own accord, and those needing only a small amount of assistance, would be shipped out to Japan. This group was to include all officers, doctors, and corpsmen.

The enormity of the proclamation did not escape Myers. It was beyond reason to assume that the Japanese doctors and corpsmen would care for the remaining POW patients. If the medical personnel left behind those who were so sickly that the Japanese didn't even want them for slave labor, they would surely die. As bad as not having enough supplies to care for patients was to Myers, abandoning them was completely unbearable.

Furthermore, Myers knew that the Allies were closing in on Manila. He'd heard the distant rumblings of the big guns and the reports of plane sightings each time a group of prisoners came back from work detail outside the camp. But if they were shipped to Japan, out of the grasp of the returning Allied troops, God only knew how long it would take the Americans to rescue them. The only thing left to do was what he'd been doing all along: keep believing that help was on the way.

As they lay on their mats the stormy night of December 11, Myers, Tex, and Tarpy talked about when, not if, General MacArthur would return. They argued over how many days were left in their current three-month block, the measurement they'd used for nearly three years as the timing for their liberation. Myers said if he had to put his money on a date, he was sure it would be within the next few days.

By 1800 hours the next day, however, Myers' hopes began to fade. A runner had arrived from Japanese headquarters in Manila with orders to ready the final draft of prisoners for Japan. Each prisoner was issued soap, toilet paper, and "dobie" cigarettes and told to be ready to move out the next morning. The prisoners were also issued various and sundry articles of clothing for a colder climate. Eighty cases of Red Cross medical supplies were set aside to be loaded on the ship, six of which were designated for the prisoners' use.

The POWs' chief medical officer protested vigorously to Nogi. He wrote the Japanese doctor a letter stating that moving the men at this late date in the war was rife with risk. But Nogi's reply was that there was no danger involved; otherwise the Japanese would never have suggested the move in the first place.

Sleep was out of the question that night. All of the prisoners had the impending journey to Japan on their minds. The night was heavy and, as usual, alive with mosquitoes.

"I'll bet the Jap ships in the bay have taken quite a beating from our planes," Tarpy said quietly.

"Yeah, ain't it a bitch!" Tex said. "All along we've wanted our boys to give the Japs hell, and now we want 'em to hold off 'cause we're gonna be riding on their targets."

"If MacArthur's as close as I think he is," Myers told them, "he's sure to step up the bombing again, probably before the Japs can get us loaded. A few good bombing runs will scare 'em back into foxholes. We just need to buy a little more time."

It almost happened that way. At 0400 hours on December 13, the men were rousted off their mats, given their breakfast ration of repulsive and slimy rice, and at 0800 were told to fall in. The 1,619 POWs, which included 37 Brits, were forced to line up for the march out of Bilibid. They would leave behind approximately eight hundred prisoners who were so physically incapacitated that they couldn't be moved. Myers knew without question that they would suffer slow starvation. It truly seemed that at this point, a quick mercy killing at the hands of their captors was a gruesomely attractive alternative.

The guards roughly shoving the men into place were of a grim pedigree. They were mostly Formosan and included a lance corporal named Kazutane Aihara. The men from Cabanatuan knew him all too well. He had a penchant for sneaking up behind a prisoner and then beating him relentlessly with a bamboo staff. Once he acquired his reputation at Cabanatuan and came near a group of prisoners, someone would yell "air raid" and all of them would take cover to avoid being beaten. Thus they had nicknamed him Air Raid.

The guard commandant was Lieutenant Junsabura Toshino, who was never without his hunchbacked dwarf, Shusuke Wada. Wada served as interpreter. The two had a record of savage brutality at Davao Prison Camp.

Under the watchful eyes of the brutish guards, the columns of POWs were about halfway out of the prison yard when the air raid alarm sounded. They were quickly reversed back into the yard and rushed to the Big House.

The men, crouched in a tight knot and looking through the building's cracked shutters, could see American planes peel off over the prison rooftops and let go of their ordnance, stick by stick. The Japanese answered with anti-aircraft fire, and that, combined with the bombs falling and shells exploding, created a deafening clamor. Although the men were terrified of dying from their own country's bombs, the anticipation of an ensuing battle and maybe even freedom was overwhelming.

"The port area is catching hell!" somebody shouted. "Our Yanks are back!"

A short time later, however, the POWs watched dejectedly as the Allied planes flew away. Around 1030 hours, the columns of four were re-formed and the march began again, first out the prison gate, then into a continuous line around the prison walls, and finally out onto the streets of Manila.

When the half-naked columns reached the waterfront, Myers saw the masts of Japanese ships poking through the surface of the bay, evidence that the American bombers had done their job. Three or four ships had been sunk while tied to the piers and several others floated on the water like soulful apparitions, their fire-gutted hulls gaping at the newly arrived POWs. Despite the fact that nearly ninety percent of the port area installations had been destroyed, the Japanese were able to protect seven ships in Manila Bay, including troop transports, a cruiser, several destroyers, and the passenger-cargo vessel named the *Oryoku Maru*.

The *Oryoku Maru* had no markings to distinguish it as carrying prisoners of war; the Japanese claimed that their shipping losses didn't allow them the luxury of designating ships for the exclusive purpose of carrying POWs. The ship's size and shape reminded Myers of the *Henderson*. He calculated that her top speed would probably be around twenty knots. That would have them on Japanese soil in five days.

The men also took notice of the fact that she had been outfitted with anti-aircraft guns. This sight brought with it the terrifying realization that the ship they were about to be forced onto could very well be a target of their own air force. The men scanned the skies, hoping for the sight of American aircraft that might prevent their loading, but no winged messengers of reprieve appeared.

A large group of Japanese women and children, Imperial seamen, and stevedores were milling around the pier waiting to board. From the looks of the miscellaneous bundles, packages, and suitcases piled around the gangplank, it appeared to Myers as if the Japanese were leaving in a big hurry. He couldn't tell exactly how many people there were in total, but it must have been well over a thousand, and he figured they were going to fill pretty much all the space topside. The only remaining space was in the cargo holds.

The prisoners were divided into three groups and then ordered to wait some more while the Japanese boarded. Around 1700 hours, it

was the POWs' turn. The first group consisted of about eight hundred men, most of them high-ranking officers. The same men who
had courageously led troops in the defense of the Philippines were
now being driven at bayonet-point like worthless vermin. They were
crammed into the aft cargo space through an eight-by-ten-foot hatch
opening and down a decrepit ladder. These holds had no ventilation
system, and this one had no air circulation because of bulkheads fore
and aft. The hatch was the hold's only source of air and light.

A man is capable of holding his breath for two or three minutes,
maybe more if he's well practiced at it and in good physical condition. These men were neither. They had watched so many from
among them die, and had lived such wretched lives the last three
years, what remained were only shells of the men they once were.
They weren't prepared to be shoved into the bowels of a ship with little oxygen, and the feeling of near-suffocation panicked them immediately.

The second group of POWs had six hundred men. They were
pushed into the forward cargo hold with ruthless efficiency. These
men faced a lack of oxygen, too, although it was somewhat less acute
than in the aft hold. Nonetheless, the guards kept driving the men
down into the hold as if they were a herd of animals, ignoring the
protests that there was no more room. As he watched both processes,
Myers heard the guards yelling and the distinctively familiar crack of
wood and bamboo thrashing against human bodies.

The final group of 219 men was somewhat better equipped both
medically and spiritually. Myers, Tarpy, Tex, and the majority of the
medical crew, along with seven chaplains, were herded into the amidships hold. The space had been previously used to transport horses,
and on three sides, the compartments still held grain. The foul-
smelling space had an air conditioner that had been used to make the
animals as comfortable as possible, but Lieutenant Toshino refused
to turn it on for the prisoners.

The last man to be jammed in had to perch on the edge of a shelf
suspended from the bulkhead. It was immediately evident that if the
other men on the shelf had inhaled and expanded their chests at the

same time, or moved collectively in any other way, this last man would have been shoved off the edge onto the men crowded below him. Suddenly the whole structure gave way, crushing the men below them. No one was seriously hurt, but the episode provided an apocalyptic beginning to the journey ahead. Around 1900 hours, the convoy shoved off, sailing out of Manila Bay and into the China Sea under blackout orders, hugging the coastline.

The masses of humanity were packed into the holds so tightly that one man's bones ground against his neighbors' if he tried to reposition himself. Some of the men made arrangements to take turns in positions, trading between four hours of sitting and four hours of standing. The example caught on and spread to other areas of the hold. Many of the prisoners struggled to find a position that would afford them more air. But none of them gained anything, and the whole group suffered: the movement increased the temperature. The heat from the men's bodies, along with the heat outside, brought the holds' temperatures to more than one hundred and twenty degrees. Dehydration and suffocation competed for supremacy. Those commanders who were able shouted for the men to remain calm and hold still, but they were powerless to manufacture oxygen, and hysteria began to build.

The men farthest from their hold's hatch openings began to panic and were well on their way to being crazed from the oxygen deprivation even before the ship was out of Manila Bay. They all begged and screamed for water and more air. The cacophony enraged Wada, who threatened to close the hatches if the noise didn't subside. Finally, in retaliation to his orders being ignored, he slammed the cover over the aft hold.

Just before dark, the guards lowered buckets down to the men, some containing a seaweed-rice mixture, and some for *benjo* use, as much-needed toilets. Those who had mess kits or containers scooped up what they could of the food. But in the dark, it was impossible to determine what a bucket might contain. Myers heard several men near him tell another prisoner they were handing him food. When the man scraped up a mess kit full of excrement, the jokesters' laughter sounded more like rabid animals' howls than anything resembling human mirth.

The cries of men who were half mad from suffocation and claustrophobia jarred the nerves of those who were still fairly mentally intact. Wada shouted down threats that he'd order the guards to shoot into the holds or lock up the hatches, making them airtight, if they didn't quiet down. The wailing, he insisted, was frightening the women and children on board.

In the inky black space, the men lost all track of time and direction. They were so hot that they stripped off all of their clothing. They argued savagely about taking one another's food or space. They begged the Japanese and one another for something to drink. Some realized they could drink the blood of those who had already suffocated to death. Others saw this and, not willing to wait for their neighbors to die, slashed the throats and wrists of living men who had drifted off to sleep. Still others, maddened by their desperate circumstances, drank their own urine after which they choked and vomited.

Almost every man suffered from diarrhea or dysentery. Those who weren't able to move quickly enough to get to the *benjo* buckets soiled themselves and their neighbors. It mattered little, because even those who did reach the buckets soon found them overflowing. The guards resolutely refused to empty them or send down more. The stench from excrement was intense. But the stench of death was even greater. Nearly fifty men died that first night.

As daylight came slowly on the morning of December 14, Myers looked closely at Tex and Tarpy. They were both alive but their skin was wrinkled as if they'd been in water all night. Looking at his own hands and arms, Myers saw his skin resembled a prune, too.

"Must be from the humidity of us all sweating and breathing cramped into such a small space," Myers said, his breath shallow. The other two feebly agreed, watching men lick condensation off the bulkhead like rabid dogs lapping up a mud puddle.

The commanding officers who still had a presence of mind tried desperately to restore order. They enjoined that every effort be made to separate the men who were still alive from those who were dead, and that the latter be put under the hatch opening. As soon as possible, they planned to ask the Japanese for permission to haul them up on deck and give them a burial at sea.

The prisoners did as they had been commanded. Two men hauled a dead buddy through the masses and laid him out. The area underneath the hatch had more air circulation than the back of the hold where the men were so tightly packed. Given this chance at a little oxygen, the man who had been presumed dead revived and crawled back to his former spot in the hold.

No water was issued that morning, but buckets of steamed rice and fish were lowered around 0700. The men had just about divvied it up when a commotion developed topside. The Japanese seamen started yelling and ran to their battle positions, while the men in the holds froze, knowing that either a sub or a plane had been spotted. Within seconds, the Japanese anti-aircraft guns began to chatter and the planes from Admiral Halsey's 3rd Fleet answered.

The prisoners in the *Oryoku Maru*'s holds were helpless. The American pilots performed brilliantly in the skies above the ship. This was what they had trained for; they had no possible way to know that fellow countrymen were aboard their target. Bullets ricocheted off the ship's sides, and the concussion from bombs dropping around her in the water was deafening. On the one hand, the prisoners wanted to cheer their ace pilots on. If the Japanese were all killed, the prisoners could be freed. On the other hand, the firepower necessary to kill the Imperial forces on board would also most likely kill them. Bullets whizzed through the ship, hitting several doctors and corpsmen in Myers' hold.

The civilians and gunners up above the holds were hit hard. Their blood seeped through the cracks in the deck and into the hatch, spattering the POWs below. Myers thought for a minute that Tarpy had been hit and then realized he was covered in the blood raining from above.

After twenty-five minutes, the bombing run ended. Wada screamed into the amidships hold that doctors were needed up on deck and a group, including Myers, went up the ladder. Carnage lay all around them. The only ones not writhing in pain were the dead. The wounded women and children moaned and sobbed, while those not hurt screamed in terror and confusion. One of the doctors asked Wada if he might also be given supplies to take back to the hold to treat the wounded American prisoners. Wada refused, and then in a fit of anger had the medical crew he had just hauled on deck beaten with gun butts and bamboo sticks.

"Americans are sinking Japanese ships!" he shrieked at them.

Myers endured several licks across the back with a bamboo stick from a nearby guard. But he snuck a look out across the water nonetheless and saw one of the transports burning. And the rest of the convoy had disappeared.

The *Oryoku Maru* limped along slowly. The planes' bombardment had badly damaged her steering gear and there was considerable damage to her superstructure. By a small miracle, she had not sustained direct hits to any of the holds. Late in the afternoon, the ship was so badly crippled that the captain dropped anchor not far from shore, where they remained until almost dark. Once the Japanese appeared satisfied that the attacks had ceased, the ship again got underway and pulled into Subic Bay on the west side of Luzon to anchor.

Wada announced to the prisoners that all Japanese nationals who had occupied the upper decks and all Japanese wounded would disembark immediately. The prisoners were to be taken off as soon as an assemblage of guards could be arranged. Myers spent that night in tortured frustration, trying to comfort and care for the wounded in his hold. There were only filthy, ragged pieces of clothing for bandages and no medical supplies of any kind. The best he could do in most cases was call for one of the chaplains. If all of them were busy, he said a prayer over the dying men himself.

While the civilians were being removed from the crippled ship, the POWs' temptation to rush the hatch grew. It was there, wide open. They envisioned somehow being able to blend in with the Japanese passengers and make their escape. The commanding officers pleaded with their men to discourage them from doing so. The guards had already threatened to shoot anyone who attempted escape. The men shoved one another as they tried to get closer to the ladder leading up on deck, which generated more heat in the already sweltering holds. Finally, several men were unable to contain themselves and made a rush up the ladder. Fellow prisoners managed to pull back some of them, but others eluded the life-saving grasps and were gunned down before their feet ever reached the deck.

Myers was shoved over toward another pharmacist's mate he recognized from Bilibid. The man was in a very bad way, raving and completely unmanageable. The night before, he and Tex had taken turns holding him down, keeping him away from other prisoners. But by now, Myers' strength and stamina were waning. The man got away from Myers and was also shot by the guards as he climbed the ladder.

After all of the Japanese had been removed, it was nearly 2400 hours. A doctor, who had been tending to the enemy's wounded up on deck, came back down into the hold and told the men near him that he believed the ship was about five hundred yards offshore of Olongapo Naval Station. Myers overheard him and again thought briefly of Stover, his buddy from the Shanghai hospital, who'd been assigned there.

Wada's piercing shouts broke through Myers' thoughts like a razor. The prisoners, Wada said, would swim ashore at sunrise. They were to take only the clothing they were wearing and to remove their shoes, but could carry them. This, Wada explained with a taunting voice, was so that the prisoners would not try to escape once they arrived on dry land. With sandpaper throats, the men begged him for water, but he ignored their cries and moved away from the open hatch. Some of the medical personnel still had emergency dressings and varying amounts of medicines, Myers among them. The POWs dug these out of their bundles in preparation for smuggling them on shore. All of them sifted through their meager belongings, deciding which of the precious pieces they would most need in the coming

days and leaving behind the heavy Japanese clothing they'd been issued.

When the sun peeked over the horizon on December 16, the
Oryoku Maru was dead in the water. She was littered with bodies:
dead Japanese up on deck and another fifty dead in the holds, American victims of their own country's bullets.

Chapter Eleven

★

Caged Rats

Myers had catnapped during the night, fearing he'd be killed by a bloodthirsty POW if he fell completely asleep. Once awake, he wasn't sure whether the *Oryoku Maru* had been reality or nightmare. Within seconds, he realized it was both. The men around him still struggled to breathe and the mad ones were still raving. All of them suffered from what psychologists often call "crowd poisoning." The phobia is similar to what some Christmas shoppers suffer in a crowded store: stale air, heat, and too many other bodies. Here, the affliction could be deadly.

It was a study in human psychology to see who had lost control and who was maintaining a sense of normalcy. Men whom Myers had come to know over the past years were no longer recognizable. The calm major from a wealthy Connecticut family had slit his wrists the day before rather than wait for what new terrors the Japanese might impose. The cheerful, freckle-faced private from Kansas threatened anyone who came near him with his mess kit knife, as if he'd been a hardened killer all of his life.

Equally peculiar was the size of the average survivor, in camp and now on the ship. The big, brawny men, like the ones Myers had admired on opposing teams in high school, didn't seem to fare as well as those who were smaller. The men with more compact builds, like his own, seemed to have an advantage over the Charles Atlas, muscleman types.

Myers heard the waspish whining of aircraft overhead. The planes didn't attack, apparently on reconnaissance for the fighters. Shortly after the sounds faded, Wada screeched at the doctor who was in charge of Myers' hold.

"No shoes, only shirts and pants to wear. Must leave packs but can take food kit and canteen," he said in broken English. "Japanese soldiers very good with guns. Will kill any man who tries escape. All men be very careful. You go twenty-five at one time. Must swim to land."

The doctor protested, saying that some of the men were wounded and wouldn't be able to swim. Wada was visibly angered by this complication and went off to consult with Lieutenant Toshino. He came back and agreed to allow the wounded to go ashore in lifeboats. Men were chosen to act as lifeboat oarsmen, including Tex.

Around 0830, as the first lifeboat was about to shove off, the day's initial wave of bombers, six in all, arrived. There would be no resistance from the Japanese since all of the gun crews had been killed the day before. Toshino signaled frantically for the lifeboat to leave. The prisoners believed he was hoping it would draw the Americans' fire. Toshino dove for cover along with the other POWs left on deck. The planes' first target was, indeed, the lifeboat. They flew low, strafing the water as they screamed by, and blew the little boat apart like a toy made of balsa wood.

More of the wounded prisoners were brought out of the holds as the next group of bombers arrived. The first bomb they dropped was a direct hit to the aft hold, crashing through the deck and killing nearly three hundred prisoners. The coal dust in the hold ignited and the floorboards gave way, dropping the survivors and dead alike into the filthy bilge water of the compartment twenty feet below.

The POWs in the hold with Myers screamed in terror and agony, and men began to rush up the ladder. The guards standing duty over the hatch fired down into it. The man closest to the top on the ladder was hit in the face and died instantly. Then obeying their captain's orders, the Japanese guards abandoned ship. The prisoners remained below for another ten minutes before they realized they were no longer being guarded. When they timidly poked their heads through the hatches and saw other Americans wandering around freely, they dashed up the ladder, pouring out of the holds. The stronger helped the weak, and every living prisoner was removed from the holds.

Myers and the other men who had just climbed on deck faltered, dazed by their circumstances. A piece of luggage had broken open and brown sugar poured out of it. The men crammed what they could of the sugar into anything available: pockets, mess kits, canteens, and their mouths. Some dove over the side of the ship. Others began scavenging throughout the ship.

The POWs were not alone, however. Both Toshino and Wada were still on board, as were several other Japanese officers. They, too, were collecting final items to take with them and were shooting on sight any Americans caught scavenging. Myers was able to avoid any run-ins with the Japs, and shoved edibles into his mouth as he pawed through boxes looking for medical supplies. Everywhere were caches of American cigarettes and candy, remnants of the Red Cross packages that had never made it to the prisoners.

Scattered around, too, were the mutilated bodies of dead Imperial soldiers and civilians. Myers stumbled across the corpse of a Japanese child, maybe seven or eight years old, lying facedown in a pool of blood. The only emotions that stirred within him were satisfaction and relief. This small victim of the madness of war, helpless as he was, meant there was one less Japanese to worry about. These feelings were foreign to Myers; they surprised and frightened him. Estel Myers had sworn to God that he would hold the care of the sick and injured as a privileged and sacred trust. He had sworn that he would not knowingly let harm come to any patient. Where had his strong commitment to this covenant gone? What kind of man was he becoming?

Myers struggled to rationalize his feelings. Perhaps if that child had grown to adulthood, he might have been forced into another emperor's mandatory military service. He might have become a hate-crazed enemy, just like those who had made the American POWs' lives pure purgatory for the last three years. This satisfied his conscience. Myers turned his back on the little corpse and ran for the main deck.

Prisoners were still roaming about in a state of confusion. Japanese officers screamed orders at them, but the POWs didn't comprehend. In frustration the officers shot them where they stood. The American planes made another few strafing runs and then regrouped for another pass. This time they came in low with the *Oryoku Maru* dead in their sights.

Calls of "She's on fire!" began to ring out through the smoky haze. The ship was burning furiously at the stern, and ammunition was exploding everywhere. Myers found Tarpy through pockets of flames and told him they'd better get going. By this time, the non-swimmers who hadn't found life belts had thrown in anything that would float and jumped in after the debris. Myers remembered a man who had once claimed that he'd flunked his swimming test in basic. He saw this man in the water now, desperately churning his arms as he kicked toward a floating plank, a living example of how fear can overcome inability.

The first group of POWs to leave the ship was now reaching water shallow enough to stand in. They looked up and saw the bombers returning for a third raid. One man began to shout and wave, frantically screaming for everyone who had his feet on the sand to do the same thing. The pilots were flying low enough to realize that the bodies floundering in the water beneath them were not Japanese but Americans, many wearing nothing but their dog tags. One of the planes tipped its wings as a signal that they'd been seen and flew off. That pilot was the first free American with whom any of these prisoners had been in communication for nearly three years.

Looking over the burning deck, Myers could see the sheer cliffs of Bataan several hundred yards to the southeast. To the northwest, at a greater distance, was the Old U.S. Navy Yard and the little town of

Olongapo. Because of the way the *Oryoku Maru* was listing away from the Bataan side, Olongapo was farther but easier to reach. Myers checked to be certain that the emergency can of meat he'd been saving for months was buttoned safely in the remaining pocket of his tattered shirt and plunged into the water. He fell for what seemed like a very long time before he abruptly met the water and sank down in the dark, cool sea, surrendering himself to it.

Myers' thoughts turned to swimming on hot summer days, in creeks and ponds and rivers back on the farm. He and his brothers, along with other guys from school, held a competition to be the first one in the water every year. Sometimes they even had to break the ice on the surface in order to be the all-important "king of the hill." The best times, though, were when girls would come down and watch them swim. The fellows did their best to look strong and powerful. They dove with grace and swung out over the water on vines like miniature Tarzans. Once in the water, they'd hold their breath and see who could stay under the longest. These antics were performed for one purpose: to garner the attentions of the young lady spectators.

Suddenly Myers realized where he was and that he was on the verge of passing out under the water. He fought to gain control, but his malnourished extremities refused to perform as they had in better times. Struggling through the green ocean, Myers finally surfaced and gasped for breath. He looked around to get his bearings and recognized a man from Bilibid off to his right. The man was out of his mind with pain from burns on his face and shoulders and probably from other injuries not visible. Myers tried to help him, but the man fought him off. Finally Myers gave up and began the swim toward shore.

In reality there was no shore at all, just ankle-deep water that lapped against a four-foot seawall. The men who had reached the shallow water first were wading toward the seawall, laughing and yelling, ecstatic just to be alive, feeling the cool sea water on their dehydrated bodies.

Myers had gone about half of the five hundred yards when the shouts were broken with the staccato sound of bullets hitting the

water. He flipped to his back to see if the planes had returned, but
the sky was empty. Returning to his fatiguing breaststroke, he figured
out where the gunfire was coming from. Machine guns were set up a
short distance from the water on top of the seawall. They were
manned by Japanese marines who were spattering bullets at the prisoners. The marines' intent seemed to be to keep the POWs in the
water, and thirty were immediately gunned down while laboring to
get to shore.

When he finally reached the shallow water, Myers took deep
breaths and crawled on his hands and knees to the seawall, waiting
for Tarpy to catch up to him. Suddenly, he heard more blasts of
machine-gun fire, and two men who had been trying to climb onto
the seawall threw themselves down onto the POWs who were scram-
bling below.

"Stupid SOBs up there are shooting at us!" one guy who fell near
Myers sputtered. "Don't they remember we're already prisoners?"

Myers looked out toward the bay. A lot of men were having a
tough time making it, either because they were hit or were in such a
feeble state they were exhausted. On top of that, the pounding
machine-gun fire forced them to frequently dive deep under the water for cover, with some not making it back to the surface. Myers followed a small group of men who swam back out across the water and
helped drag in those who were struggling. One of them was Tex, who
despite his fear and fatigue, had been shocked into a state of surliness.

"Sit still!" Myers ordered him after they had hauled themselves up
to the base of the seawall.

"Screw you! I'm climbing up there," Tex said, pointing to the top
of the wall.

"Look, you stupid son of a bitch," Myers told him, "you already
had one close call today. You're no cat and you don't get nine lives.
Climb up there and you'll be dead."

"The hell you say," Tex retorted and stood to begin his climb.
Tarpy dragged another man in just then, inadvertently knocking Tex
off his feet. The corpsman was so spent he didn't even try to stand up
again, let alone give the wall another try.

"Here, thought we could use these." Tarpy swung a couple of pairs of boots off his shoulders and tossed them to Myers. He'd tied the laces together and swum with them all the way from the sinking ship. "The Japs I took 'em from aren't gonna miss 'em a bit."

The survivors from the doomed Japanese ship were forced to remain in the water until 1300 hours. While the sea had at first been a godsend on their parched skin, it now chilled their scrawny bodies. A rumor circulated among the men that the shooters on top of the seawall were the JNLP, Japanese Naval Landing Party, Imperial marines well known for their ruthlessness during the war with China.

Although the prisoners had been under the control of the Japanese navy while on board the *Oryoku Maru,* on land they fell under the Japanese army's jurisdiction. The bulk of the army from Olongapo had been sent to Leyte to fend off the Allied advances there, so in their absence the JNLP were on watch at the Old Navy Yard. Toshino was only too happy to turn over the stinking rabble of POWs to the JNLP for a time. Only a handful of his guards had survived the American attacks and he needed to find additional men in Manila.

From the water, the POW commanders negotiated with the JNLP and finally convinced them to allow the feeble group to climb the seawall and rest in the sun. But it would be under watchful eyes and warm gun barrels. As the men straggled over the seawall, the commanders tried to explain to their new Japanese guards how they had been without water for two days. The guards begrudgingly agreed to let a few five-man details go to a nearby faucet for water.

The prisoners were at first grateful for the hot Philippine sun as it warmed their bones, numbed from their immersion in Subic Bay. But after two hours, their unprotected skin began to burn. Meanwhile, the former medical officer and other doctors from Bilibid organized an aid station. The medical staff pooled the first-aid supplies they'd managed to salvage. Myers, Tex, and Tarpy were only an hour into the job of assisting the most wounded when the Japanese ordered that they break camp and get ready to move.

The Imperial marines formed a line from the beach to their head-quarters half a mile away. They stood one hundred feet apart and brandished their rifles, convincing the POWs that any who tried to escape would be shot without hesitation. But the prisoners were far more concerned with holding one another up than escaping. Weak, most of them naked and barefoot, they marched with difficulty along the coral-encrusted path. If one of them stopped to rest or pull a shard out of his foot, he was immediately goaded with a bayonet or clubbed with a bamboo pole.

When they arrived at the gate of the Old Naval Station, the harried prisoners were again told to sit down, which they gladly obliged. Myers watched as the JNLP began a heated discussion amongst themselves with much shouting and pointing. It seemed evident that the marines hadn't expected the POWs' arrival and were in no way prepared for it. Keeping a large group of men under control, no matter how frail they were, would be no small task.

While another long wait ensued, Myers and Tex lay exhausted in the grass.

"They're starting to get to me," Tex said. "I'm tired, Myers."

"I know, pal," Myers answered. "I'm tired, too, but we're still on Philippine soil and now we know for sure the Yanks are on their way. It won't be long now."

At last the JNLP decided that a concrete tennis court was to be the new prison area. In the early part of the century, when the Old Naval Station had been occupied by the Americans, a tennis court had been constructed, along with theaters and nightclubs. Much like the other base areas in the Philippines, Olongapo enjoyed an ambiance of lighthearted gaiety. That was back in the days when life in the service on the islands was more like duty at a country club.

In the old days, the tennis court had undoubtedly been the site of lively games. Now it caged a collection of dirty, bloodied, bearded men. They were shell-shocked and ravaged by disease, and many had been wounded by friendly fire. Many were confused and all were starving, having had nothing to eat all day and practically nothing the day before. Droves of mosquitoes stung their unprotected skin.

The only overhead shelter on the court was a tall referee's platform; the only water source was a single faucet. As they had done aboard the ship, the commanding officers tried to organize the tightly packed group. After a great deal of arguing and shouting, the prisoners were somewhat assembled and roll was called. Their number had dwindled from the original 1,619 to less than 1,300.

The incomprehensible plight that Myers and the others found themselves in was not unique in the Pacific war. The Japanese had begun shipping prisoners from their captured islands as early as 1942. The ships' eventual destinations were Japan, China, Manchuria, and Korea, and they had earned the moniker "hell ships" for the nightmarish voyages that ensued. The prisoners were moved for one reason: the Empire needed as many laborers as could be found to support the Japanese war machine. The POWs proved to be an enormous asset.

The Japanese claimed they did not treat the POWs any differently than they treated their own fighting men when it came to transport by sea. It was true that Japanese forces did not have it easy; they, too, were packed into ships like broiler chickens, on their way to their next battle. But when POWs shared the old, disreputable freighters with Japanese troops, the former were always stuffed in the most tightly and kept down the deepest in the holds. Measured by the number of bodies crammed into airless holds, the hell ships were as bad as the slave ships that came from Africa in the eighteenth century.

While the seas were still controlled by the Imperial Navy, the transports were at least safe from Allied attack and spent only days on the water. The first hell ship, the *Argentina Maru,* a passenger ship, sailed from Guam with her human cargo on January 10, 1942. There were no prisoner deaths for any reason during her voyage. As the Allies drew closer, the Japanese began moving POWs out of the islands in greater numbers. They used transports bearing Red Cross markings for their weapons while the ships carrying prisoners of war were unmarked and targeted by American carriers and submarines. In

1943, the prisoners began suffering casualties aboard the hell ships, and 1944 was the worst year of all.

A total of nine hell ships made their way out of the Philippines that year between August and December. Only the first one, the *Noto Maru,* which left Manila on August 24 with 1,035 POWs aboard, arrived in Japan with all her human cargo still alive. On board all of the other ships, POWs died at a horrendous rate, some from lack of water, food, and air, and others as victims of American firepower.

On September 7, 1944, American torpedoes hit their target, the *Shinyo Maru.* As the prisoners fought their way off the sinking ship they were fired upon by their Japanese guards either while coming out of the holds or after they had made it into the water. Of the 750 Americans who began the voyage, only 82 made it ashore. On October 10, the *Arisan Maru* left Manila with 1,800 American prisoners on board. Eight days later she was torpedoed by the USS *Snook* during a typhoon. The ship sunk rapidly, taking with her 1,792 men still locked in the holds. Eight men managed to escape and survive. Meanwhile, on October 16, an unnamed ship left Manila Bay only to be torpedoed on October 22, resulting in 1,100 prisoner deaths. Before Myers had even set eyes on the *Oryoku Maru,* 3,852 prisoners of war had already suffered needless and malevolent deaths.

Most of the POWs not shipped off to slave labor didn't fare much better. On the Philippine island of Palawan, work details had been toiling at a feverish rate to build an airstrip. Soon it became evident that the work would not be completed by the time the Americans arrived.

The prisoners had been forced to build their own air-raid shelter, a deep burrow half underground in a small bunker. It was perched near a cliff overlooking the ocean. Contrary to their orders, the men built the shelter with two openings: one in the front that the Japanese knew about, another secret opening in back. The 140 Americans from the work detail were herded into the shelter on December 14, 1944, the same day the prisoners aboard the *Oryoku Maru* were praying to be spared from the first wave of American bombers.

When all the POWs were inside the shelter, the Japanese doused the opening with gasoline and threw hand grenades to ignite the gas. A few frantic men made it out the back entrance, and as the rest tried to escape the flames through the front, guards peppered them with machine-gun fire. One prisoner decided in a frenzy that if he was going to die, at least one enemy was going with him. He ran out of the shelter, his body ablaze, and bear hugged the nearest Japanese soldier, dragging him back into the inferno to die with the rest of them.

The men who escaped out the back tumbled down the steep cliff toward the beach, hiding in caves or behind boulders. The Japanese suspected that some of the men might have escaped and a search was mounted but ultimately abandoned. Eight men of the original 140 survived.

Stories circulated throughout prisoner groups that any men not moved from the Philippines to Japan would be killed. Some thought this was the enemy's plan to prohibit the prisoners from ever relating stories about their mistreatment in the camps. Others just assumed these events were one final act of brutality. In all, thousands died during these final chapters of an already unspeakably barbarous theater of war.

An average tennis court measures 78 by 36 feet for a total of about 2,800 square feet. Arranging thirteen hundred men in such a small concrete space was like the nightmare of the ship's holds all over again. At least now they had air. The officers finally decided that the men would sit in rows of fifty-two across, twenty-six rows on one side of the net and another twenty-six on the other side. They sat with their knees pulled up under their chins. The only alternative was sitting spread-eagle, with each man's haunches in the fork of his neighbor's legs.

Myers, Tex, and Tarpy had managed to regroup on one end of the court. Survival was the prime consideration of most and the medical corps, through force of habit, did what they had been trained to do. Again, they had designated a hospital area occupying the fifteen-foot strip of space beyond the tennis court's baseline. The corpsmen collected various garments from among the uninjured, stringing some overhead to serve as protection for the wounded against the burning sun, and reserving others for use as bandages. They managed to pull up bamboo shoots growing under the tennis court's board fence to use as splints. Beyond that, the hospital was no different than the rest of the court. Enough supplies had been collected to start another of their now famous improvised aid stations. The Japanese, of course, furnished no medical supplies.

"Here they come again," Myers yelled. The men around him looked skyward to see a surging contingent of three American planes. "Hit the deck!"

The men crouched as best they could, given their tight space, not sure whether they would be strafed or ignored. The first plane headed for an anti-aircraft gun mounted on the knoll beyond the tennis court. The second plane headed straight for the *Oryoku Maru,* dropping its ordnance in a direct hit. The third plane's bomb hit off target, but by this time the ship burned furiously.

Standing on tiptoes, Myers was able to see the ship ablaze and the explosions from the remaining ammunition on board. The *Oryoku Maru* sank completely after a couple of hours, taking with her the remains of the dead POWs.

Myers and the other corpsmen had absolutely nothing with which to relieve their patients' pain. They regaled those who hadn't seen the final attack with tales of the burning ship and the likelihood that they would be liberated long before they could be reloaded to continue their trip to Japan. The goal was to take the patients' minds off what, for some, was the inevitable: excruciating pain followed by a grisly death.

Dysentery and diarrhea still plagued many of the men. There were no drugs to alleviate this situation. Many of the men were in stages of nutritional decimation; their bodies would have been unable to tolerate nutritious food even if it had been available. Those, Myers among them, who had tried to save brown sugar from scavenging aboard the *Oryoku Maru,* would now have found it of no use. The Japanese had allowed them to dig straddle trenches for latrines outside of the tennis court fence but would only allow two or three to go at a time. Consequently, the stream of men there and back was continuous. Those who couldn't wait had no choice but to relieve themselves on the tennis court, the stench drawing flies in tremendous swarms.

The men carefully filled canteen cups from the worn-out, rusted faucet at one end of the court and distributed the water four spoonfuls per man. The future did not look hopeful, however, as the trickle of water from the tap grew ever more scant. Sitting in the full sun as they were, with some of them nearly naked, made their thirst ever more powerful.

Myers and the other corpsmen worked feverishly among the injured, nearly to the point of their own exhaustion, cleaning faces and wounds as best they could. Many of the men from the aft hold were badly burned; other prisoners' bodies were covered with the ship's oil that had been floating on the surface of the water. Their beards popped through in spots and were matted down in others, causing them to resemble grotesque cavemen.

The severity of their wounds varied. There were slashes and puncture holes caused by the shrapnel from the bombs. There were burns of assorted degrees, although those with the severest burns had already died. Some POWs had been crippled by debris falling into the holds. And many of them had wounds that had occurred before they'd boarded the ship. These were now infected from exposure to septic conditions.

Two men with ragged arm injuries were in such a horrible state that the doctors determined they had no choice but to immediately remove the limbs. The patients had a high likelihood of dying from the crude surgery, as there was no sterilization, anesthesia, or instruments. The only usable equipment the doctors had was a pair of tissue scissors, a hemostat, a razor blade, and a mess kit knife sharpened on the concrete surface of the tennis court. But without the amputations, the men were certain to die.

Myers happened to be near one of these men, a young Marine corporal. The doctor who was working on the Marine told Myers and another corpsman they would have to assist him with the surgery.

Myers knelt next to the young Marine and asked, "How goes it?"

"No sweat," the Marine answered. "They gotta take the arm"—he jerked his head toward the blood-stained strip of uniform shirt he was using as a bandage—"but shoot, I got another one." He grinned feebly.

Myers had seen enough carnage over the past three years to know that the Marine's situation was grave.

"I haven't got anything to sterilize the instruments with," the doctor said as he fumbled in his mess kit. "And nothing to cauterize the stump."

Myers got up and walked cautiously toward a guard watching from the edge of the tennis court. The prisoners knew the guards were cooking, they could smell the campfires. Myers talked this guard out of a burning stick to use during the surgery, promising to return it as soon as they had finished.

One of the other corpsman fastened the hemostat to the tattered skin on the Marine's arm, pulling it back and revealing the wound in full.

"Most of the muscle is already exposed," the doctor said. "Getting through it will be easy." He looked at Myers and motioned toward the burning stick. "You're going to assist." Myers picked the stick up as the doctor handed the knife to another corpsman. "I'll use this when we get to the bone. And both of you need to keep the patient calm and still." Then he looked at the Marine. "Ready, son?"

"Yes, sir," the Marine answered, as positively as if the doctor had asked if he enjoyed cold beer.

All of the surgeries Myers had assisted in thus far in his career had been performed in a far more stable environment. Even the hospital at Bilibid now looked like a top-notch medical facility. He felt his empty stomach lurch. It wasn't looking at the shredded tissue of a human body that bothered him; it was the fact that the Marine was completely conscious that made Myers uncharacteristically squeamish. He'd been good at soothing animals on the farm when they'd been injured or were giving birth. His current task wasn't dissimilar except that the outcome of this procedure carried a much higher price—that of a human life.

Myers spoke to the Marine, whose eyes alternated between being squeezed tightly shut and looking around wildly.

"Keep looking at me, buddy," Myers told him, holding the mangled arm steady under his knees. "Pick out a scar or a mole or something on my face and just stare at it as hard as you can."

The Marine did as he was told and never took his eyes off a spot on Myers' left cheek. Myers spoke in a tempered, steady voice, quoting Bible verses and song lyrics and anything else he could think of to fill the Marine's mind, just as he'd done with the animals in distress. His strategy was working and the Marine never made a sound. As improbable as the idea of doing delicate surgery in such bizarre and underequipped surroundings seemed, it was going relatively well. All of the men, from doctor to corpsmen to patient, had already seen and endured so much. How could this possibly be worse?

As the doctor sawed through the man's arm, Myers cauterized each section with the burning stick. When the arm had been completely removed, they rebound the stump, using a fresh, albeit not clean, bandage made out of the Marine's cutoff pants. Myers stayed with him through the night, providing him with as much water as possible, including adding a portion of his own ration to the Marine's. He opened the emergency can of meat he still had tucked in his shirt pocket. The Marine choked some of it down, Myers had some, and the rest was shared with other nearby patients. The Marine survived the night and awoke clear-headed.

Other men fared less well that night. After watching the breakdowns aboard the *Oryoku Maru* of fellow prisoners who had been friends, every man regarded the man next to him suspiciously. None of them were quite sure they could trust their neighbor and carefully guarded whatever possessions they had. The beginnings of an "every man for himself" philosophy pervaded. It was a study in witnessing civilized men return to their primitive, base instincts.

The men's physical discomforts were as intolerable as their emotional ones. The surface of the tennis court, which was like a hot griddle that had seared the prisoners in the full sun, lost its heat and became almost glacial at dusk. The men with the most severe sunburns developed chills, hugging themselves to stop their violent shaking.

Toshino's remaining Formosan guards mingled with the JNLP around the tennis court. The Formosans had all spent the war guarding other camps and they recognized some of the prisoners who were once again suffering under their watch. A few among them exhibited rare flashes of compassion. They threw a couple of shirts over the fence and shoved casaba melons and cigarettes through the broken wooden slats.

Given their interlocking positions, the men in rows on the court all had to lie down, or none of them could. The rows that chose to lay did so on their sides, fitting together like spoons in a drawer. When the cold, hard concrete became too painful for their unpadded bones on one side, someone would yell, "Turn over, boys," and the whole line would roll to the other side. The fact that so many had to use the latrine during the night, coupled with their hunger, thirst, and disheartenment, allowed very few to get much sleep.

When morning arrived, during the brief period in which they were no longer freezing and not yet burning, they again began the tedious process of roll call, with an officer shouting out names from up on the referee's stand. The Japanese were fastidious record keepers and had supplied the commanding officers with their lists. It took nearly two hours as arguments routinely broke out over whether or not a man was dead or alive.

A commanding officer would yell out, "Smith?"

"He died on the ship," someone would respond.

"No, he didn't. I saw him yesterday," another would chime in.

"You'd think you saw your mother yesterday."

Finally, the man in question would answer: "Here, sir."

The process continued until the group had determined that another six men had died during the night. The clothing was removed from the bodies to be used elsewhere, and the JNLP allowed some volunteers to bury the corpses down near the seawall.

Later in the day, the prisoners received their first food since arriving at the tennis court. Each prisoner was given two spoons of raw rice. Wada was lurking around and they begged him for more food but were reminded he had no control over the situation for "jurisdictional reasons." Wada said it was of no matter to him if all 1,300 starved; they were now the army's problem.

The men shared what few articles of clothing they had with one another. A man who had a full set of trousers or a long-sleeved shirt gave the legs or arms to other men who were less protected from the elements. A load of cast-off clothing arrived by truck from Bilibid, and by the time it was all distributed nearly every man had at least one article in the form of a shirt, pants, or hat.

The medical staff was finally able to persuade their captors to let them move the most badly injured among them to a grassy, shaded area outside of the tennis court. Only one hundred were allowed outside; the rest were ordered to remain in the sun. And those who were moved outside had to be brought back onto the tennis court again at night.

On December 18, the prisoners again received food. The next day, they received nothing in the morning or at noon, but two more spoonfuls of raw rice were distributed at night. Finally, on December 20, a convoy of nineteen trucks arrived. The Japanese removed about eight hundred of the thirteen hundred prisoners on the tennis court and loaded them into the trucks.

Myers, Tex, and Tarpy remained on the tennis court, mustering meager curiosity about where the other group had gone.

"Bet those bastards are tired of messing with us. We're dead weight, too much trouble. They're probably gonna kill those other guys," Tarpy spat out as they huddled together on the cold concrete that night. "Probably kill us, too."

"I don't know," Myers said. "The Japs need us—we're their slave workforce. I was thinking maybe they took 'em back to Bilibid to put 'em on another ship. I think we got a fifty-fifty chance. That's better than no chance."

The next morning the truck convoy returned and loaded up the remaining five hundred prisoners before heading north. Each time the Japanese guards heard or saw American planes overhead, the trucks veered off the dirt road and hid under the canopies of trees until the threat passed. Eventually, they arrived in San Fernando Pampanga, about two hundred miles from Manila. The trucks drove by a prison yard, where the prisoners saw the first group encamped. Both groups of POWs were so relieved to see that their comrades had not been executed, they hooted to one another as the convoy passed. The trucks drove on to the town's theater, where Myers' group was offloaded.

The prisoners took stock of the last five days. They'd been bombed, shot at, and exposed to the elements. Several hundred had died. Those remaining had lost more of their rapidly ebbing strength. But they were still in the Philippines. And MacArthur was still on his way.

CHAPTER TWELVE

★

A Feast Before Hell

San Fernando Pampanga's dilapidated theater was the closest thing to paradise the POWs had seen in years. The building was filthy, its seats removed from the sloping floor. Nothing was provided for the men to sleep on save the cold concrete floor, but in an amazing act of humanity, the Japanese set up equipment to cook rice. On December 22, the prisoners received their first hot meal since the morning of December 14.

Half a canteen cup full of cooked rice, with a little steamed *camote* alongside, was served from a sheet of corrugated roofing material to Myers and his fellow prisoners. The Filipino yams made him think of a yam concoction his mother made to accompany all of the family holiday meals. Those thoughts led him to wonder who would be present for dinner at his parents' home this Christmas, which was only days away. Then he wondered if he would ever be present at one of those meals again. Quickly, he forced the fear out of his mind. He ate the feast currently before him slowly, in tiny bites, to draw the pleasure out as long as possible. The prisoners also had water available to them from the theater's toilet intakes. The line to get water had been continuous since they'd arrived at the theater, and it moved at the same speed as the water flowed: slowly. Many men fell asleep waiting before their turn came.

As if miracles would never cease, a few Red Cross boxes arrived that night from Manila. They contained much-needed drugs, which dwindled to next to nothing by the time they were divided among thirteen hundred men. The medicine arrived too late for the young Marine corporal who had bravely endured amputation on the tennis court. He died that night in the theater, as quietly as he had suffered over the previous several days.

Early the next morning, good news traveled to the prisoners from a few Filipinos who had surreptitiously snuck up outside a theater window: the Yanks had landed at Batangas, a town less than two hundred miles south. But the men's high spirits soon plunged when Wada and several Japanese guards stalked through the theater, looking each man over carefully.

After the contingent passed him, Tex muttered, "Assholes!" Wada talked for a few minutes to the two group commanders, who relayed his orders to the corpsmen. Fifteen men in the worst physical condition were to be removed and, as Wada benevolently explained it, sent back to Manila where they could recuperate. The doctors and corpsmen were to choose the men.

"God, I hope they make it," Myers wished out loud.

"I'm telling you, we're getting to be too much trouble," Tarpy told him. "Japs'll probably finish 'em off here. They're no good as slaves. They're probably better off wherever they're going. They won't be hungry or sick or scared no more. I kinda wish I was goin', too."

"Cut that crap out right now!" Myers demanded. "Only way we're gonna get through this is because we want to. Don't stop wanting it, Tarpy."

Tarpy hung his head.

At 0500 on December 24, the men were rousted out of the theater and were joined by the group from the prison. The entire assemblage was counted and then recounted before being marched to the town's railroad station. Even in the early morning light, the bullet holes that riddled the narrow-gauge locomotive which awaited them were visible. Attached to the engine was a string of freight cars, each six feet wide and twenty-six feet long. The first few cars were loaded with ammunition, the next seven or eight were designated for the prisoners, hardly enough to carry them all. Wada explained the next leg of their journey.

"Injured men to be put on top of cars. If American planes fly overhead, wave bandages to show that you are POWs. You are protection for the prisoners inside the cars. Wave bandages so your friends up there will recognize you."

His wicked, twisted mouth imitated a smile and every prisoner understood Wada's rationale. The men on top of the cars would also protect the three that were loaded with ammunition. The guards were ordered to begin loading the cars. One hundred and fifty men were stuffed inside each car, with another fifty on top. A guard rode inside each car, as near to the door as he could position himself to avoid having to breathe the foul stench exuded by the prisoners. Two more guards went up on top.

Someone saw planes engaged in a dogfight in the distance and the news spread through the crowd of men around Myers. While they waited their turn to enter a car, the men silently cheered on the American pilots. To do so out loud would have antagonized their captors and meant sudden death. Finally, the guards reached Myers, Tarpy, and Tex, and they were pressed into a boxcar along with a hundred and twenty others.

The heat within the boxcars was as intense as it had been aboard the *Oryoku Maru*. The men's sweat quickly plastered their tattered clothing to their bony frames. There was no water available, and except for near the open door blocked by the guard, the air became stifling almost immediately. The train moved out around 1100 hours. Predictions of their destination circulated through the rank air.

"We're goin' to Cabanatuan."

"Naw, Camp O'Donnell."

"Bilibid for supplies."

Most bets ran in favor of a return to Bilibid. When the train finally did pass the switch to Cabanatuan, their legs ached from standing. Another dogfight broke out overhead but the Allied planes did not threaten the train. Headed northward through the mountains, the train at times was forced to creep through still smoldering wreckage of Imperial aircraft and tanks. This was yet another cause for silent celebration among the POWs.

The train rumbled to a slow stop, and it soon became obvious it was a dinner stop for the guards. Myers smelled the cooked rice, and as vile a substance as it had become over his three years of imprisonment, he was so hungry he would have gladly accepted a serving of it. Some of the more able-bodied prisoners conjectured on their chances of making an escape through the enemy-infested hills. No one gave the idea very favorable odds and the suggestion was dropped.

The train got underway again, and by the time they passed Camp O'Donnell the men's lips were parched and quite a few passed out from the lack of air. When they did faint, the car was so crowded they couldn't fall to the floor. Instead they were passed overhead, hand to hand, until they arrived at the boxcar door, where the increased air circulation revived them. When night fell, the air turned cold again. The men on top begged to be brought down and the guards did make a few exchanges during another brief stop. Once the train started up again those who hadn't been moved begged to be brought down, too. The guards became irritated and threatened that anyone else making noise would be shot immediately.

After a journey of more than sixteen hours, the train pulled into a station at San Fernando La Union in the early hours of Christmas morning. Thirteen hundred men tumbled out of the suffocating boxcars and onto the station's platform. It appeared as though no one had died during the bone-jarring train ride.

They immediately all lay down on the cinders to rest, but their respite was brief—they were ordered to their feet moments later and herded to a small, single-story trade school, half a mile away on the outskirts of town. The men arranged themselves throughout the schoolyard, grabbing handfuls of leaves and flowers from the hibiscus bushes on either side and devouring them. The building itself became the ever-present dispensary, in name only, for the most seriously ill. The doctors and corpsmen had little help beyond their hands and their heads in their pathetic attempts to ease suffering.

Wada announced that water was available, but they would have to dig for it. When the prisoners found some, they used iodine to purify it.

"What is this place?" someone asked, shivering in the cold and dark. He was answered, and soon much speculation began.

"I saw a sign at the station; we're at San Fernando La Union."

"That's a shipping port. We're on the Lingayan Gulf."

"Oh, God, another ship?"

"Won't happen."

"How in the hell do these stupid Japs think they're gonna get us outta here? There must be a Yank blockade of subs surrounding this entire island."

"Bet they'll be here in short order."

It was Christmas day. On previous holidays celebrated in their respective prison camps, many had shared stories of Christmas back home. They were long past the stage where they missed the details that meant home to each of them. Their most compelling drive now was to simply survive.

Nonetheless, the chaplains prayed in ironic recognition of the day the Prince of Peace was born. The prisoners were fed a half cup of steamed rice with a couple of pieces of *camote*. They were given rust-colored water to drink from a nearby carabao wallow teeming with mosquito larvae. They were exhausted, and yet sleep was impossible; they were once again exposed to the blazing Philippine sun.

As dusk fell, the POWs were lined up in ranks of four and marched again down a road paved with shards of coral and shell. The chalky white road soon became streaked with crimson, as the road's surface sliced at the feet of the men without shoes. Only an air-raid alert gave them a brief chance to nurse their painful, bloodied feet.

Three miles later, around 2100 hours, they arrived at a beach and were grouped near a loading dock covered with boxes, where they were expected to remain for the night. They could see the lights from several ships anchored out in the bay. As on the tennis court, the temperature swung from a furnace-like day to the numbing coldness of night, making sleep on the wet beach unlikely. Some of the men tried to bury themselves in the sand for protection from the cold wind and discovered as they dug that hundreds of drums of gasoline had been buried under the beach.

On the morning of the 26th, the prisoners were roused at an early hour. The day's first meal consisted of a lump of rice the size of a tennis ball. Myers and the other corpsmen tried to assist in serving, but any organization soon broke down. Consequently those who were strong enough grabbed several lumps of rice; the weaker ones received none.

Myers watched in disgust as the men around him continued to sink to their basest instincts. Taking food from a fellow serviceman was bad enough, but Myers saw officers taking from enlisted men. This was strictly against all the rules. It appeared that some of the men, however, had not only abandoned the rules of the military, but all other rules for decent human behavior as well. The brutality of the enemy combined with the courage of the captives brought out the very best in some men, and as he was witnessing, the very worst in others.

The rising sun again seemed to ally itself with the Imperial troops, as it reflected off the sand and the bay, to fry the men's skin. For all their thirst, the prisoners were issued only the equivalent of two tablespoons of filthy water from the carabao wallow. The commanders saw the toll the exposure was taking. The men around them were parched, their dehydration not even allowing perspiration.

The Japanese were finally impressed by the suffering, and in the afternoon the prisoners were finally shown mercy when they were allowed to go down to the water's edge in groups of one hundred. The groups were each given five minutes to bathe, splash, and do whatever they could to rejuvenate themselves in the stinging salt water. Those who were the most dehydrated scooped the water up and drank it. As one group was being marched back up the beach, an Army captain broke ranks and ran back into the water to drink up more. The guards raised their rifles to their shoulders, but some men quickly dragged the captain out again, saving him from certain execution.

Their brief ocean dip began to work against them as soon as they began to dry. The salt from the water clung to their bodies and intensified the sun's piercing rays. A few hours later, the commanders again implored their captors for relief from the hellish effects of the afternoon sun. This time it came in the form of one canteen of water for every twenty men. The water was divided into four tablespoonfuls per man, and enough was issued for each man to receive his share every ninety minutes.

Japanese activity reached a fevered pitch that day. Enemy reinforcements, horses, and supplies came ashore from anchored ships in droves. Myers, Tarpy, and Tex watched the goings-on with only mild interest. It appeared as though the enemy was preparing to defend the area down to the last man. And for the prisoners, the next days spread out like the vast Pacific Ocean. But surely, they had already experienced the worst suffering they would ever see.

The troops of General MacArthur's army had found no more time to celebrate the holiday season than Myers had, although they at least had a hot meal, a warm bed, and their freedom. In December of 1944, the battle for the island of Leyte wasn't over, but it had already been decided in the Allies' favor. With the victory undoubtedly would come supremacy throughout the Philippines. Japan had consolidated her forces from other islands and redeployed them in Leyte to fend off the two hundred thousand American combat troops on the island. This redeployment would likely cost the Japanese in their defense of other islands.

The significance of the Leyte defeat did not escape the Imperial powers. The price would be half of their empire. Radio Tokyo reported that the Battle for Leyte Gulf was not only important in deciding "whether we lose one corner of the Philippines" but also "whether we lose our sea routes to our southern regions. . . . We cannot withdraw even a single step, for we have burned our bridges behind us."

Allied landing craft began cruising close to the shores of other Philippine islands, offloading patrols whose job it was to root out the enemy from wherever he may be hidden. Loudspeakers on the landing crafts announced in Japanese that giving up was the wisest thing to do. There were promises of good food, clean beds, and bathing, far more generous than anything the Japanese were providing the Allied prisoners. The Japanese troops were told that this would be regarded as an "honorable surrender." The vast majority of those troops within earshot, however, clung to their belief that there was no such thing as an honorable surrender, and very few accepted the Americans' offer.

By December 19, the Japanese abandoned their organized fighting on Leyte although resistance continued well into 1945. It was the first step toward the American goal of liberating the Philippines from the Japanese. But the enemy still controlled air bases on other islands, and the only facilities that would allow the Allies to wipe out those bases were located on the island of Luzon.

MacArthur's forces passed through the Mindanao Sea and northward to Mindoro, where they landed on the southwest shores of the island. There they began work on two airfields from which the all-important next step to Luzon could be taken.

The American forces were zealous in their desire to liberate the American prisoners of war known to be held in the Philippines. One morning, just off a Philippine shoreline, Army Staff Sergeant Henry Telker tried to force his eyes to penetrate the thick fog enshrouding the island. He noted his compass reading and wrote in his logbook: "Location doubtful, chart little or no help."

Telker's orders had been to deliver caterpillar tractors to the beachhead via landing craft, and he was a man who obeyed orders. Once Telker and his detail had come ashore, they were met by throngs of ecstatic Filipinos. But when Japanese planes strafed them, Telker was confused.

After asking one of the Filipinos for their location, Telker discovered he had inadvertently invaded Mindanao, a Philippine island still exclusively and thickly held by the enemy. The sergeant and his party abandoned that particular beachhead immediately.

Myers and his fellow POWs would have been astounded to learn how plentiful the Yanks were in and around the Philippines, and equally astounded at how close they were to liberating them. Mac-Arthur's plans for the initial invasion of Luzon included landings at Lingayen Gulf, practically on the same spot where the Japanese had landed during their initial invasion in 1941. He set the Lingayen landings for December 20, but a combination of seasonal rains, lack of air cover, and the success of the kamikazes caused the landings to be rescheduled for January 9, 1945.

The Luzon campaign was to be the longest and most difficult of the entire Pacific war. The Lingayen landings alone were larger in size than the combined invasions of North Africa, Sicily, and southern France; more than two hundred thousand troops had been made available for the offensive.

Lieutenant General Tomoyuki Yamashita, called the Tiger of Malaya for the success of his invasion of that peninsula and ultimate victory over the British troops there, was the Imperial officer in charge of the defense of the Philippines. But Yamashita was not to have the kind of success he had previously enjoyed. Again the rivalry between the Japanese army and navy came to the forefront. And again, as it had when they begged Wada for food on the tennis court, the rivalry had a crucial impact on Myers and the rest of the POWs.

The twenty-five thousand Imperial naval troops on the island of Luzon obeyed only their commanders and, from the moment Yamashita arrived, the troops ignored his orders. This, combined with the fact that a significant portion of the Japanese troops had left to defend Leyte, prompted Yamashita to offer only a token defense of Manila when the Allied troops began their December reconnaissance flights, followed by the frequent bombing runs. Had the Japanese been able to muster more protection for their POW transports, Myers' plight and that of his fellow prisoners might have had a very different outcome.

Wada and Toshino had taken note that the Allied planes had not bombed the prisoners on the tennis court nor those tied to the top of the train. Using the men to protect the Japanese goods and equipment appeared to have a guaranteed outcome.

"Be warned," Wada said, "you are sitting on much gasoline. If planes bomb, well . . ." He shrugged, leaving the prisoners to use what was left of their imaginations.

"I think he's on the level," Myers told Tex. "I heard a guy from the Two Hundredth Coastal Artillery say he'd spent the night sleeping on top of a gas drum. He'd dug into the sand and there she was."

As night fell on December 26, a detachment of Japanese soldiers arrived in trucks, shovels in hand, and dug up the buried drums, loaded them into the trucks, and drove away. More war materials were unloaded from ships at the docks and piled neatly on the nearby shore by Imperial troops.

Myers fell into a tormented sleep on the cold, wet sand until he was awakened by kicks by a sentry's hobnailed boots. The prisoners were told to get ready but were never instructed exactly what they were readying themselves for. Word floated among the men that they were going to be taken out to the two freighters they had seen anchored in Lingayen Gulf the day before.

As a constant among them, the men were only vaguely aware of their hunger and thirst as they huddled together on the cold sand. It didn't appear as though any preparation was being made to give them anything, and even the commanders were too cold and exhausted to attempt any kind of entreaty with the guards. About 65 prisoners had expired since the train had arrived at San Fernando La Union, bringing their number to about 1,234. Some had died from exposure, some from their myriad injuries and diseases, and a couple at the guards' hands. The guards hadn't been any crueler than they had previously been, but blows the prisoners had been able to sustain only weeks earlier were now fatal on their infirm bodies.

An hour and a half later, the prisoners were ordered to march along the waterfront to the dock loaded with Japanese supplies. They were marched out to a wharf which jutted out from the shore. On the way, they passed inbound Japanese troops who had been told these were prisoners recently captured on Leyte. The POWs stretched out their hands to the Japanese troops begging for a morsel of food. The only response they received was sardonic laughter as the Imperial soldiers made fun of the foul-looking Americans.

The landing boats were having difficulty in coming alongside the wharf due to a choppy sea. Suddenly, the Japanese in charge of the prisoners' loading became agitated and shouted at the prisoners to get on two barges tied up at the dock.

"Speedo, speedo!" Wada screamed, running among the POWs.

Some of the prisoners moved too slowly to suit their captors and were literally shoved off the dock and onto the unstable barges. Fragile bones splintered when the gaunt prisoners landed on the decks below. Nothing deterred the guards on the barges, who immediately began pushing the prisoners back with rifle butts and the flats of swords.

"Back, speedo! Speedo!"

The barges sputtered away from the dock with their loads of hollow-eyed and bewildered prisoners. Miserable as they were, the sailors among the POWs knew that ships always considered themselves relatively safe from air and submarine attacks at night, since the visibility is limited. What they did not know was that during the course of this war, the Americans had become adept at night attacks, putting Japanese ships at risk nearly twenty-four hours a day.

"Something's got these Nips scared," Tarpy observed.

"Maybe it's MacArthur; I'll bet MacArthur's landed somewhere close," Myers told him.

Tarpy shook his head sadly, looking across the deck of the barge to the two freighters looming like ghost ships in the dark ahead of them. "Too bad he's too late."

CHAPTER THIRTEEN

★

The Price of Sugar

In the predawn gloom of Wednesday, December 27, 1944, it appeared as though Estel Myers would be leaving the Philippines once and for all. A Japanese barge was ferrying him in the dark across a turbulent Lingayen Gulf, approaching the awaiting two freighters. Drawing closer, he could now see a covey of other ships hovering around as well, presumably for protection similar to what the *Oryoku Maru* had had.

At exactly the same moment that Myers was being rudely jostled against fellow POWs on the barge, his younger brother Ken was weathering the waves only a few hundred miles to the south aboard the hospital ship the USS *Bountiful*. The ship had tended to the wounded from the Battle for Leyte Gulf and was now cruising north toward Mindoro and Luzon. Her next destination would be determined by when and where the Allied landings began in the impending fight for the Philippines. Estel, of course, had no idea that Ken was stationed on a ship so near, or that he was even in the war at all. Ken, on the other hand, had a powerful belief, one of epic proportions, that it wouldn't be long before he'd be reunited with his brother.

Ken Myers hadn't ever been the type of guy easily duped into believing anything contrary to what his own senses told him. Years ago at a state fair, he was the one who had figured out that the side show magician wasn't really disappearing; he had simply installed a fake floor in his magic trunk. Ken was also the first to inform the kids in the neighborhood and his younger brother, Bert, that there was no Santa Claus and never had been. But as a seaman in the U.S. Navy, something happened that overwhelmed his previous unyielding skepticism.

While crossing the Pacific months earlier, it was the job of the *Bountiful*'s crew to ensure that everything was shipshape before they arrived at the battle zone. Ken had been ordered to clean out some lockers, and at the bottom of one of them he came across a placard that read USS *Henderson*. Ken recognized the name from Estel's early letters describing his first night at sea aboard the *Henderson*. Ken took the placard to his petty officer and asked him what connection the two ships had.

"This ship was the *Henderson* up until a year ago, seaman," the petty officer told him. "After the war started she was refitted and became the *Bountiful*."

Ken was positive this news had to be more than just a coincidence. It was a sign. Fate had seen to it that he was assigned to the same ship his brother had been on. To Ken, that was a sure sign that Estel was alive and well, and relatively close.

It was true that Estel was close, and that he was alive, but he never would have described his condition as completely well. He'd been suffering from a case of diarrhea just like all of the others had. Although he'd long ago become accustomed to ocean swells, this barge trip, brief as it was, made him feel dreadful.

The freighters weren't marked with names. Instead, one ship had "No. 1" painted on her funnel and the other had "No. 2" on her superstructure. The prisoners learned later that the ships were officially the *Enoura Maru* and the *Brazil Maru,* respectively. They bore no distinction that would alert any pilots who might happen by overhead that they carried human cargo. The ships' props were running, the engines' chugging sounding as impatient as the Japanese guards' shouting voices.

"Speedo, speedo!"

The first barge began offloading its prisoners onto the *Brazil Maru,* the larger of the pair. Then the second barge began to offload onto the same ship; Myers, Tex, and Tarpy were among this group. Myers estimated the vessel was about eight thousand tons and that her little sister was probably two or three thousand tons less. The off-loading went slowly, of course, since so many men had to be helped up the gangplank. The impatient captain directed his sailors to move the Americans along faster, but it just couldn't be done.

After exasperated jabbering at his guards and anxious glances at the morning sun beginning to rise in the sky, the captain finally ordered that the transfer to his ship be stopped. The guards had counted off one thousand men. The remaining 234 prisoners were to be loaded onto the *Enoura Maru.*

For once, the Japanese did not procrastinate in getting underway. They didn't even take the time for one of their famous *bangou.* The last man was being pulled over the bulwark railing when the entire convoy weighed anchor and set off along the coast of northern Luzon.

While the prisoners aboard the *Enoura Maru* were immediately herded down into the holds, Myers and the others aboard the *Brazil Maru* were surprised to be held in groups on the deck, watched closely by the vulture guards perched overhead. A Japanese officer had singled out a ten-man crew of POWs and explained in broken English that they were to go down into the hold to clean something. It wasn't clear what the Japanese expected, since the POWs weren't given any kind of tools to clean with.

While they waited, a couple of prisoners spied water dripping from one of the steam cylinders that powered the deck winches. The prisoners ran their tongues along the length of the cylinder to lap up every drop of greasy water they could before a guard caught them and beat them back into line.

Myers watched the scenario as it played out in front of him and was bewildered. Those prisoners hadn't threatened the guards in any way. They hadn't done anything to cause any alteration in whatever the next plan of action might be. In fact, there was no obvious reason for the guards to repeatedly refuse these men the food and water. The only conclusion Myers could arrive at was that the Imperial guards just took pure pleasure in the prisoners' deprivation. Myers had never before known anyone capable of doing that; he had never conceived of the possibility that someone might want to.

As had happened nearly every step of their arduous journey, the POWs were again obviously moving too slowly for their Japanese captors and were again the subjects of their impatient rage. The officer screamed, "No clean!" and ordered that the prisoners be jammed into the midships hold.

If a man didn't move spryly enough to suit the guards, the latter lashed out at him with a rifle, broom, or the broadside of a sword. As some of the POWs began climbing down the ladder into the hold, the guards shoved them. Although the force might not have been enough to make them lose their footing under normal circumstances, in the prisoners' frail condition it caused them to tumble onto the men below them. Between the beatings and the falls, a number of the prisoners would begin this leg of the journey with open wounds.

After he'd been shoved down into the hold, Myers forced his eyes to focus in the new dark and fetid surroundings. The hold was constructed with two levels and a repulsive odor assaulted his nostrils. Myers recognized the stench instantly.

"This place stinks like horse manure," he told Tarpy. "That must have been what the Japs wanted those guys to come down and shove around. And it smells like there's gallons of horse pee someplace."

"Japs use it for chemical manufacturing," a major near them offered. "I'll bet they had cavalry horses in here and saved all the pee. It's probably down in the bilges."

As on the *Oryoku Maru,* this ship had a ventilation system for the animals' comfort, but the Japanese shut it off as soon as the prisoners began loading. Unlike their first ship, however, this one at least had adequate space so that each man could lie down.

Besides the overpowering stench of the place, it was filled with enormous, vicious horseflies. They had been drawn to the animal excrement first but must have taken delight in the load of fetid hu-

Estel Myers in 1922, at twenty months of age. (Courtesy of the Myers family)

The Myers children, 1929. From left to right: Estel, Orville, Iola, Ken, and Bert Jr. (Courtesy of the Myers family)

The Myers family, 1937.
Estel, age seventeen,
is on the far left.
(Courtesy of the Myers family)

Estel and his dog, Pos,
taken in 1941 just prior to
Estel's being shipped off to
Shanghai. (Courtesy of the
Myers family)

The USS *Henderson*, the vessel that carried Estel to Shanghai, and then to the Philippines. (Courtesy of the National Archives)

The USS *Bountiful*—formerly the USS *Henderson*. The vessel was transformed into a naval hospital ship on which Ken Myers, Estel's brother, served. (Courtesy of the Naval Bureau of Medicine and Surgery)

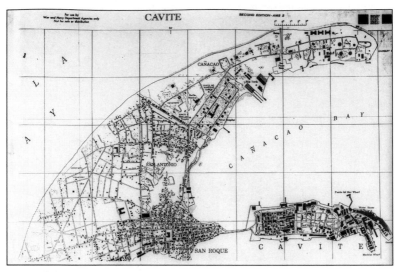

Map of the Cavite Naval Yard. (Courtesy of the Naval Bureau of Medicine and Surgery)

An aerial view of the Canacao Naval Hospital compound before it was bombed by the Japanese. (Courtesy of the Naval Bureau of Medicine and Surgery)

Just across the bay from the Cavite Naval Yard, Canacao Naval Hospital was the largest Navy medical facility west of Pearl Harbor when the Japanese closed it down and imprisoned its staff in January 1942.
(Courtesy of the Naval Bureau of Medicine and Surgery)

Sangley Point after the Japanese attack of December 1941. Note the half-sunken ships in the harbor.
(Courtesy of the Naval Bureau of Medicine and Surgery)

The Jai Alai Club was a nightclub that was converted into a hospital after the initial Japanese bombing of Manila.
(Courtesy of the Admiral Nimitz Museum of the Pacific War)

The aftermath of the Japanese bombing of Manila, December 31, 1941.
(Courtesy of the National Archives)

American troops surrendering by waving the white flag on Corregidor
outside the Malinta Tunnel, May 8, 1942. (Courtesy of the National Archives)

A captured Japanese photo of surrendering American troops, May 1942.
(Courtesy of the National Archives)

Pier Seven, where POWs boarded the infamous hell ships such as
Oryoku Maru, *Tattori Maru*, and *Arisan Maru*, was bombed extensively
by the Allies in their efforts to retake the Philippines. (Courtesy of the
Admiral Nimitz Museum of the Pacific War)

A captured Japanese photo of the Bataan death march—POWs carry the injured on makeshift gurneys of blankets and bamboo poles. (Courtesy of the National Archives)

The *Oryoku Maru.* (Courtesy of Arch Ford)

The entrance to Bilibid Prison. (Courtesy of the Naval Bureau of Medicine and Surgery)

Bilibid Prison
Manila, P. I.

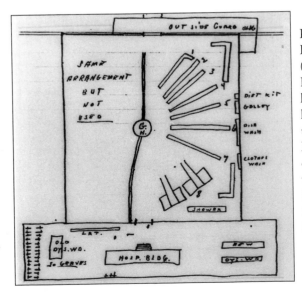

The Navy staff of Bilibid Prison, 1942. The medical personnel came from Canacao Naval Hospital in Cavite. Photo was taken by the Japanese. Myers is in the right-hand side of the third row, wearing a white shirt and looking between two officers' shoulders. (Courtesy of the Naval Bureau of Medicine and Surgery)

Lt. George T. Ferguson, MC, USN (deceased), sketched Bilibid Prison's layout in a diary he kept while interned there. Lt. Ferguson later perished on one of the hell ships, a victim of friendly fire. (Courtesy of the Naval Bureau of Medicine and Surgery)

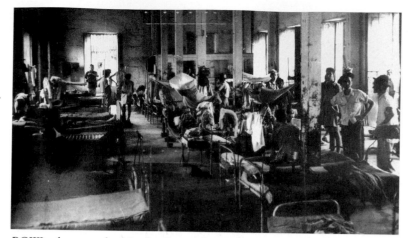

POWs photographed in the gloomy hospital in Bilibid Prison. The Japanese refused to issue medicine or laboratory facilities to the doctors and Navy pharmacist's mates caring for the suffering; as a result, the death toll was staggering. (Courtesy of the Naval Bureau of Medicine and Surgery)

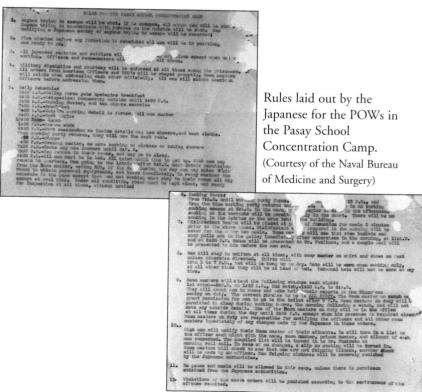

Rules laid out by the Japanese for the POWs in the Pasay School Concentration Camp. (Courtesy of the Naval Bureau of Medicine and Surgery)

A crematorium at Moji, Kyushu, Japan, near one of the POW camps, where prisoners' remains were cremated. (Courtesy of the Naval Bureau of Medicine and Surgery)

A POW holds in his hands three jars—one with rice, one with corn, and the third with soybeans. The contents, which barely cover the bottom of the jars, represent more than one day's rations awarded to the prisoners. Soybeans were added to the POWs' diet only days before the first advancing forces of the U.S. Army reached Manila. (Courtesy of the Naval Bureau of Medicine and Surgery)

Thinned to the point of emaciation by malnutrition and illness, POWs pose for photographers at Bilibid Prison. (Courtesy of the Naval Bureau of Medicine and Surgery)

U.S. troops retaking Manila, street by street. (Courtesy of the Admiral Nimitz Museum of the Pacific War)

"Forgive them, Father. . . ." All that remains of a bombed church in Manila. (Courtesy of the National Archives)

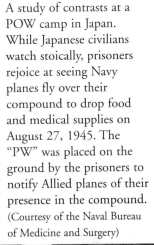

A study of contrasts at a POW camp in Japan. While Japanese civilians watch stoically, prisoners rejoice at seeing Navy planes fly over their compound to drop food and medical supplies on August 27, 1945. The "PW" was placed on the ground by the prisoners to notify Allied planes of their presence in the compound. (Courtesy of the Naval Bureau of Medicine and Surgery)

Dropping provisions to POWs after the surrender. (Courtesy of the Admiral Nimitz Museum of the Pacific War)

Prisoners cheer wildly, waving flags of the United States, Great Britain, and Holland, as Allied rescuers arrive with clothes, food, and medical supplies. Taken near Yokahama, August 29, 1945. (Courtesy of the Naval Bureau of Medicine and Surgery)

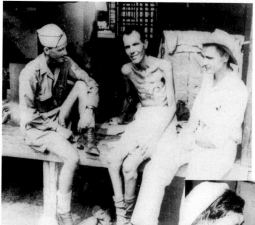

A newly liberated POW suffering from severe malnutrition. (Courtesy of the Naval Bureau of Medicine and Surgery)

A stretcher case aboard a harbor craft in Japan, August 30, 1945. The POW is too emaciated and weak to walk and will be transferred to a Navy hospital ship waiting in Tokyo Bay. (Courtesy of the Naval Bureau of Medicine and Surgery)

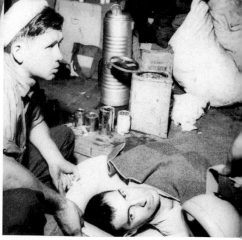

A Navy nurse inspects the Bilibid Prison graveyard shortly after the war's end. (Courtesy of the Naval Bureau of Medicine and Surgery)

Going home—POWs boarding a ship bound for the States. (Courtesy of the National Archives)

Returning POWs, Aeia Hospital, Hawaii, in the fall of 1945. Their haggard, drawn expressions only hint at their horrific experiences. (Courtesy of the Naval Bureau of Medicine and Surgery)

Estel Myers receives the Bronze Star from Capt. John H. Lewis, January 18, 1947. (Courtesy of the Myers family)

mans. The flies began biting the men's bare backs and legs immediately, while the prisoners tried to shoo them away, but finally gave up
and settled for keeping their eyes and mouths closed.

It was not practical for the medical staff to do that, however. They
had patients to tend to and went to work right away. The upper deck
of the hold was designated as the sick bay, and the deathly sick men
were segregated from the rest of the rabble who were less ill. There
were far more patients than there were medical staff members; the
doctors and corpsmen couldn't physically be with everyone at all
times. Several of those who were afflicted the worst became delirious
that first night and rolled off the upper deck into the main hold below, woefully aggravating all their ailments.

The main bulk of the prisoners divided themselves into groups of
twenty, with each group designating one among them to be the food-
and-water man. It was this man's job to secure the sustenance for his
group. The plan was that the position would rotate so no one man
would be overtaxed. The designates would receive their groups' rations
from the officers, who in turn reported to the hold's commander.

The officers chose a lieutenant colonel to continue to act as the
entire group's line of communication with the rancorous Wada and
Toshino. The prisoners, though, were ordered to first speak with the
two Formosan guards posted in the hold. This arrangement proved
intolerable. Anything the Formosans tried to convey to the Japanese
was completely ignored since the Japanese viewed the Formosans as
only a small step above the prisoners in order of significance.

The merchant crew under whom the ship ran had not been forewarned that they would be taking on this large draft of prisoners.
The crew had no way to feed the POWs and as had become par for
the course, no provisions had been made by the Japanese officers
back on Luzon, either.

For two days the ship made her way northward while the men in
her hold languished without food or adequate water. Finally the lieutenant colonel made a bold decision to climb up the hold's ladder to
the deck and speak to Wada man to man about their dire situation.

"Look," the American said to the surprised interpreter, "these men are dying from lack of food and water. We won't be of any use to you sick or dead. We're not afraid to work for our lives. All we ask for is a chance."

A nearby guard overheard the American and sneered back, "We don't care if you do starve! We hate you! Your submarines are sinking our ships!"

Wada spat out something harshly in Japanese, and the guard cowered and slunk away. Toshino and Wada conferred and finally gave in to the request. At first they sent food down into the hold, but a short time later, although they had been afraid to let the prisoners up on deck, six-man chow details were allowed to go to the galley for food. There was rice enough for each man in the hold, along with a canteen cupful of hot soup. The Japanese would not, however, let the POWs keep the buckets down in the hold long enough to adequately divide their rations. Some of the prisoners still had raincoats, befouled from having been dragged from ship to ship, so they dumped the rice out on them. When the raincoats overflowed, the rice was dumped directly onto the manure-encrusted floor.

Myers was on duty up on the sick deck and as time permitted watched the wretched men stumbling below clutching their tiny allotment of rice. Their hair and beards were matted with blood and dirt, and teeming with vermin. Their legs were stained from their own waste. They ate from scraps of cloth or their hats or their grubby hands, all the while trying to keep the flies from getting mixed in to the sticky rice that was their meager meal. The men Myers had admired since he'd arrived at the Philippines, doctors and commanding officers, were now reduced to living like savages.

"I hate the Japs," one of the patients near Myers said weakly. "I hope we get 'em. I hope we kill 'em all, old ones, women, children, every last one of 'em."

"There's some bad ones among them, that's for sure," Myers told him. "But killing the innocent ones makes us just as bad as they are."

As soon as the words were out of his mouth, Myers recalled the child's corpse he had regarded so callously on the *Oryoku Maru*. The horrors of his plight kept him bouncing from one extreme to the other. He was laboring to keep his sense of morality and civility all the while he was surrounded by people and events mutating him into an inhuman degenerate.

"Come on, corpsman," the patient objected. "Don't tell me you don't hate these yellow little sons of bitches and that you wouldn't kill one if you got the chance! After all we've been through?"

"Yeah, okay, I hate 'em. But it's not easy for me to say that," Myers confessed.

"How come?"

"I dunno. My mother tried to teach my brothers and sister and me that hate was evil. Something Satan thrives on. I can quote you ten Bible verses she drummed into us about loving your enemy like yourself. In all my life, I don't think I've ever heard my mother say she hated anybody or anything. She never even said she disliked anybody. 'Bout all she'd admit to was that some people were a little 'different' than the rest of us."

"Yeah, but look around you," the patient persisted. "How can you believe that stuff now, here, in this stinkin', rotten ship?"

Myers sighed. "That's the part that bothers me most. After hearing all my life that I should be kind to other people, it's damn near impossible when you're surrounded by nasty bastards who enjoy torturing you."

Tex had brought up a scrap of cloth with enough rice on it for himself and Myers to share. "I don't think there's gonna be any winners in this war," Tex said. "We'll beat these stinkin' Japs, that's for sure. But if I make it outta here, I don't know how I'm ever gonna feel like a winner. I've spent three lousy years takin' crap from 'em instead of dishin' it out."

A deafening thunder shuddered through the hold, and then another. Some of the men said it sounded like torpedoes, near misses that had exploded along Luzon's shore. The fact that they missed was gratifying, Myers thought. The threat of being attacked again by their own Navy or Air Corps shrouded the hot and heavy air of the hold. Suddenly the idea that he would remain alive and uninjured if the ship was bombed was just too fantastic to even hope for. He felt himself slipping into the kind of depression he'd seen in other men. They hadn't survived it, he warned himself. *If I'm not careful I'll suffer the same fate. God help me survive this trial.*

All through that night, death's finger jabbed at members of this pitiful group. Some died of dehydration; their dysentery combining with the lack of water shriveled them up like deflated balloons. Myers figured they were dying at the rate of one per hour. The Japanese allowed the chow crews back up to the ship's galley to get rice sacks to use as shrouds. Once again the dead men's clothing was stripped from their bodies for use among the living, and the rice sacks were hoisted up through the hold carrying the dead men's remains.

As the number of bodies multiplied, Wada ordered that they could no longer be removed from the hold immediately. Rather, he said, they had to be stacked on the floor in groups of eight, where he could see them. When eight had accumulated, he would give permission for them to be hoisted topside. By this time, the prisoners had run out of rice sacks, so they tied a bowline around each corpse's feet and a half hitch around his head. A couple of prisoners stationed above would hoist the dangling body as the rest watched from below and contemplated how long it would be before it was their turn.

"You ever think about dying, Myers?" a seaman asked, as they watched the procession of dead men swinging up through the hatch. "I mean, you ever wonder how much longer you've got?"

Myers put into words the thoughts he'd been forcing himself to believe. "I'm not gonna die here."

"Well, I don't want to die, either," the seaman said. "But it looks like our days are numbered."

"That's not what I said, pal," Myers corrected. "There's a difference between not wanting to die and making up your mind that you're not gonna die. One's just a wish. The other's a choice. I made my choice; I'm not gonna die. Not here, not now."

"I want to die," another voice whispered. "It's my time."

"Ah buddy, you don't mean that," Myers said, crawling across the deck to where an emaciated, bloody figure lay. The man had a sullied bandage over one eye, and the other eye was so caked with dried gore that he couldn't move the eyelid to open it.

"No, I do mean it," the man assured him. "I've thought about it and I think it's really my time. But I don't want to die alone. Will you sit with me for a little while, so I'm not alone?"

"Sure thing," Myers said. It seemed cruel to argue about living and dying with a man in this guy's condition.

"Wasn't that you I heard talking about the Bible before?" the dying man continued. "I remember when my granddaddy died, the pastor in our church read a psalm. Do you know any psalms?"

"I know a couple," Myers told him, reflecting on the hours his mother had required him to memorize Bible verses. "I guess my favorite's the twenty-third psalm, the one that starts, 'The Lord is my shepherd.'"

"That's it, that's the one they read. Do you know the rest?"

"Sure do. In Sunday School, when I was a kid, we got a little gold star every time we could recite a Bible verse from start to finish."

"Will you say it for me?"

Myers cleared his throat and began again, softly.

"'The Lord is my shepherd, I shall not want; He maketh me to lie down in green pastures.'"

The meadows around the Myers' farm had been green, the most glorious verdant color. After every spring rainstorm, the grass smelled so sweet, the earth so rich. Myers desperately pined to recapture in his mind the smell of living things.

"'He leadeth me beside the still waters. He restoreth my soul. He leadeth me in the paths of righteousness for His name's sake.'"

Myers believed in God. He had been taught that possessing the strength to endure, come what may, was a divine gift. It was not for him to question life, no matter how difficult it might be. There was a plan. How it came together was for God to know and Myers to find out along the way.

That didn't mean it wasn't hard to keep the faith under such oppressive conditions. That was why another Bible verse had come to mind so often during the last couple of years: *Father, why hast thou forsaken me?*

The dying man reached out and touched Myers' arm. Continuing the psalm, Myers grasped his hand.

"'Yea, though I walk through the valley of the shadow of death, I will fear no evil; for Thou art with me. Thy rod and thy staff, they comfort me.'"

Several other patients had tilted their heads in Myers' direction. Some were looking at him as he spoke; others bent their heads in prayer.

"'Thou preparest a table before me in the presence of mine enemies.'"

The man tightened his grasp on Myers' hand. His body seemed to tense, his breaths became gulps.

"'Thou anointest my head with oil; my cup runneth over. Surely goodness and mercy shall follow me all the days of my life.'"

Now the man's breathing was so shallow, Myers could no longer hear it, but he saw his hollowed-out chest barely rising and falling. The man took one last rattling breath as his grip on Myers' hand loosened. His head lolled over to one side slightly, and Myers gently laid the hand down next to his thin body.

"'And I will dwell in the house of the Lord forever.'"

Quietly, from the shadows, a voice said, "Amen."

By December 31, the two ships and their convoy had made the Formosan straits. With their northerly course, the air temperature had changed dramatically. It was the dead of winter, and frigid wind blew violently off the China Sea, through the hatch, and into the ships' holds. The hard metal floor, already intolerable to bodies no longer cushioned with fat, became a conduit, conducting the cold to the prisoners' very core. The men had been without food for so long their hunger pain became just one more ache in an ever-lengthening list of ailments. But the lack of water was the death knell for many. They were occasionally given a quarter canteen cupful a day. Their number was down to 1,184.

Some time New Year's Eve, the convoy was attacked by submarines. The POWs felt the concussion from the torpedoes, exploding so close to the ship that chunks of rust fell from the walls and into the hold like New Year's confetti. The *Brazil Maru* had not been hit, but the men in the hold tensed, wondering how long it would be before she was. They wondered among themselves whether any of the other ships had been hit, most notably the one carrying the balance of their group.

The ocean waves beat relentlessly against the ship's hull and the cadaverous men were tossed like rag dolls. Although the pitching and rolling exacerbated their previous wounds, it seemed like a small sacrifice if it would make them a more difficult target for the Allied subs prowling below.

Myers awoke on New Year's Day to silence; the engines were no longer churning and the ship was no longer moving. Word spread through the hold that they had arrived at Takao, Formosa. Rumor also had it that the only other ship in the convoy to survive the repeated submarine attacks was the one carrying the balance of the prisoners. The chaplains in the hold, still clear-headed enough, offered a prayer of thanks for the obvious miracle.

And it appeared as though that wasn't the only miracle to occur on the first day of 1945. The Japanese deemed a celebration for their safe arrival was in order, and five pieces of *terro-pan*, finger-sized Japanese hardtack, were issued to each prisoner. It was stale and moldy and full of weevils, but Myers didn't care. It was a small nourishment for his languishing body, and he figured the weevils provided an element of protein just as the cockroaches had back in Bilibid. For washing down the hardtack, the Japanese charitably issued half a canteen cupful of water to each man.

The sanitary conditions in the hold were beyond salvaging, but it still seemed to some that an effort should be made. The commanding officer asked for *benjo* buckets and the Formosan guards told him that the men could use a hole in the aft, which dropped to another hold below. The prisoners used it for their latrine for two days until a Japanese maintenance crew discovered the mess while inspecting the ship for leaks. Wada and Toshino were informed and enraged at the situation. Wada told the American commanding officer that it made no difference that the Formosans had told them to use it, and the POWs were ordered to clean up the muck. Ten men were selected for the odious job and the Japanese agreed to provide five buckets to the more than one thousand men for *benjo* use. But the captors permitted those buckets to be emptied only once a day.

The two freighters with their load of POWs sat in the Takao harbor. Once more the prisoners' water rations were inexplicably cut off. The tiny hoard of medicine the doctors and corpsmen had brought on board with them was gone. The pile of bodies in the center of the hold grew steadily. They were down to 1,150 men from their original 1,619.

Those still lucid and aware of their surroundings couldn't guess what was taking place topside. The days crawled by. January 2 became January 3, although in the ship's hold, activities never varied from day to night. Myers halfheartedly acknowledged that it was his twenty-fifth birthday. January 4 dawned and some of the more stalwart men talked feebly about escape. They should try, while they still had any strength left, some said. Where would they go, others asked. A Caucasian would be easily picked out in Formosa. And the water was too cold to chance swimming. The suggestions swelled and faded like the tide around them.

Several times a day a noisy duel occurred between the Allied planes overhead and the anti-aircraft batteries. Some of the prisoners callously regarded the fighting as of little consequence to them. Myers heard one of them say, "What's the use? If we don't get bombed, we'll starve to death anyway." He went on to say that a quick death was preferential anyway.

Between air raids, the Japanese on deck amused themselves by dropping cigarettes into the hold and watching the prisoners drag themselves to retrieve them. The soldiers above mocked the American chaplains, too, as they led the prisoners in daily devotions. Several times a day, when one of them would rise to lead the men in the

Lord's Prayer, nearby Japanese guards would taunt, "Your God isn't here to save you. You believe in the wrong God. Buddha is powerful. He has taken care of the Japanese."

The fifth day, the prisoners were fed a half canteen cupful of rice and a quarter cupful of water. Then another day crawled by as the pitiful coterie in the hold crowded closely together for warmth, contemplating the filth on them and around them. They were at the most sordid depths of human existence. It couldn't get worse.

On January 8, all of the men on the *Brazil Maru* were hauled up on the deck after their morning ration of rice. They were searched by the guards before being allowed to make the climb, and any possession they had with them, such as rice sacks or straw mats, were confiscated. Tex was still in possession of his mother's wedding ring, although he had moved it from just above his rear to beneath his armpit. He was spending so much time at latrines and *benjo* buckets, he was afraid he'd lose it. They were made to sit shivering in the cold on deck while a considerable amount of conferring went on between Wada and Toshino.

Wada then announced that since some of the prisoners had died aboard the other ship, there was now room for them all to be on one ship. While the POWs waited, a larger ship pulled alongside and began unloading cargo onto the *Brazil Maru,* including two-hundred-pound bags of coarse brown sugar. When the ship couldn't take on any more of the sugar bags, the rest was unloaded onto the *Enoura Maru.* Wada made sure every prisoner understood that if any of the sugar was touched, the perpetrator would be beheaded with haste.

The order came to move to the new ship and they were loaded onto a barge for the transfer. When they arrived at the *Enoura Maru,* five hundred of the men, including Tex and others of the medical crew, were ordered into the *Enoura Maru's* forward hold. That hold had previously carried horses like the hold on the *Brazil Maru.* The men were already crowded and covered with their own filth, oblivious to the flies crawling all over them. Myers and Tarpy were ordered to descend into the middle hold, which was less crowded but no less repulsive.

After the POWs were situated on the *Enoura Maru,* a new rumor circulated. Some among them had been unable to resist the temptation of the sugar. They had found a way to get to it and had gorged themselves on it all day long. Eating it after having been without food for so long made all of them sick, yet they continued their looting. The Japanese knew about the thefts, but by this time none of the guards was willing to spend any length of time in the putrid holds with the prisoners to catch the thieves.

Finally, in frustration, Wada announced that the thieves had to be sufficiently punished. "Men who steal sugar must come forward. Until then, no more rice or water for the prisoners. If all die, so be it."

This new turn of events was the most grave the prisoners had faced. Those who hadn't yet expired were barely existing on the meager rations they were getting. To go without meant certain death. The commanding officer asked for two volunteers. He told the prisoners that these volunteers would most probably be tortured and then executed. If by some miracle they survived, he personally would see to it that they would never be without food or water for the rest of the voyage to Japan, even if it meant giving up his own share.

Myers' arm went up. "I'll go, sir," he announced firmly.

"What the hell are you doin'?" Tarpy demanded. "Have you got a screw loose?"

"Nope," Myers told him. "Most of these men'll die for sure without food and water. I think I got a chance of making it through a beating. Unless those Japs haul out their swords."

By this time several others had volunteered, too.

The commander turned to Myers. "Son, that's very brave of you, but we can't risk losing any more medical people. Your knowledge and skills aren't replaceable." He selected two of the other volunteers, an American and a Brit, the hardiest appearing of the group. The men shook hands with the commander and a chaplain prayed with them. Then the commander led them up the ladder to the deck and delivered them to Wada.

The commander returned and they all waited for the sounds of brutality and screams of pain. But they heard nothing. Shortly, one of the prisoners was sent up on deck to empty a *benjo* bucket. He returned with the news that he had seen both men, and that they were still alive. They had been forced to kneel between a couple of guards and were being subjected to kicks and blows. Each time a man slid down, he was hauled back up to his knees and hit again. Eventually the guards got bored with their game and tossed the two back into the hold, beaten but alive.

That afternoon the Japanese made good on their promise of continuing to feed the prisoners if they produced the sugar thieves. Slimy, water-thin rice soup was distributed. For most, the soup acted like a laxative. As they ate, the prisoners heard a hubbub in the distance—the American Air Corps had returned and their strafing was being met with return fire from the Japanese.

The unmarked freighters were sitting ducks in the Takao Harbor, and had been for eight days. Thus far, they'd been left untouched. But the prisoners knew that was just a matter of time before the ships would be selected as targets. When, in the late afternoon, one of the men assigned to empty the *benjo* buckets returned with the news that a destroyer had tied up alongside them, the POWs figured that time was about to run out.

About 0800 hours on January 9, just as the prisoners were finishing their morning rations, the distinctive sound of anti-aircraft fire shattered the icy air. Shortly afterward, the drone of plane engines became audible. The *Enoura Maru* and the destroyer tied up next to her were the pilots' targets. Almost simultaneous with the engine sounds came the whistle of falling bombs. The first bomb to hit the ship ripped down the bulkhead between the forward and amidships compartments. Seconds later, two more bombs fell directly on the forward hold, crushing fragile bodies like eggshells under the weight of fragmented wood and metal.

Myers and Tarpy had both been knocked to the floor of the hold from the first bomb's concussion. After the second one hit, Myers was knocked out cold for a few minutes. When he came to, he moved his extremities in an effort to check his condition. Everything worked, and aside from some lacerations on his arms and legs, he appeared to be uninjured. He pulled himself up to his hands and knees. Other men were stirring, too, among inert bodies and torn, bloodied parts of bodies. He was facing in the direction of the forward hold and he strained through the dust to survey the bombs' devastation. He saw no movement, only corpses.

Myers heard moaning, and then a voice in the forward hold yelled, "Get us some bandages!"

In the amidships hold, those who were able pulled themselves to their feet and began to pick their way through the debris toward the sound of the voice.

"We need everybody's clothing for bandages!" came another shout. "Rip off your pants legs and shirts. If you're cold, get a sugar sack."

Moving automatically to the hoarse order, Myers and the other men did as they were told. He only had one pants leg left; the other had been donated for bandages days ago. As he ripped the pants leg into sections, Myers realized an eerie yellow glow was rising through the hold. It was clinging to the hair and skin on the guys around him. The thought that maybe he was dead and looking through some kind of celestial mist crossed his mind.

"What the—" Myers began.

"It's ammonia picrate gas!" a man next to him yelled. "The horse pee in the bilges musta caught on fire."

Myers floundered through the wreckage toward the forward hold with his bandage contribution. *This could not get worse,* he thought to himself.

A pile of debris blocked his progress, making passage into the hold impossible. Looking into it was not. And that was when Myers saw Tex. His friend was lying on his back, close to the hole that the first bomb had blown between the two holds. A mammoth wooden beam lay across Tex's midsection and the expression on his face was one of peace: his eyes were closed, his mouth relaxed. A shock of black hair had fallen onto his forehead, as it always seemed to do. He looked as if he was sneaking forty winks amidst all the death and destruction.

Myers tried futilely to shove aside the splintered beams to get to

Tex. But he couldn't muster the strength to make any headway. He sank to his knees, feeling impotent, and began to cry. Such a good man, such a god-awful waste.

"I need help here!" a man yelled, his voice cracking in desperation.

Myers dragged himself up and mumbled, "I'll be back for you, buddy."

The survivors in both holds were helpless to aid any of the wounded who had more than minor injuries. It was a bloodbath, the screaming and groaning of those trapped beneath debris bouncing eerily off the metal bulkhead of the stricken ship. Myers thought it was surely what the gates of hell must look and sound like.

It was hours before the POWs could do a final tally. Forty men had died in the amidships hold, another 200 were wounded. Half of the men in the forward hold, 250 in all, had been butchered, jumbled together with the rest, all of whom were gravely injured. Nearly all of the medical corpsmen and doctors in the forward hold had been killed, drastically diminishing the number of men capable of providing any kind of relief to the other survivors. Their number had now been diminished to 850.

CHAPTER FOURTEEN

★

From One Benjo to Another

In the hours following the harbor attacks, the Japanese showed no interest whatsoever in assisting the POWs. Takao, Formosa, was a fairly substantial city with doctors and hospitals. None of these were offered. The prisoners would have been helped immensely with any kind of medical supplies, even minimal contributions. But none were forthcoming.

The prisoners' injuries ran the spectrum of what an emergency room doctor might see during an entire career. There were fractures of femurs and crushed vertebrae. There were hundreds of less serious breaks, such as arms and ankles. Some men had been struck with fragments of flying wood and steel, splinters from the ship's hull and bulkhead. Myers figured that the wounds were so numerous and severe from the bombings, they would have been beyond the medical staff's capabilities even if they had been fully supplied.

There were only a few medical personnel in the forward hold. Although the Japanese had ridiculously ordered the prisoners in Myers' group not to try to communicate with or even look at POWs in the forward hold, Myers did anyway. One doctor was working frenetically one minute and keeled over the next. A corpsman tried to revive him until he realized the doctor undoubtedly had internal injuries and, knowing he was dying, had kept on, literally working himself to death. The only other doctor Myers recognized appeared to have sustained some kind of shrapnel wound to the back of the head. Blood dripped down his neck and shoulders, but he pressed on helping those in far worse shape than he was.

Passage between the two holds was not possible because of the rubble. The only way the corpsmen and doctors could get aid to the survivors in the forward hold would be to enter from topside. But the Japanese resolutely refused to allow the prisoners on deck. Nor would they allow the Americans to remove their dead from the holds. Several prisoners who were alive after the bombing died tortured deaths before sunset.

For Myers and Tarpy, who had suffered facial lacerations during the carnage, caring for the men in their hold meant not much more than a comfortable position for them and soothing words. The corpsmen were able to stop hemorrhages with dirty strips of clothing taken from the dead. They used the same cloth for dressings. Fractures were splinted with pieces of the fractured timbers. But there was no morphine to ease pain and no water for dry lips.

The next day, January 10, a small group of Japanese medical department corpsmen arrived at the ship. They didn't attempt to go into the forward hold. From their expressions and agitated chatter, Myers gathered that the bodies and rubble were too offensive to them. But they did descend into the middle hold and ordered that all those with minor wounds line up and pass by for dressings. They stopped after giving only half of the men in line the promised bandages. They would not work on the seriously wounded at all, but before they left the ship, the corpsmen sent down a few boards to be used as splints, a dozen roller bandages, a bottle of iodine and another of mercurochrome, three triangular bandages, and less than a pound of cotton. These would be the last medical supplies issued to the prisoners on board the ship.

There was no way of knowing for sure, but it seemed to Myers that at least two thirds of the men in his hold were suffering from dysentery. He and Tarpy were fortunate: thus far they'd managed to avoid it, but he was certain they'd be doomed to contract it now. Between the flies, filth, and lack of water to clean anything, he told Tarpy, he'd be surprised if every one of them didn't catch it.

It was now more than twenty-four hours since the ship had been hit, and the corpses of those who'd died immediately had become bloated, the stench unbearable. The POWs pleaded with Wada for permission to remove them. He went off to confer with Toshino but didn't return to the hold the rest of the day. The prisoners spent another night amidst their mangled, decaying compatriots. It wasn't until the morning of January 11, two full days after the harbor attacks had occurred, that the captors agreed to let the prisoners bury their dead.

Gaining permission, however, was only a part of the problem. The removal of hundreds of swollen bodies would have been a challenge even for healthy men under favorable conditions. These survivors were malnourished, disease-stricken, and in shock. They had no equipment with which to lift the bodies the twenty feet up to the ship's deck. The Japanese guards tossed down some one-inch-thick ropes, but nothing more.

Details of the most able-bodied corpsmen took up the gruesome chore, which they began in the amidships hold. The more frail among the prisoners first removed any remaining scrap clothing from each corpse, which would later be redistributed to the living. Next came identification, which frequently proved to be a near impossible task. Not only were the men emaciated shadows of who and what they had once been, many of the bodies had been mutilated in the bombing, and were in an advanced state of decomposition.

Corpsmen down in the hold then tied ropes to the stripped corpses' ankles while others on deck pulled the bodies up one by one through the hatch and laid them gently on the ship's deck. The grotesque sight of naked, emaciated, blood- and feces-smeared bodies, twirling upside down at the end of a rope over their heads, broke even the most intrepid officers in the hold.

Removing the dead from the forward hold was going to be more difficult because of the sheer number of them. Hauling them out singly wasn't an option, so the prisoners were given a wire cargo net to haul them out in batches. Myers and Tarpy were on deck for this operation, and it was sheer agony for them to watch the group of corpses, including Tex, to be hauled up. Not that it would make any difference to their fallen friend at this point.

"I'm not sure who's the luckier," Tarpy huffed in exhaustion after they'd laid Tex out on the deck, "him or us."

"Don't do that to yourself," Myers snapped at him. "And don't do it to me."

Soon the stack of bodies topside took on titanic proportions. There were three hundred and fifty dead men in all. While those who had died previously on the journey had received a burial at sea, such a ceremony was now not practical. The Allied bombing had made certain that the *Enoura Maru* was no longer seaworthy. She had sustained hits to her stern as well as to her forward and amidships. Some of the more senior Navy men said they thought she was already sitting on the bottom of the shallow harbor. It was obvious to both the Americans and to the Japanese that she could not be moved.

Mass burial in the Takao Harbor was out of the question since such a vast number of decomposing corpses would surely trigger the spread of disease, and the Japanese feared disease almost as much as Allied gunfire. The only solution was to organize a POW burial detail and take the bodies to shore. Wada announced that thirty men would be allowed to volunteer for the detail.

Myers volunteered and so did Tarpy. Like every other man on the burial detail, while they were sincere in their desire to provide the dead men an appropriate farewell, each hoped there might be an opportunity to get something to drink.

A barge came alongside the *Enoura Maru,* and as many corpses as possible were loaded onto it. The barge traveled to the breakwater, and from there the prisoners were ordered to carry the bodies ashore through the waist-deep water. The suggestion was ludicrous since it was questionable if the men on the detail possessed enough stamina to wade through the water at all. As distasteful and disrespectful as it seemed, the burial detail finally decided to drag the corpses to the breakwater.

They made two trips that day, loading the bodies onto the barge, dragging them to the breakwater, and hauling them up on land to be lined up in neat rows. At sunset, the ragged detail saluted in unison and began the barge trip back to the crippled vessel that was their prison.

A couple of guys crouched on the barge deck near Myers and Tarpy asked them if they knew a guard on the ship named Ah Kong.

"Yeah, I know which one he is," Tarpy told them.

"Well, I was on chow detail the morning of the attack, see," one of the men said. "And Ah Kong was supposed to be guarding us. Except when the bombers started dropping their eggs, he drops his gun and takes to his heels to hide. Murph, the guy with me, says, 'Holy shit! Those Japs see us without a guard and they'll mow us down for sure!'

"So I grab the rifle and run after Ah Kong. You know where I found him?"

The men shook their heads.

"In the latrine, between the crappers, peein' his pants. He puts his hands up when he sees the rifle 'cause he thinks I'm gonna shoot him."

"Yeah, and you should have, you moron," the man's buddy chimed in.

"Right, and when the Japs found me they would have killed me for sure. I walk over to Ah Kong and give 'em back his rifle. Then I tell him to get his ass back out on deck and guard us like he was supposed to do."

The men smiled; they were so exhausted from the work it was the most they could muster. This story gave birth to others.

"I was just about to take a bite of my morning rations," a man said. "The guy sitting next to me got hit. Top of his head was blown clean off. Little bits of bone and pieces—I don't know, skin or brain, or somethin'—landed in my rice." He paused, closed his eyes, and shivered. "I looked at my rice, but I was so hungry I gulped it all down before the next bomb hit. It didn't even matter. I probably ate part of his brain along with my rice."

On the morning of January 12, the burial detail made a final barge trip with the remainder of the corpses. Then they loaded them all onto wagons and hauled them to a nearby crematorium. The detail gave a final salute and rendered the dead men to ashes.

Had the landings at Lingayen Gulf occurred on December 20, 1944, according to MacArthur's original schedule, Myers would never have been part of the burial detail at Takao Harbor. There would have been no need for burials. The Japanese would probably never have been able to move the POWs off Luzon. Although some prisoners may have become victims of friendly fire in the Allied arrival, others would have been spared the tormented existence and agonizing death aboard the *Brazil Maru* and the *Enoura Maru*. But fate chose to play a different hand, and the POWs' futures, including those of Myers, Tarpy, and Tex, were radically altered.

According to the new schedule, the Lingayen Gulf landings were set for January 9, 1945. For their success to be realized, two significant military goals had to be accomplished in the first eight days of January.

Of primary importance was the continued Allied bombardment of Formosa from the air bases that had been established in China. The Imperial Air Force used Formosa as their staging ground for all replacement planes heading to Luzon. Despite the huge losses of aircraft in 1944, and Allied bombardment of Japanese industrial cities, their factories still churned out planes at a steady rate—fourteen hundred in the month of January 1945. The kamikaze pilots flew the planes from Japan to Formosa, where they awaited their target assignments.

The American 3rd Fleet, now the most powerful naval force ever assembled, mounted the Formosan attacks. The fleet was also charged with pinning down Japanese airpower on Luzon itself, especially those Imperial planes on their way to attack supply convoys prior to and during the Lingayen landings. Planes from the 3rd Fleet kept up the bombing of both Luzon and Formosa throughout December and January, but still did not shut down the kamikaze operations entirely.

MacArthur's second goal was to establish a beachhead on the northern shore of the Philippine island of Mindoro, fifteen miles to the south of Luzon. Control of the entire island was strategically important to the Allies; it would allow sea traffic on its way to central and northern Luzon to pass between the two islands, saving both distance and time. The northern Mindoro beachhead was secured on January 2, placing American troops just ninety miles from Manila.

As powerful as the 3rd Fleet was, the ships were not impervious to the disastrous effects of the kamikazes. For five days, until January 7, the suicide pilots struck cruisers, carriers, and destroyers. But while all of these attacks took place miles to the west of Luzon, the Japanese completely ignored the forty-mile-long convoy cruising along Mindoro's northern coastline before it turned northward and on to Lingayen Gulf.

At 0700 on January 8, the largest group of American military personnel ever assembled in the Pacific stood ready to retake the island of Luzon. Preliminary bombardments of targeted beaches along the gulf were successful, and at 0930 on the ninth the landing of more than two hundred thousand Allied troops began.

Thirty days had passed since Myers and Tarpy had been marched out of Bilibid and been forced into the hold of the *Oryoku Maru*. When they left Manila, they had numbered slightly over sixteen hundred. Now, sitting in a crippled ship in a Formosan harbor, a little over eight hundred remained. Nonetheless, the journey would continue.

Wada ordered that all the POWs, regardless of their physical condition, be transferred by barge from the *Enoura Maru* back to the *Brazil Maru*. Even for those who were not wounded or deathly ill, the transfer would be difficult. But for those who were in the severest shape, moving meant taking a step closer to death.

To make the transfer as gentle as possible, the corpsmen fashioned a bos'n's chair out of the same ropes they had used to haul out the bombing victims. They then began lifting the living skeletons out of the hold. Those who were unable to sit upright were tied to a plank and pulled up horizontally. The men were all loaded onto a waiting barge to be taken the short distance to the *Brazil Maru*.

The wounded men screamed, some even slipped into a coma from the bouncing and jerking, while those moving them exerted themselves to capacity. It took hours to get them aboard the new ship and into the hold and was a nerve-wracking experience for the corpsmen as they listened to the bones of the fracture cases grating against one another. Fourteen men never made it into the hold, dying on its deck instead. The rest of the wounded were lowered into their new prison in the same way they had left the last one.

It was dark and cold before the grueling procedure was complete. Through it all, Wada seemed to take great pleasure at the prisoners' struggles, his sadistic smile never fading at their travails.

Once again the POWs were impossibly forced into a single hold near the ship's stern that was insufficient in size for their number. The hold was divided into bays fifteen feet long by ten feet deep, previously used to transport cargo. The commanding officers still possessing any strength arranged the POWs into twenty-man groups. Each group could decide on one of two body positions: they could sit with their legs extended, or lie with their knees drawn up. Standing fully or lying down flat were not options, and everyone in the group had to assume the same position.

The wounded were arranged in the only open space available in the hold, the hatch cover leading to another hold below. Having the patients concentrated in a single area would make it easier for the medical corps to care for them.

Under a blanket of darkness on January 13, the ship slipped out of the Takao Harbor.

On the day that Myers and the others were beginning the next leg of their blighted odyssey to the Home Islands, Hirohito had been Japan's Emperor for eighteen years. The Japanese people had never heard his voice, nor could they print or utter his name. No one was allowed to look at him and all heads had to be bowed if he passed. The Emperor rode a white horse, therefore no one else in Japan could own one. It was also forbidden to look down upon the Emperor, so no buildings taller than the palace could be built in its vicinity.

The traditions that fostered the Emperor's existence were completely alien to Americans. Even a basic understanding of them might have shed light as to why Wada and Toshino, Homma and Yamashita, in fact most of the men in the Japanese military behaved as they did during the war.

The Japanese Emperors were direct descendants of Emperor Jimmu, who founded Japan in 660 B.C. They were the inheritors of the divine command known as *Hakko Ichiu,* the bringing together of the eight corners of the world. The emperors were neither men nor gods. Rather, they were the country's spiritual institution, the center of its energy, loyalty, and morality. The Emperors were the physical incarnation of the state. They were Japan.

When Hirohito became Emperor in 1926 at the age of twenty-five, his character was unusual for a Japanese Emperor. The bespectacled, diminutive man played tennis and golf, although he was indifferent to both. He studied marine biology and wrote poetry. Most important, he was bored by foreign policies and army maneuvers.

Hirohito, consequently, adopted a mythological status, choosing not to be involved in his government's actions or decisions. With no one at the helm of the country's foreign policy, an oligarchy developed, the power vested in two dominant forces.

One faction, a small, select group of successful industrialists, sought to make certain that Japan was run in a manner that would be most advantageous to their bank accounts. The other faction, a band of top-ranking generals and admirals, strove to maintain Japan's military supremacy at home and abroad.

The two groups' goals always conflicted, but their motivations were startlingly similar. Both were self-serving, and based their decisions on greed for wealth and power. They vied for control of Japan, yet they were forced to cooperate. The wealthy industrialists knew they did not possess the skills to oversee an army; the military powers reluctantly realized they could not run the factories. And the one who could have been the deciding factor in all issues, the Emperor himself, deliberately absented himself from any decision-making.

The two power-hungry groups cleverly used the Emperor's absence to their respective advantages by inventing the *Kodo-Ha,* the "Way of the Emperor." The *Kodo-Ha* was used as the reason behind all Japanese government actions. It made the Emperor responsible for all decisions, although he wasn't involved in any of them.

The *Kodo-Ha* developed long before the war had escalated to its ultimate global proportions. In the early 1930s, the Japanese military strongly opposed a disarmament treaty. The industrialists realized open armament would risk alienating their important foreign trading partners. So to thwart the military, the industrialists invoked the *Kodo-Ha,* asserting that it was the Emperor who supported the disarmament.

In a like manner during the late thirties and early forties, when the Japanese military wanted to join the Rome-Berlin Axis, withdraw Japan from the League of Nations, and declare war on the United States, they employed the *Kodo-Ha.* The military assured the members of the Japanese government that these actions were the Emperor's wishes. The name of the Emperor was sacred in Japan. It was the name, not the man, that carried the weight.

By the time Japan was fully immersed in World War II, the industrialists' power had evaporated, leaving the military in total control. It was convenient for the military to continue the charade of the *Kodo-Ha* throughout the war. In doing so, they never had to be accountable for their actions. The decisions made by every one of them, from top generals to the lowliest prison guards, were always attributed to the *Kodo-Ha,* the will of the Emperor.

CHAPTER FIFTEEN

★

The Death Hatch

The *Brazil Maru* joined with a convoy of ancillary vessels at about 2200 hours on January 13 and headed out across the East China Sea. For the POWs in her hold, there was little difference between the nightmares of sleep and those of the waking hours. But one thing Myers knew for sure as he drifted in and out on that first night out of Formosa: he was more determined than ever to survive. He may have suffered to the limit of his endurance, but he told himself that to give in to death now meant that all his suffering would have been for naught.

As medical personnel moved among their patients, their attempts at comfort were mostly psychological. Caring for physical ailments was not possible; instead, the doctors and corpsmen aspired to give hope to the sick by pointing out that since they were aboard a ship at sea, they were considerably safer than when they had been a motionless target in the harbor. In addition to that scrap of bright news, Myers attempted to encourage all the POWs, patients and not, by telling them that this was certainly the last leg of their journey, and that there would be very little more they would have to endure. He wasn't certain if it made any difference to his fellow prisoners, but each time he said it, he believed it a little bit more himself.

In reality, this was to be the worst trial these men would face. Because of the lack of sanitation, all of the men, including Myers and

Tarpy, were stricken with dysentery or some other form of diarrhea. The prisoners were allowed to empty the scant number of *benjo* buckets only when the Japanese would authorize it. This authorization had no relation whatsoever to when the buckets became full. They overflowed and the feces were walked through and further spread as the ship churned through the waves.

The cruelest irony was that the prisoners were surrounded by water and still forcibly dehydrated. When the ship left Formosa, her water tanks had been filled to the brim, but the first two days out of Takao, the prisoners received nothing to drink. Neither would the Japanese give them seawater with which to clean themselves and their mess utensils.

The air temperature dropped rapidly as the ship made her way northward. The hatch cover had to be kept open if the prisoners wanted any fresh air, plus it was their only source of light. But this meant they left themselves exposed to the elements—the frigid winds, freezing rains, and driving snow. The problem of the elements was made worse by a ventilator located in the hold, which caused a powerful draft of cold air to blow over the scarcely clad, trembling Americans. The POWs begged Wada to allow them to stuff the ventilator with one of their straw sleeping mats, but the answer was always the same: "No need."

The wind and cold temperatures brought with them a new enemy to the men's already weakened immune systems: pneumonia. A prisoner who contracted the disease, as many did almost immediately in their immobile state, could drag himself to where the draft was strongest and bring his suffering to a permanent conclusion. Before long, the prisoners began calling the cold the "Wind of Death."

After a day on the *Brazil Maru,* Tarpy mumbled weakly to Myers, "Bastards! What the hell is the point? Isn't it bad enough that they've beaten us, shot us, tortured, and suffocated us? Now they're trying to kill us from thirst and exposure? Makes no sense."

"Give up on making sense of this," Myers told him. "Just keep thinking about surviving."

Everything in the hold, the floor, the walls, the sleeping bays, was constructed of steel, which immediately became as frigid as the air. There were some straw mats available to use for protection from the cold steel, but there were only enough for about a third of the men. Groups of friends huddled together under a single mat, trying to fend off the frigid temperature settling over the hold.

The seriously ill and wounded suffered the most from the radical drop in temperature. The plan to use the hatch cover as the hospital area seemed practical in Formosa, but once underway, the patients near it were exposed to the cold air and snow.

Finally, on January 15, black, salty, unpalatable water was doled out to the POWs, one canteen cupful to be divided among eight men. Next came their ration of rice, one canteen cupful for every four men. The men received these allotments twice a day.

In the face of the myriad of threats, it was soon obvious to most that only the strongest would live. By common consent, the commanding officers decided that since the medical staff was doing most of the physical work, their ration should be greater. The inequity was immediately distasteful to Myers, who argued the point with the officers. He was only convinced when it was pointed out to him that the medical staff needed to maintain as much strength as possible since they were responsible for more than just their own lives.

The death rate rapidly escalated. The first day out, Myers counted fifty dead. In addition to the Americans still trying to keep track of their living, the Japanese were now also calling roll each day. The guards stood imperiously at the edge of the hatch, calling out with great difficulty the unfamiliar names. Their voices droned on for nearly two hours at a time.

If an American didn't answer to his name, Wada simply drew a line through it on his manifest, silently and without question. He was not interested in how, or even if, a man had actually died. He was concerned only with the total number. While the logical assumption would be that the fewer men there were to feed, the more food each man should receive, Wada stubbornly refused to make the adjustment. The galley still produced only enough rice for a quarter cupful per man.

There was madness evident in this hold, too, as there had been aboard the *Oryoku Maru*. Some of the cases stemmed from the crowded conditions. The men were less violent than previously, but still made verbal threats of murder, the result of arguments over space, rations, or a ludicrous claim like whose mother made the best cakes. But no one had enough strength left to do bodily harm to anyone. Other cases of madness were the result of disease and deprivation, manifested in the men who were muttering incoherently, or lying quietly, their glazed eyes rolling, seeing nothing.

The morning of January 16, Wada inadvertently sent down some good news into the hold. He announced to the prisoners that anyone caught stealing from this ship's cargo would be severely beaten and then shot to death. He promised not to be as lenient with would-be thieves as he had been previously. This was good news. It meant that there was something on board that was worth stealing, and those who were able began an immediate search for it. It wasn't long before the cache was discovered.

"Hey, Myers," one of the prisoners called later in the day. "There's sugar in the hold below this one. You better get yourself some."

Although the offer sounded tempting, Myers wasn't sure his system could take it. Pretty soon, though, he saw prisoners in every bay licking the unrefined sugar out of their grubby paws. Myers gave in to the temptation. He asked one of the guys who had originally found the stuff for a handful. That proved to be a foolish request. As he had feared, Myers' body could not digest anything so rich as the sugar after having been deprived of food for so long and he had violent diarrhea for several hours.

Tarpy took care of him, sharing his next ration of water to replenish some of the fluids Myers had lost. It was the closest brush with death Myers had had, but it also gave him an idea.

Once he regained his strength, he sought out the prisoner who'd offered him the sugar the day before.

"Hey, fella," Myers said when he found the man, "that sugar in the hold below us, is it in bags?"

The man told him it was.

"Well, we sure could use the bags to keep some of these guys from freezing to death. Think you could haul a few of 'em up here?"

Several intrepid POWs volunteered to go into the sugar hold with the first man. They returned hauling as many bags as they were able to. That started an entire lineup of men bringing up the bags of sugar, looking like a colony of ants that had just found a picnic to feast on. They dumped the sugar onto the floor of the hold and covered themselves up with the bags.

The best element to this thievery was that no one feared retribution. Wada's threat of death was not much of a deterrent, since the men figured they had been living with that threat since their capture. Furthermore, the prisoners knew this sugar theft would never be discovered. The sty in which they lived was so vile, the Japanese were afraid to descend into it for fear of catching their diseases.

On January 18, after four days at sea, some of the corpsmen remarked that they hadn't seen Lieutenant Toshino in quite some time. He was supposedly still the man in charge of this prisoner movement but had made himself scarce. Someone wondered out loud if he'd been the victim of an American shell. If not that, then perhaps he was sequestered in his quarters trying to figure out an adequate excuse to give his superiors for the dismal condition in which his cargo would arrive.

The men were packed into every square inch of the hold, including the hatch in the center of the hold, which was always left open and was the coldest spot. The remaining commanding officers made the difficult decision that only the most seriously ill would have to endure it. It became their Zero Ward, but they called it the Death Hatch, the place where those who were beyond help were brought to die.

The corpsmen and doctors continued their care of these hopeless cases, but the medical staff was barely clinging to existence themselves, and not immune to the effects of the cold and the wind. So they kept their vigil over their failing companions in shifts. They listened to feverish mumblings, held dirty, frail hands, and promised to get word to families back home. The last faces these dying men looked upon were those of the medical staff, and the enormity of that fact didn't escape Myers. Never would he have dreamed that by following an innocent recommendation to join the hospital corps, he would be a witness to so much needless death, and be so powerless to prevent it.

Each time Myers took his shift at the Death Hatch, it challenged his effort to maintain a positive attitude about his own future. Gradually, he reached the point where he felt he was beyond being able to withstand any more of the anguish and unanswerable queries that crowded his mind. There was a recurring challenge whose answer, Myers feared, would rock the very foundation of his faith: what, in the end, was God's ultimate purpose in this war?

Myers' question to his Maker was far more profound than that of a simple patriot. He understood that the United States was waging war against Japan in the name of freedom. But why, day after miserable day, had he been chosen to continue dragging himself through this bondage while others slipped through his fingers into eternal sleep? And from the depths of that dung-laden hold, the largest imponderable of all was whether he was surviving because of the grace of God or a curse of Satan himself.

On Saturday, January 20, 1945, Franklin Delano Roosevelt celebrated his unprecedented fourth inauguration as President of the United States. In deference to the hardships the war had caused, he delivered his inaugural address without fanfare from the south portico of the White House.

In the days and in the years that are to come, we shall work for a just and honorable peace, a durable peace, as today we work and fight for total victory in war. We can and we will achieve such a peace. We shall strive for perfection. We shall not achieve it immediately—but we still shall strive. We may make mistakes—but they must never be mistakes which result from the faintness of heart or abandonment of moral principle.

These strong words of conviction propelled the United States forward in the crusade to reestablish freedom in the Pacific Theater of the war. As the Japanese steadfastly refused to withdraw from the islands they had captured without bloody, protracted fights, it became apparent to American government and military officials alike that the only solution to end the fighting would be an invasion of Japan herself.

So the Allies pulled more vigorously on the ever-tightening noose around Japan's Home Islands. Japan's defense was still keenly centered in the Philippines, primarily Luzon and Formosa, and these, along with the Home Islands themselves, became principal Allied targets. Huge carrier task forces commanded by Admiral Nimitz sailed closer and closer to Tokyo, while American B-29s rained fire and death upon Imperial troops and citizenry alike below.

The B-29 had become the ultimate air weapon of war. It was capable of flying, fully loaded, for sixteen hours without stopping. Airdromes large enough to accommodate the Superfortresses were carved out of jungle on the islands that the Allies recaptured. Thirty-eight-year-old General Curtis LeMay, who had taken command of the XXI Bomber Command on January 19, led daylight, close-formation raids. These raids inflicted terrible damage, hitting the aircraft factories and harbors of mainland Japan. They hammered the main cities, one by one.

The Imperial commander-in-chief of the Philippine operations, General Yamashita, determined that to defend Japan he must defend Luzon. He had carefully studied the mistakes made by the Allies when Japan invaded the Philippines three years earlier. Troops and supplies spread too thinly were not wise. Yamashita chose to divide his more than two hundred fifty thousand forces between three mountain strongholds on Luzon.

The most important stronghold was located north-northeast of Lingayen Gulf. From his headquarters in the town of Baguio, Yamashita would command these one hundred fifty-two thousand men himself. His second concentration would defend southern Luzon from the hills east and northeast of Manila. The eighty thousand men encamped here would be led by Lieutenant General Shizuo Yokoyama.

Yamashita's third force was in the Zambales Mountains, west of the Central Plains. From a network of air bases, including Clark Field, Major General Rikichi Tsukada would command thirty thousand men. Yamashita felt confident that his defense plans were sound and dug in with the purpose of exacting the maximum number of casualties possible on the Allies.

For the retaking of Luzon, MacArthur had chosen Lieutenant General Walter Krueger and his 6th Army, along with Nimitz's 7th Fleet. The forces would begin with the landings at Lingayen Gulf in nearly the same spots that the Japanese had landed in December 1941. The Allied landings began on January 9, 1945. Two corps, containing four assault divisions, landed side by side on twelve separate beaches. As Yamashita had no intention of sending troops to defend the beaches from his mountain strongholds, the landings went virtually unopposed.

By noon on landing day, an infantry regiment was six miles inland and another had pushed through the town of Lingayen. By evening, the Allies had sixty-eight thousand troops ashore and a beachhead on the gulf twenty miles wide and nearly four miles deep. Over the next two days, the Allied troops moved cautiously farther inland. MacArthur and Krueger's plan for retaking Luzon was complicated, calling for strategies and counterstrategies.

Yamashita's men had been progressively weakened throughout the month of January by continuous Allied bombardment and frequent attacks by the Filipino guerrilla forces that now infested Luzon. These, combined with the sophisticated American offensive, proved too much for Yamashita's forces and the Imperial defense of Luzon soon began to crack.

This weakening was exactly what MacArthur and Krueger had hoped for. The race toward Manila was on, with one clear goal in mind: to liberate the Allied prisoners of war they knew were somewhere in the city.

*   *   *

To Myers and the other men in the hold of the *Brazil Maru,* their imprisonment in Manila felt like an experience that had occurred in another lifetime. They were absorbed only with their survival in the present. That meant, among other things, the constant effort to keep from freezing to death. The barely surviving POWs eyed the clothing of those on the Death Hatch like vultures observing prey in the desert. The addition of more clothes of any kind would surely help assuage their cold. They wanted to be close at hand when death finally and inevitably came, and the scraps of cloths would be redistributed to new owners.

In a feckless attempt at the equitable division of the clothing, the prisoners selected a committee whose job it was to remove the clothing from the corpses and redistribute it in accordance with the survivors' need. But oftentimes men died during the night and some of the more clever prisoners were able to get the best clothing before the committee even realized they had a new corpse to contend with.

A notable discovery was made on January 21. One of the men found a few life vests hidden in a corner that had been overlooked by the Japanese when they made a final search of the hold before the prisoners were loaded. The POWs tore the vests open and pulled out the contents, stuffing it into the arms and legs of their shirts and pants, if they still had them. Their appearance was instantly transformed from raw-boned and grimy men to fat, dingy teddy bears.

One of the overstuffed prisoners, scratching ferociously, dragged himself over to Myers as he sat next to a dying man on the Death Hatch.

"Hey, Doc, I itch all over," he complained in a raspy voice. "What the hell's wrong with me now?"

Myers surveyed the stuffing protruding from the man's pant legs. "Those life vests, who knows how long they've been down here," Myers told him. "They're probably full of lice or some kind of critters."

The man pulled up a pant leg and squinted at his dirty shin in the dim light coming from the open hatch. After a couple of minutes he looked back at Myers and said, "Good diagnosis, Doc." He got up and stumbled away, still scratching, and cursing the lice, the life vests, and, most of all, the Japanese. Before long, several other men who'd stuffed their clothes with the filling were doing the same.

The prisoners were now perishing at the rate of between twenty and thirty a day. Wada had permitted a burial detail to be formed and allowed the detail to perform the odious task of burying the dead at sea on a daily basis. Each time the detail returned to the hold, it was with a new tidbit of information.

The first news flash, which had come in three days after they'd been out of Takao Harbor, was that the *Brazil Maru* was traveling in a submarine zone. The burial crew had noticed that they were now towing a crippled ship, probably victim of a torpedo. They continued towing it for a day, which further hampered their already slothful progress. Just as the disabled craft was picked up by a smaller, more nimble ship sent to haul it in, the *Brazil Maru* was ordered to turn back toward the direction she had just come for yet another vessel in distress. This one was towed for two days. The backtracking and slow speed levied a heavy price on the prisoners: the longer they were at sea, the higher the death toll would climb. It reached forty dead men on January 21 alone.

The second fact that the burial detail discerned was that the ship's course did not appear to be set straight across open sea for Japan. Rather, the men said, they were cruising by a series of ugly, barren islands, surrounded by nasty yellow mud.

Two naval officers guessed they were hugging the Chinese coastline. Myers overheard them and weighed in with his opinion.

"I'll bet we're near the mouth of the Yangtze or Whangpoo Rivers. I was stationed in Shanghai back in forty-one." Myers shook his head. "The ugliest, stinkingest rivers God ever made are in Shanghai."

"I saw that shit out there," another prisoner said. "All this time I thought dying was the worst thing that could happen to me. It ain't. The worst thing is dying here and being tossed into that Chinese muck for all eternity."

Each time an officer or doctor got the chance, he pled with Wada to increase the prisoners' food and water rations, which Wada flatly refused to do. He informed them that there wasn't any more of either available. But while the Japanese had no water, food, or cigarettes to give the prisoners, they had plenty to sell. The transactions took place through the open gratings, the same ones responsible for the Wind of Death that blew through the hold. After three years in captivity, the Americans had very few possessions left. Most of them had held onto whatever it was they treasured the most, a wedding ring or West Point ring.

These items the Japanese couldn't resist. A thick, heavy, solid gold wedding ring bought five canteens full of water. The military rings were a poor second to the wedding rings, initially bringing in four cigarettes, and later, as the market became glutted, only two. A lieutenant from Albuquerque had guarded a heavy Navajo turquoise ring through all his trials. By this stage, though, he gladly traded it for two straw mats to save his own life and that of another officer.

A pair of the prisoners' shoes was good for two cans of tomatoes or salmon, or a handful of tangerines. The prisoners were most in need of heavier clothing, since anything they had was inadequate to fend off the fierce Manchurian wind blowing through the hold. Clothing, however, was never a commodity the Japanese had enough of to trade.

Most of the time, the men huddled as far back in the hold's putrid corners as possible. They didn't move, they didn't speak. Those who were still in possession of their faculties remained still to conserve as much energy as they could. The others were no longer capable of anything but staring dully into the void around them. The only consistent sound was that of raspy coughs from parched throats.

The morning of January 23, a lieutenant colonel caught the attention of a Japanese guard staring down into the sorry pit of humanity. The American knew the guard could understand a little English.

"Listen," the lieutenant colonel implored, "can't you get us some water? If these men don't get water, they'll all die!"

The guard sneered back, "Everybody *potai,* dead—okay, okay."

He dismissed the American with a wave of his rifle and the officer sank back down to his straw mat in dejection.

Each morning, as the *Brazil Maru* journeyed on while trying to hide from prowling submarines, POWs who had seemed fairly hardy the day before would be found dead in their bays. It soon became so commonplace that the corpsmen made rounds every day, shouting to bay leaders, "Roll out your dead."

One bay, which had been the home to some of the strongest prisoners in the early stages of this part of the voyage, had lost a third of its men. In other bays, the counts were much worse. Often the corpses would already be stripped naked, leaving nothing for the clothing committee to do but shake their heads.

The remaining few chaplains gathered the men together each night to pray before the evening rations arrived. They prayed for strength over their fear of death. Myers couldn't imagine his own death; it didn't seem feasible to him to die after being in captivity for so long. Yet he and some others had developed a rather callous attitude toward it. If you made it, you made it. If not, you died. That was all there was to it.

One chaplain consistently gave away his rations of food and water to the sick, telling the protesting corpsmen that he felt fine and would keep his next ration. But he would give the next one away, too, making the same promise until finally, after praying with the men on January 24, his weakened body gave out.

Other brief glimpses of human decency occurred amid the rancor and despair. Two brothers were among the POWs. After one passed away on the Death Hatch, the corpsmen prepared to haul his body over to the stack where the dead were kept before being hauled up on deck for disposal.

"Handle this one with care," Myers whispered to the others. "His brother's watching from the upper bay."

The surviving man stood feebly over his brother, his matted head bent in mourning as he climbed slowly back into his bay. A brief time later, he, too, died.

For the prisoners who had enough remaining strength, the search for water became an all-consuming task. Sometimes, if the snow fell heavily enough and the ship slowed a little, the tiny, pristine flakes fluttered through the hatch and into the hold. Prisoners struggled to their feet, clutching their mess kits, or whatever fouled containers they possessed, and waved them in the air to catch what ice or snow they could. If they had no container, they held up a shred of cloth and licked and sucked on it when it had been dampened enough by the snow. Those who had no possessions at all turned their filthy faces skyward and tried to catch the flakes on their tongues like little children.

Dead bodies that created obstacles for the men in their quest for the snow were tugged out of the way to clear a path. Invariably, the corpses would then block the paths of other men, who would move them again. Frequently the bodies would have been dragged back and forth under the open hatch several times before the corpsmen could stack them with the others.

The concentration of snow and ice was greatest up on deck. Those who volunteered to empty *benjo* buckets would furtively scoop up handfuls of snow from the ship's deck and shove it into their mouths on their way back to the hold. This only helped a few men, since no more than six were allowed on deck at a time. Others had discovered a steam winch that stood on the deck near the hatch. One of the pipes dripped and a clever man could capture anywhere from a few spoonfuls to an entire flaskful of water.

Getting to the steam winch also required getting permission from the guards to come on deck. Some of the men asked to relieve themselves over the side, while others were able to convince the Japanese they were *toxan bioki,* very sick. Both groups positioned themselves so that the winch was between them and the guard, and while pretending to urinate or vomit would capture as much of the dripping liquid as they could.

On January 25, the POWs had been at sea on this leg of the journey for twelve days. Wada proclaimed that he would allow the men one bucket of seawater per day for the POWs to clean themselves and the hold in which they lived. The prisoners begged him to re-

consider, telling him that was not nearly enough to make the remaining five hundred or so clean. Washing mess kits and canteen
cups was out of the question. What a senseless, tyrannical rule to
deny them additional seawater, especially when their number was
dwindling. After all, they were afloat on the world's largest ocean.

The prisoners thought that if they took their case to Toshino, he
might rule in their favor. They asked Wada for him and the interpreter refused. They shouted loudly for Toshino and Wada came to
the edge of the hatch.

"If you do that," he screeched down at them, "I get guards and
order them to shoot into the holds."

This threat, which once had carried some weight with it, was now
without power over the prisoners. One of them yelled back, "To hell
with you! We're all going to die anyway, aren't we?"

CHAPTER SIXTEEN

★

To Suffer and Die

For the men clinging to their tenuous strand of life aboard the *Brazil Maru,* thirst was the greatest menace of all their ailments. Those who finally succumbed to it suffered horribly the last twenty-four hours of their lives.

The thirst victims went completely out of their minds at the end. They stumbled over the other prisoners in the hold or tried to climb the ladder that led to the deck, where guards waited ready to cut them down with rifle blasts. The POWs appointed a stair guard to keep these men from wandering up on deck, but one day a prisoner managed to get up there without permission anyway. Before the guard could raise his rifle, the man threw himself over the side of the ship.

In their thirst-driven madness, some men held one-sided conversations with friends who had died days earlier. Some discoursed with inanimate objects: the remains of a life vest, a canteen cup, or a *benjo* bucket. To watch a man in this condition was a particular hardship to the corpsmen still functioning in their hospital duties. Myers, Tarpy, and a handful of others from the original Canacao group worked ceaselessly to comfort and aid their fellow prisoners. But when yet another man slipped into the dark recesses of thirst-driven madness, the corpsmen all felt as though they weren't working hard enough to save those around them. They redoubled their efforts, pulling long shifts on the Death Hatch throughout the night, working in total darkness, with patience and kindness. They were rewarded with very little sleep during the day because of their increased activities in the hold.

The POWs who were crippled relied solely on the corpsmen for their base existence. They shifted bony, feeble bodies into less painful positions, although there was no position of actual comfort for these poor men. They carried the *benjo* buckets around to those in need, helping the dying men use them. The corpsmen listened to the incessant babbling of some, and answered all the questions and requests of others, even those which were impossible. An eternity ago, as freshly graduated hospital assistants, the corpsmen had made a solemn promise in their oath, saying, "I dedicate my heart, mind, and strength to the work before me."

The corpsmen may have questioned themselves and their God, as Myers did, asking what benefit would come of the sorrowful anguish around them. But they never complained that their job was too difficult, too strenuous, or too odious to perform. The closing line of the corpsman's oath was the creed they lived by still: "I shall do all within my power to show in myself an example of all that is good and honorable throughout my naval career, so help me God."

One of the doctors squatted down next to Myers on the morning of January 28 and said, "Well, I figure we've lost more than a thousand men. Last count the bay leaders took came out to about five hundred."

Myers looked at those who remained. They looked more like feral beasts than men. Their four weeks' growth of beard and their hair was matted with one another's excrement; their skin was drawn tightly over their bones; their eyes were hollow and glassy.

Myers couldn't think of an appropriate response to the doctor's comment but the doctor hadn't waited for one, anyway. He had shaken his head and moved on.

The men continued their quarreling, one of the most contentious disputes being how often to change positions in the bays. They were no longer interlocked in their bays because of crowding but for warmth. Still, they all had to turn over at the same time or none of them could. Some of them were wounded on their right side and didn't want to put their now insignificant body weight on their wounds, while others didn't want to lie on injuries on their left side. So the arguments continued.

The thieving among some of the POWs had never ceased, even in their infirm conditions. Burglars, stronger than the rest because of their thefts, prowled the hold day and night. Some could sit down next to a sleeping man, open his canteen, and drink all the water in it without making a sound. Even the prisoners who tried to sleep with their fingers locked around their canteen's plug weren't immune. Every morning someone would sit up, yelling, "Where's the dirty bastard who stole my water?"

The stealing from the Japanese never ceased and they were now taking the coarse brown sugar from the hold below with great abandon. Those who ate measured amounts were able to digest it, but those who gobbled up handfuls at a time always paid for it as it made their chronic diarrhea worse.

Their only food alternative was the Formosan rice provided by the Japanese. It was rough and full of hulls and increased their diarrhea as well. So the men continued stealing and eating the sugar simply because it tasted better. One of the guards had seen a prisoner on deck mixing a handful of the sugar with snow and reported it to Wada. The hunchback interpreter told the prisoners that if the sugar heists continued, he would completely cut off all their provisions.

As he dozed during the afternoon of January 29, Myers heard wild shouts in Japanese up on deck. A short time later, a chief yeoman fell back down the ladder into the hold, practically landing on top of Myers.

"What's going on up there?" Myers asked him.

"I went up to take a whiz," the chief yeoman told him, "and I saw the most beautiful icicle hanging, just hanging, all sparkly in the sun. I couldn't help myself; I just reached up for it. Jap sentry saw me and came at me with his bayonet." Tears formed in the man's eyes.

"I had a snowball for a backup, too, but when that son of a bitch came at me with his pig sticker, I ran. I didn't get the icicle, and then I dropped the snowball when I fell."

He sat down and licked the few droplets of water still clinging to his filthy hands.

As the ship continued her northerly course, snow fell more frequently. It melted on the deck during the daylight hours and seeped down into the hold, making it treacherously slick. Falling down on the hard steel floor of the hold was painful for these sickly men, but sometimes it had far worse consequences. Since the Japanese refused to allow the prisoners' three or four *benjo* buckets to be emptied more than once each day, they were always full. If a man landed in a *benjo* bucket when he fell, he was destined to remain encrusted in waste. With no water, washing it off was an unfulfilled luxury.

Myers witnessed one man fall into a *benjo* bucket. The sullied man refused any comfort from the corpsman. Without a word, he climbed up to his bay, picked up his canteen, and struck himself in the brow with it, slumping over dead.

On January 30, two men who had been up on deck to relieve themselves spread word through the hold they had seen land. They were positive that the ship must be just off the coast of Japan. Sometime before 2300 hours that night, the silence in the hold was shattered with the sound of American torpedoes. The prisoners had known all along that subs lurked close by, but this was the first time since Formosa that they'd been fired upon. Having already witnessed the carnage from the other American attacks, the pathetic clutch of four hundred ninety men was terrified.

"Look at the bright side, lads," a keen sailor near Myers remarked. "If the Yanks are firing torpedoes at the Japanese coastline, the end of the war must be close at hand."

A private leaning against a large chief yeoman expressed what they were all thinking.

"Oh God, we're so close. We're the survivors; we've made it through everything else. We can't go down now! And I ain't even ever been baptized." He looked at the chief yeoman. "I don't think they'll let me into heaven since I ain't been baptized."

The private crawled over to where the two chaplains still alive were lying. They were so weak, he couldn't make them understand that he wanted to be baptized on the spot. The chief yeoman called him back to where he still sat and offered to perform the ceremony. Neither of them had any water, so they used the only liquid they had available—the chief yeoman's saliva. The newly baptized man was so relieved that he curled up in a ball and went to sleep. He never awoke.

At dawn on the morning of January 31, 1945, the *Brazil Maru* crept into the harbor of Moji, Japan, on the most southerly Home Island of Kyushu. The ship had no more than dropped anchor when a group of Japanese military, their capes flying and polished sabers flashing, came aboard to inspect their recently arrived human cargo. Myers heard the Imperial officers scream down their orders, demanding that the senior American officer present himself on deck.

Slowly, painfully, the American made the climb out of the squalor below. His hair and beard were clotted with festering scum in which he'd been living for seven weeks. What clothing he had, no more than dirty rags, barely covered his decrepit form. The American gave a feeble salute and sank back, exhausted from the exertion, against the bulkhead behind him.

The Japanese officials were stunned as they took in the deck scene illuminated before them in the clean morning light. Surrounding the debilitated POW were rank-smelling slop buckets, full to the brim, and a stack of naked, emaciated dead men, some gawking with sightless eyes at their new wardens.

Unsure of what their next move should be, the officers shouted orders and a cadre of medical personnel materialized. After a brief discussion, the doctors decided the rest of the prisoners should be brought up on deck for disinfection before they disembarked. To convey that order, two lesser-ranking men descended the ladder into the hold.

Myers and his fellow POWs, whose eyes were accustomed to the darkness of their fetid home, watched listlessly as the two officers paused at the base of the ladder and puffed up their chests with the all-importance accorded them by the Japanese Empire. Moments later, when their eyes adjusted to the dim lighting, the air of supremacy became breathless horror. Another fifty-two more naked corpses were piled off to one side. And the living were the most wretched-looking human beings they had ever seen. The sight and oppressive smell of urine and feces caused the two to stagger backward as if slapped by the flat side of a giant sword. The officials in Moji had expected to find a thousand healthy men, ready for work. Instead, a gaunt, stinking lot languished before them.

The two officers scrambled back up on deck and shouted down the order for the prisoners to report. The medical detail made ready their disinfectant spray gun and used it immediately on the stumbling, squinting POWs pouring out of the hold. Myers and Tarpy helped load those too weak to walk onto a wooden platform, which was unceremoniously hauled up onto the freezing deck. The corpsmen followed their patients and were instantly hit with the icy blast of liquid disinfectant. Absolutely no attention was given to wounded men's feeble condition, and they, too, were summarily sprayed.

The same mingled feeling of dread and curiosity accosted Myers as it had that first day when the Japanese contingent had arrived at the Manila hospital. The frigid wind blew across the harbor and onto the ship, penetrating his drenched and sparse clothing. He trembled uncontrollably, trying to focus on the dock scene beyond the deck. They had finally arrived. Four hundred and twenty-seven men out of an original 1,619 had been delivered from their tormented existence aboard a ship of death.

Coinciding with the arrival of the *Brazil Maru* in Moji, Japan, another momentous arrival was underway, as Allied troops stood poised to retake the city of Manila. A riptide of liberators had spread across Luzon, surrounding the Imperial troops with the ultimate goal of concentrating them in the center of the island. In their fight to regain the 450-mile-long Luzon, American forces touched every landmark that Myers and his fellow POWs had passed through on their hellish expedition out of the Philippines.

After the successful Allied landings at Lingayen Gulf, the troops began moving eastward toward the main Japanese defenses. As with the virtually deserted Lingayen beaches, Yamashita was hardly contesting the route to Manila, either, still holding fast to his plan of the three defensive strongholds. Meanwhile, MacArthur and Krueger continued steady pressure on the Japanese lines.

On January 24, Krueger's 40th Division had advanced toward the ridges and hills overlooking Clark Field. His major task was to capture the four airstrips in the area. The battle was fought in short, slow advances in the face of heavy Japanese mortar and machine-gun fire. It took the Americans three days to gain a thousand yards, but by 1800 hours on the 28th, Clark Field was once again in Allied hands.

Further north, thirty thousand more troops landed at Lingayen on the 27th and pushed their way into Zambales Province without opposition. On January 29, they recaptured Olongapo and the Old Naval Station on Subic Bay. They began an offensive to capture the important road and rail center of San Jose Pampanga on January 30, and on the 31st, the 11th Airborne Division landed twenty-five miles south of Cavite.

With the Allied troop movements, the Bataan Peninsula was eventually sealed off. For the Philippine guerrillas who were part of this offensive, it was a chance to exact revenge on the enemy. These guerrillas had formed a complex underground network when the Philippines had been wrested from American control three years earlier.

Throughout the war, the underground guerrillas blew up bridges and railroad tracks and surreptitiously sank enemy boats as they floated in the harbors. They picked up Allied pilots who had been shot down and Allied prisoners who had escaped from camps. They operated weather stations, the information from which helped not only the landing troops but the ships and planes out at sea that were involved in bombing runs against the Home Islands. To assist the Filipino underground, the Americans sent submarines, which brought more arms, ammunition, and medical supplies. The subs brought more spies, too, both American and Filipino.

The guerrillas' value was immense, and their heroism often went well beyond the call of duty, even where death was inevitable. It was with great pleasure, then, that these men, who had taken to the hills at the start of the war, were now able to hunt down the one thousand ruthless Japanese soldiers left on Bataan. These were the same Imperial soldiers who had forced the guerrillas' comrades to make the grueling Death March.

On the same day, January 30, two prison camps were opened to the outside world for the first time since the fall of the islands. In a daring raid carried out by the guerrillas and a group of American Rangers, five hundred nearly starved Americans were freed from Cabanatuan Prison Camp. A short distance away, reconnaissance units came upon Camp O'Donnell, about sixty miles north of Manila. The Americans surmised that the Japanese had left just the day before, after torching the buildings. Not a living soul was visible.

Two burial grounds had been established, one Filipino, the other American, each containing more than a thousand crosses. In an effort to affect benevolence, the Japanese had erected a rough cement monument which carried the inscription "In memory of American dead. O'Donnell War Personnel Enclosure erected by Imperial Japanese Army."

A few minutes past midnight on February 1, the 1st Cavalry Division was in position on the northern outskirts of Manila. Twenty thousand Japanese troops were prepared to defend the city and had laced the streets with mines. They blew up square miles of the metropolis, including MacArthur's former penthouse suite at the Manila Hotel. They massacred civilians, whites, and Filipinos alike, determined to wreak as much death and destruction as possible. Under an Imperial military directive, they were to hold on or die trying.

True to form, MacArthur would not be deterred from his goal of taking back the capital city. "If we run out of bullets we will use grenades," he told his troops before they began their crusade. "If we run out of grenades, we will cut down the enemy with swords; if we break our swords, we will kill them by sinking our teeth deep in their throats."

Two days later, on Saturday, February 3, nine Marine pilots flew over Santo Tomas University, located on the north side of the city, dropping leaflets that read: "Roll out the barrel. Santa Claus is coming to town Sunday or Monday." But the 1st Cavalry chose not to wait. Moments later, there was a roar of engines and a voice shouted, "Where's the front gate?" A Sherman tank crashed through the wall and liberated approximately thirty-seven hundred prisoners.

At virtually the same moment, the 8th Cavalry was seizing Old Bilibid Prison. One thousand twenty-four men were clinging to a meager subsistence. They were the remnants of those who had been left behind, determined to be too sick or disabled to depart for Japan aboard the *Oryoku Maru.*

Had they been the least bit capable of doing so, the *Brazil Maru's* survivors wouldn't have bet a plug nickel that the guys they left behind in Bilibid survived long enough to be liberated. Instead, Myers and the rest of the men were still focused on what had been their singular purpose for the last forty-nine days: survival. They were huddled together in little clutches, struggling to share whatever body heat their pitifully gaunt frames radiated.

Meanwhile, the Japanese doctors had discovered the rampant dysentery that most of the POWs had. All men, they said, had to be tested. A regiment of Japanese corpsmen arrived with cases of glass rods. The rods were inserted into the prisoners' rectums and samples were taken.

Simultaneously, the dead were now being brought up from the ship's hold. The Japanese had been putting the corpses into thin pine-board boxes. But now that dysentery had been discovered, the Imperial doctors ordered that the dead be tested as well. So the rude coffins were opened and the deceased were tested with the glass rods.

Myers and Tarpy viewed these actions with disgust.

"What difference does it make if those guys died of dysentery or not?" Myers whispered. "They're dead either way."

"They got names for people who mess around with corpses," Tarpy whispered back. "I just can't think of the word."

"No talking!" Wada screamed, scurrying over to where the two corpsmen were standing. He pulled out the slender club he had stuck in his belt and swung at Myers. Wada was standing too far away from him to inflict any great injury but caught Myers in the buttocks, which sent him sprawling forward.

A Japanese officer saw the commotion and strode over to Wada. He looked down on the hunchback and uttered words from deep in his throat. Wada began to shrink back, and the officer grabbed the club with a white-gloved hand and heaved it overboard. Myers hadn't understood a word the officer said, but judging from Wada's reaction, he had probably threatened the interpreter with his life should any further damage be done to the already damaged cargo.

A little clothing was distributed among them, and some shoes, but not nearly enough was provided to completely outfit all of the men. Most stood shivering and barefoot on the snow-covered deck. The last muster aboard ship was called and the prisoners were marched down the dock. As had become customary during the forced marches, the guards ran up and down among their ranks yelling, "Speedo, speedo." Those who fell and were unable to rise under their own power were beaten with a rifle butt until they either got up or were pulled to their feet by fellow POWs.

They were marched through the streets of Moji, while Japanese children spat at them, and arrived at a large, empty, unheated theater building. Some blankets and overcoats were handed out to fend off the cold air. The men were so weak and exhausted that they sunk to the floor, caring little that it was bare concrete.

It appeared that a new exercise in Japanese bureaucracy was being organized, and Myers used the brief respite to consider the consequences of the time the prisoners had spent aboard the *Brazil Maru*. They had begun with 1,619 men when they left Bilibid. Between Manila and San Fernando Pampanga, 659 prisoners died or were killed. Another 533 lost their lives between San Fernando and Moji.

A total of 1,192 men had given away all of their tomorrows in the name of freedom today.

Myers became cognizant of the activity taking place around him. As with all the previous musters and Imperial organizational activities, the men were not given any food or water before or during the process. They were being sorted into three groups. The first group divided out was the "hospital group," those who were determined to be too infirm to begin work right away, if indeed they ever would at all. During the sorting process alone, Myers personally tended to three men who died on the floor of the theater.

The remainder of the prisoners—Myers guessed there to be around three hundred of them—were divided into two groups considered the "well" men. He and Tarpy managed to stand closely enough together to be assigned to the same group. The well men were told to fall in and, as they did so, a fleet of ambulances arrived to remove the hospital group. Myers wondered to himself why no corpsmen had been chosen to go with this group as caregivers. The Japanese had steadfastly refused to care for the prisoners any other time, and Myers couldn't imagine that the status quo was going to change now that they were in Japan. The obvious answer to this pondering was not long in coming to Myers. The hospital group of men were in such dire condition, they were never going to recover. The Japanese probably figured there was little point in wasting able-bodied men by sending them with the doomed. Myers' conjecture proved to be correct. Of the one hundred men who were taken to a hospital in the nearby town of Kokura, seventy-six never went any farther.

The prisoners were marched to a train station and loaded into cars with wooden benches. All of the window blinds were pulled tightly shut. Several gutsy Americans managed to sneak peeks at the Japanese landscape. The devastation was tremendous, caused, the men divined, by American air power. As this news spread through the train cars, the POWs could only guess that their guards didn't want them to get any ideas of impending liberation. As long as the prisoners were kept ignorant they could be forced to continue to submit to their captors' demands.

The trip took about five hours, and the men still hadn't been given any rations. When the train pulled to a halt and the doors opened, the men staggered out onto the tracks. Myers looked up at a sign on a nearby building that had English written alongside the Japanese characters.

"That says 'Kashii,'" a tall man beside him said. "I know where we are, I've heard of it. This is an industrial area. Manufacturing and coal mines, too." Myers turned to ask him how he knew so much, but the man blended in with the others stumbling along. He decided it didn't matter whether the information the man gave him was accurate or not, since it was more information than he'd had.

From a platform near the long building that ran along the tracks, a man in tattered clothing was speaking loudly, and it took Myers a few minutes to realize the man was speaking in English. The newly arrived men were to stay with their groups. Group One, which had 173 men and included Myers and Tarpy, was to follow him to trucks; the second group was to wait for the other Americans to arrive to take them to another camp.

All during the sorting process in Moji, the train ride, and now on their way to the trucks, the Japanese guards brandished their weapons as if the men might at any moment rush and overpower them. The concept was ludicrous given their physical condition, but evidently this hadn't registered with the guards. Again shouts of "Speedo!" rang out as the men were herded into the trucks.

News soon spread during the short truck ride that the Americans at the train station were POWs captured at Wake Island. The group was on its way to the camp known as Fukuoka #1. Shortly after nightfall, the trucks arrived at the camp. The new prisoners were issued overcoats, courtesy of the American, British, and Australian Red Cross, and then taken to another large, unheated building. The building was fairly new, the first new structure Myers and Tarpy had been in since becoming prisoners.

But that wasn't the most surprising thing about their first night in Japan. A meal arrived a short time later, the best they'd seen in a long time, including cooked rice, hot soup, and warm Japanese tea.

Myers fell asleep soon after he'd finished his meal. It was the first time in weeks he didn't feel that the weight of other men's very survival rested on his shoulders.

There were twenty-four camps named Fukuoka, after the prefecture in which they were located. Each was numbered one through twenty-four, and some of the camps had been given additional names, denoting the area in which they were located. Myers and Tarpy's new camp, Fukuoka #1, had had three different locations during the war, and as many names. It had first been situated in Kashii, where their train ride had come to an end. Then the camp was moved to the airport outside of Kashii, and in January 1945, the camp was relocated a final time, slightly north of and inland from the city of Fukuoka. Because of the surrounding grove of pine trees, the camp became known as Pine Tree Camp.

Fukuoka #3 was located in Yawata, near the Dai-ichi Seiko steel mill. Roughly one hundred *Brazil Maru* survivors made the one-hour trip from Moji to #3. Fukuoka #17 was at Omuta, home of the Mitsui Coal Mining Company. Ninety *Brazil Maru* survivors, mostly enlisted men, were sent there, although twenty-four died shortly after their arrival, despite the fact they had been part of the prisoner group who were considered "well." Number 17 quickly built a reputation for being the roughest among the Fukuoka camps.

Pine Tree Camp was located about a quarter of a mile from the main-line railway that had brought the prisoners from Moji. It was very close to a new Japanese military installation and within a few miles of coal mines. The camp compound measured 1,000 by 300 feet and was surrounded by a wooden fence topped off with electrified barbed wire. Like all of the other buildings and modes of transportation with which Myers and his fellow prisoners had come in contact, there were no markings anywhere in the camp that might indicate that it housed POWs.

Pine Tree Camp was a melting pot of nationalities. Aside from the men who arrived with Myers from Japan, there were another 300 Americans, four of whom were civilians captured on Wake Island.

The camp's population also included 150 British, 250 Dutch, and 20 Australians, military personnel all, bringing the total population to 913.

The camp's buildings were crude, despite the fact that they were relatively new. Some were even still under construction. The twelve unheated barracks were framed of native lumber and bamboo with tar-paper roofs, and each housed between forty-eight and sixty prisoners. The buildings were sunk four and a half feet into the ground and had sand floors. The portion of the walls that stood aboveground was covered with mud plaster.

The barracks were divided on the inside by a long passageway on either side of which were the narrow sleeping bays measuring just two feet wide per prisoner. There was no heat in the buildings, but each man was issued six tattered blankets with which to make his bed. There was only one small light in the barracks and the prisoners were only allowed to turn it on after sundown. At all other times, the barracks remained in a shadowy gloom.

Because of the dire conditions aboard the *Brazil Maru*, Myers thought Pine Tree Camp might be tolerable, beginning with the fact that the entire group was allowed to remain in bed for the ten days after their arrival. On their eleventh day in camp, an Imperial doctor came through the barracks and again the prisoners were sorted by who was fit for labor and who wasn't. From that time on, those who were considered to be well were required to rise at 0630, eat their morning ration, fall out for *bangou,* and remain outside of the barracks until 1630 hours, with the exception of thirty minutes at 1000 hours and sixty minutes at noon.

The work details at Pine Tree Camp were identical in the fact that they all entailed ten hours of hard labor. The officers among the prisoners were not required to work alongside their men. Rather, their duties included the upkeep of the camp garden, although most of them were so incapacitated they were hospitalized a great deal of the time.

The three remaining doctors and a handful of corpsmen still functioning, including Myers and Tarpy, were assigned duty in the camp hospital. Only those POWs who were unconscious or dying were brought to the hospital, a structure that was a carbon copy of the barracks. The hospital had no beds; rather, each patient was allotted floor space about two feet wide and six feet long. Each was given four Japanese army blankets and a pillow bag filled with rice husks. As was the rest of the camp, the building was inadequately heated, and it seemed to Myers as though he was as cold inside as he was out in the compound.

The hospital only had the capacity for fifteen patients and it was filled on a first-come, first-served basis. Since that meant a great many men who should have been hospitalized had to remain in their barracks, Myers' and Tarpy's patients were in both the hospital and the barracks. This was relatively inefficient since it never seemed like they had what they needed where they needed it most.

The upshot was that there weren't many supplies, anyway. The fact that the building was even referred to as a hospital was a joke to Myers. Like every other situation he had been in as a POW, this hospital was very ill equipped to treat the kinds of injuries and ailments from which these patients were suffering. There were no surgical facilities and very few medicines and dressings. Many of the doctors who'd been there previously were sick themselves, and the arrival of the needy from the *Brazil Maru* strained the facility even more.

After a few days at the camp hospital, a representative from the prison camp headquarters in Fukuoka arrived to inspect the facilities and the prisoners, and he inquired what they might need. The doctors drew up a list of medical supplies and stressed the need for additional food. If Red Cross packages were available, they suggested, this was the time that they would do the prisoners the most good.

The representative's visit netted the prisoners one small Red Cross package for every three men, all of which were immediately placed under the control of the camp's Japanese medical officer, Dr. Masato Hata. He was incompetent, inconsiderate, and particularly brutal. Only after the most insistent pleadings would he allow the prisoners any additional supplies, appearing to take great pleasure in forcing the Allied medical personnel to literally beg for what they needed.

"Hey, Myers," Tarpy called to him one afternoon after they'd been in camp for two weeks. "There's a guy over there, third from the left, second row. Says he was sent over to the warehouse connected to Hata's office. Says that slimy Nip's got boxes of Red Cross medicines that he's hoarding."

Myers thought for a minute and answered, "We have to get the doctors to write scripts for the drugs before Hata'll give 'em to us, right?"

"Right," Tarpy answered.

"Why don't we double up on the number of scripts we have the docs write. You know, instead of sulfa for one guy, we'll say there are two guys. If Hata's got it maybe we can get enough that way."

Myers took his idea to the doctors, who thought it was very clever and implemented it. But even the double dosages didn't seem to help the men. It was always too little and too late for many of the prisoners, particularly those who had survived the hellacious trials aboard the *Brazil Maru*.

In fact, the ship's survivors were in such horrid shape when they arrived, the men who had already been interned at Pine Tree Camp were shocked at their appearance. They were even more shocked at their mortality rate. Malnutrition was so chronic in all prison camps it was barely given notice. But these men had each lost between seventy and ninety pounds. In addition, they suffered from a variety of injuries and complications. One doctor counted twenty-three streptococci infections on his own legs and body that ran with blood and pus.

About the end of February, a Japanese colonel came to inspect the camp and asked to meet with the doctors and corpsmen outside the hospital. Myers and the other men shivered in the cold while the colonel took his time finishing a cup of tea in the office of the camp commandant, First Lieutenant Yuichi Sakamato. When he was ready, he faced the Americans to give a brief introductory speech.

"We wish all prisoners to be cared for. Men need to work and we have work for them to do. But they must get well."

So you can work them or beat them to death, Myers thought. As

soon as he had been ordered out of his sleeping bay ten days after his
arrival, Myers witnessed the guards' brutality. In some cases it was
even worse than what he had seen up until this point. After a prisoner received his beating for his rule infraction, he was tossed into an
unheated guardhouse for a period of solitary confinement. In the
near zero temperatures, with little clothing and no body weight to
warm them, POWs often never left the guardhouse alive.

The Japanese colonel continued his speech to the medical staff.
"We will supply you with what you need to make these men well."
He then asked each medical officer what recommendations he might
have to rally the languishing patients. The responses were unanimous
and no different than they had been to prison camp representatives:
food and medicines. This time, the doctors thought if they were
more specific, their needs might be met. They requested meat, milk,
and butter, and again asked for Red Cross boxes which would contain medical supplies.

The colonel's answer was not surprising. "We understand that
you need those things, they are very important but difficult to have
during war. And we cannot give you Red Cross boxes because you are
so hungry now. If we give them to you, the men will eat the food too
quickly and waste them and they will do you no good."

He moved on to the corpsmen and asked for their recommendations. Few if any had suggestions, but Myers spoke up. "Sir, the men
need more blankets to keep warm during this cold weather."

The colonel countered with the fact that Japanese soldiers are
only given five blankets and the POWs already had one more than
that. Myers figured it was useless to pursue the argument, despite the
fact that logic dictated men as emaciated as the prisoners had no
body fat to help protect them against the chilling northern winds. It
was the old argument all over again: what was good enough for Imperial troops was more than sufficient for prisoners, regardless of the
other hardships they suffered.

CHAPTER SEVENTEEN

★

Pain Among the Pines

By the beginning of 1945, Japan's industrial foundation was crippled and her military had begun to crack. A British War Cabinet paper had even boldly stated that "Germany would probably lose the war because she had factories and no raw materials, but Japan would lose because she had raw materials and no factories."

Early in the hostilities Japan had secured what the Imperial military strategists had called the "Southern Resources Area," namely Malaya, French Indo-China, and the Dutch East Indies. But the Japanese lacked the time and means to develop these areas so as to make use of their resources. In addition, by 1945 the Allies had regained a significant number of Pacific islands formerly in Imperial hands and the shipping routes between them. Significant sea blockades were set up and the inflow of raw materials and supplies to Japan slowed to a trickle.

Aside from the lack of supplies, Japanese industry itself was in trouble. Critically important factories and manufacturing centers were packed tightly together on this island nation. That made them easy pickings for the nearly constant B-29 bombardments the Americans began unleashing late in 1944 from air bases in China, Saipan, and the Marianas. Furthermore, because Japan had sent most of her able-bodied men into the fighting arena, most recently as kamikaze pilots, production in the factories had begun to seriously lag behind

the endless demands. Children and the elderly had already been re-
cruited as workers, but still more labor was needed.

Japan drew their needed manpower from their large wealth of Allied POWs. By 1945, there were more than one hundred seventy-five
POW camps in Manchuria, Korea, and on the Home Islands. The
prisoners shoveled coal and repaired railroad tracks. They operated
blast furnaces and loaded cargo. They worked everywhere their captors ordered them to: in mills and foundries, in mines and on piers.
The hours were long, the days off infrequent, and the conditions
harsh. There were very few medical supplies and very little food.

Since Japan was unable to sufficiently feed her own population,
the prisoners were given only the most meager rations. For those
men who had fought and been captured on Bataan, they were beginning their fourth year of chronic starvation. There were almost no
animals left in Japanese zoos; they had all been eaten except for a few
surviving elephants. Sumo wrestling had been cancelled. The official
daily calorie count for Japanese civilians fell to below two thousand,
not nearly enough to maintain the sumo's weight for competition.

There was not enough fabric to make kimonos, so the women
wore *mompei,* working trousers, instead. There was no sugar and no
tobacco. Even Mother Nature added to the travails by sending
strong, cold winds blowing across the Japanese Home Islands that
winter. The cold affected prisoners and citizens alike; there was no oil
for heating homes and no gasoline for powering vehicles.

The Japanese military leaders told the struggling nation that they
were making the sacrifices necessary for the continuation of their
race. They were assured that the war was going Japan's way and that,
in the end, the sacrifices would be worth it. Imperial citizens were
forewarned that if the evil white invaders arrived on the Home Islands, they could expect massacre, rape, and pillage. The Emperor,
they were told, expected them to resist to the end. One hundred million people were ordered to all die together.

The militarists at the helm of the Japanese government were more
than a little accurate regarding their admonition about an attack on
and invasion of the Home Islands. The Allied leaders felt that, given

the tenacity the enemy had exhibited thus far, it was the only way that complete submission could be exacted from them. The invasion plans called for the operation to be divided into two parts, code-named Olympic and Coronet. It would begin on November 1, 1945, with the island of Kyushu. Nine Army divisions would be devoted to the cause, along with five thousand planes and six thousand ships. Luzon would be the supply base and staging area for the upcoming attacks.

General MacArthur was well aware of the importance of securing the Philippines. After the arrival of his troops in Manila on February 3, and their ensuing liberation of the prison camps in and around the city, MacArthur declared the city secure on February 7. Though it may have been secure, it was not surrendered. Japanese navy Rear Admiral Sanji Iwabachi was in charge of the Special Naval Base Force and had been given orders to defend the city. He and his twenty thousand troops had every intention of carrying out the order, especially since they had no means of escape.

Throughout the month of February, the Allies made building-by-building searches, fighting constant skirmishes with the Japanese. In the process the city of Manila was completely destroyed. Three quarters of the residential district in the southern part of the city had been leveled. Utilities were almost nonexistent and the business district had been wiped out. The government buildings, the churches, and the historical structures and walls of the Intramuros were obliterated. Philippine death counts topped one hundred thousand.

The island of Corregidor was also still in Japanese hands and being defended by five thousand naval troops. Because of the already successful corralling of Yamashita's troops on Luzon, the island's military value was superfluous. But it had symbolic value to MacArthur.

On February 16, twenty-four B-24s, forty-two medium-range bombers, eight cruisers, and fourteen destroyers bombarded the island. By the 24th, the United States controlled all of the island except for the last three thousand yards of the "tail." On the morning of the 26th, in a desperate suicide attempt, the remaining Imperial troops detonated an underground arsenal. This resulted in the death of two hundred Japanese and fifty Americans, and the wounding of another one hundred fifty Americans. But it was the final act in what had become a very long and tragic struggle. The next day, the Stars and Stripes were once more raised over Corregidor.

The same day, February 27, 1945, MacArthur officially restored the Philippine Commonwealth government to its rightful president, President Osmeña, who responded by saying: "We shall be redeemed from slavery. As a crowning glory to Philippine-American collaboration, we shall become a full member of the concert of independent nations."

While the fighting was winding down in the Philippines in February 1945, it was just beginning on the islands of Iwo Jima and Okinawa. It would be from these islands, which lay 800 and 350 miles from Japan respectively, that the Allies would launch their invasion of the Home Islands.

The Allies began the bombardment of Iwo Jima with B-24s and B-25s flying out of the Marianas. The missions began in late October of 1944, seventy-two days before the landing took place, making this the longest bombardment of any island in the Pacific war. To understand the translation of the island's name is to understand the significance of the attacks. Translated from Japanese, *iwo* and *jima* mean "sulfur island"; seven and a half square miles of volcanic remains. The Japanese had transformed the island into a veritable web of interconnected tunnels similar to Corregidor. The tunnels and bunkers had walls four feet thick, made from a combination of the volcanic ash and cement. In addition, natural caves were abundant on the island, some large enough to hold up to four hundred soldiers.

The defenses the military had seen in Tarawa in November of 1943 had seemed rugged, but compared to Iwo Jima's defenses they had been child's play. When American Marines first landed on Iwo Jima on February 19, 1945, harmless-looking, earthen mounds on the beach suddenly exploded with enemy gunfire. Beside these camouflaged pillboxes, the ground was sown with thousands of land mines.

On February 23, the American flag was raised on the Marines' first goal, Mount Suribachi. The fighting didn't end until March 26 and Iwo Jima was in Allied hands. The taking of this tiny morsel of real estate went down in the history pages as the bloodiest battle in the history of the United States Marine Corps, costing 6,821 American lives.

While the battles raged on land in the Pacific, the Allies continued blasting away at the Home Islands from the air. The winter winds and heavy cloud cover over Japan in 1945 diminished the effectiveness of the American high-altitude precision bombing. So in March, the B-29s commenced low-level bombing of smaller industrial targets. On the 9th of the month, the planes began a run of attacks, dropping incendiary bombs on Japanese cities, an event that drastically changed the strategic nature of the air war.

The next day, March 10, three hundred thirty Superfortresses attacked Tokyo. Sixteen square miles of the capital, nearly forty percent, burned to the ground. Eighty-five thousand people died as a result of the ten thousand tons of ordnance that were dropped.

The Allied pounding continued, and the tempo and size of the raids increased. After the Tokyo firestorm, 285 bombers struck Nagoya, then Osaka, Kobe, and Yokohama. The buildings in these cities, made primarily of paper and wood, burned instantly. Three hundred thousand people were left homeless.

American plans called for an April 1, 1945, landing on Okinawa. Because of the island's proximity to Japan, the Allies expected to encounter the most savage defense. This, in a war that had already been extraordinarily lethal. March 1945 had been the costliest month in battle for the United States with a loss of twenty thousand servicemen, an average of nine hundred per day. The war had taken a huge toll on Japanese lives, too. By the end of the same month they had lost two men for every one American, a total of three hundred thousand since the war began.

The Allied military leaders planned to use everything they had learned thus far in the war about assault landing techniques to take Okinawa. For his part, the Japanese commander on the island, General Mitsuru Ushijima, was determined to make his stand the most high-priced campaign of the war in terms of American lives.

The main American assault began with the April Fool's Day landing. Knowing that the Allies would be well equipped, the Japanese employed their one remaining strategy: suicide. Kamikaze drafts were formed at every Japanese air base. No one could refuse the assignment. Despite propaganda that insisted they had volunteered, the pilots were forced to choose either duty or the firing squad. Because many of these pilots were novices without much training, the kamikazes were often inaccurate in their deadly runs. But there were hundreds of them, and their sheer numbers made up for the inaccuracies, hitting even a hospital ship as well as their military targets.

Another ominous weapon of war was unleashed for the battle of Okinawa. Three hundred and fifty suicide boats, an assortment of small wooden craft, were heavily loaded with high-powered explosives. The boats' captains were expected to ram the sides of American ships, blowing themselves up in an attempt to sink the larger vessels.

From all appearances, the Japanese were committed to a last-ditch defense of their Empire. General Ushijima told his fighting forces that each man was to trade his life for the lives of ten Americans or one American tank. The landings on the north and south end of the island went well, as did the next four days. At that point, the Allied troops ran into the greatest concentrations of Ushijima's forces, and two things became evident. First, the Allies were going to have to slog their way across the island, taking inch by bloody inch. Secondly, the Japanese aimed to employ their strategy of suicide in every element of their stand.

Besides the kamikazes and suicide boats, the Japanese were willing to risk the lives of every one of their soldiers on Okinawa if it meant they could take the lives of Allied fighting men. The Japanese went so far as to plan a suicide for the pride of their navy. The *Yamato* was given only enough fuel for a one-way trip to Okinawa. When she arrived, she was to turn her guns on American ships while kamikazes attacked from above. A single kamikaze plane would be held in reserve, and when the *Yamato* could no longer fight, it was to sink her where she sat.

Throughout the months of April, May, and most of June, the Americans hammered at the Japanese lines. They retreated begrudgingly, until Ushijima reached his last stronghold. The Americans asked him to surrender but the Imperial general refused, committing *hara-kiri* on June 22. By the next morning, Okinawa was secured. Although Ushijima had lost the battle, he succeeded in achieving his goal. The Americans lost 20,195 men in the taking of Okinawa, while the Japanese lost a staggering 110,000. The fighting on Okinawa was indeed the most costly of the war and one of the most costly in history.

The POWs at Pine Tree Camp were well aware of the bombing runs occurring around them. Some of the prisoner work details were ordered to build bomb shelters in the Fukuoka area. When the air-raid sirens screamed, announcing potential death from the skies, the prisoners on work details outside the camp watched as terrified Japanese citizens fled into the sturdy shelters. The prisoners, meanwhile, would be herded into nothing more than flimsy shacks.

Other prisoners worked long, arduous days in the coal mines. Then, after returning to camp at day's end, they were made to dig graves, carry coffins, or take part in other cemetery duties. Almost all of the POWs were forced to work beyond their physical capabilities and were beaten for lagging behind.

After a couple of months at Pine Tree Camp, it struck Myers that his function in the hospital there was not unlike what it had been in the Bilibid Prison hospital. Living corpses arrived daily at the hospital, mostly from the coal mines. Feeble and sick, they could scarcely walk in under their own power. Human dignity and decency were absent from their lives and their feeling of self-worth had disappeared. They had been forced to become animals, with the single goal of surviving just one more day. An officer Myers had met aboard the ship from the Philippines was interned with him at Pine Tree

Camp. He told Myers one day that the camp's conditions were so bad, "a healthy pig would have died." Myers didn't disagree.

In addition to guard beatings, slow starvation, fevers, and pneumonia, the Pine Tree Camp prisoners also had to contend with the camp commandant, Sakamato, who was as odious as Hata, the camp's doctor. Sakamato had no reservations about delivering beatings to the prisoners, whether for "just cause" or for sport. Nor did he do anything to prevent the prisoners from being stoned by civilians as they plodded on their work details outside the prison walls.

Pine Tree Camp's hygiene facilities were a vast improvement over anything Myers and Tarpy had on their journey from the Philippines. But Myers decided they still were a long way from anything even the most underprivileged American had lived with during the Depression. The camp's latrine facilities were adequate although they were nothing more than straddle trenches. There was also a bathhouse; it was unheated and contained five large, square vats made of wood with metal bottoms. The vats were ten feet long, four feet wide, and four feet deep, and the water they contained was heated through the use of a fire pit beneath each of them. This was where all the men bathed, the infirm as well as those with only a meager clutch on life. Soap was only rarely furnished, and when it was it usually had to be shared between four or five men.

The bath water was changed weekly, which meant that it was fairly polluted most of the time. When Myers and Tarpy had first arrived during the coldest months, they avoided it altogether, as did most of the medical personnel.

"Don't get in that tub," Myers warned a man one day who had just recovered from a long bout with pneumonia. "You're already pretty weak. You catch a chill from getting wet, and you won't be long for this world."

"But the guards just changed the water this morning," the prisoner argued. "It'll be clean, and it feels so good. It warms me right down to my bones."

The prisoner took his bath, fell ill again within a day, and was dead by week's end.

As it had been everywhere else during their captivity, the prisoners' diet at Pine Tree Camp consisted primarily of rice, about three quarters of a canteen cup of rice daily. Here it was mixed with *koreon,* a small grain that resembled broomcorn. The rice was digestible, but the men saw the broomcorn pass through their intestinal tracts nearly unaltered.

Their daily ration also included half a cup of soup, with pieces of daikon, a large white radish, swimming around in it. Occasionally a small bun was added, and the evening meal included a few grams of dried fish. A major problem the POWs faced was a lack of salt, and the craving for it became almost unbearable. Fortunately, the men didn't sweat in the winter months, thus preventing an even greater depletion of their salt supplies.

Myers was treating a man in one of the barracks one evening and passed several prisoners bent over a small cooking fire in the compound. He stopped and asked what they were doing.

"Found some salt out near the manure piles we were working in," one of the men told him. The Japanese used their animals' manure to fertilize their crops, and the POWs had the unpleasant job of collecting and spreading it.

"Must've been left from when they salted the animals," another man added.

"You gotta be sure to remove all the manure," Myers told them. "We're already so full of parasites it's a wonder we're surviving at all. But you sure as heck don't need to pick up anything new."

"That's what we figured," the first man said. "So we separated it from the manure real careful and now we're dissolving it in boiling water. We figure we'll let it stand until all the dirt settles to the bottom and we'll use it on our rice."

Human ingenuity never failed to impress Myers.

In the absence of a mess hall, a prisoner representative from each barrack was sent to fetch the food caldrons from the kitchen and then distribute the food to the best of his ability and moral integrity.

One night during their evening meal, Myers and Tarpy were discussing that the food at Pine Tree Camp was better than they'd had since leaving Manila.

"That's not saying much for what you been through," another prisoner remarked.

"There's not much that can be said about it," Tarpy answered him.

The scant food and inadequate supplies continued to take their physical toll on the POWs. But in April of 1945, the physical deprivation took a back seat for some men and psychological deprivation became their greatest nemesis. The length of time they'd been prisoners, combined with the stress of not knowing how many more months of the deficiencies and brutalities stretched in front of them, created a very different atmosphere than that which Myers and Tarpy had experienced at Bilibid. There was no *quanning*, no making fools of the guards, no entertainment of any kind. Myers observed that they were all just barely hanging on. And when some went beyond hanging on, when the mental stress and the lack of even the most primitive comforts became too much for them, they adopted a defeatist attitude and faded away.

Dark thoughts invaded Myers' mind as well. But they were more of a pragmatic nature than panic-driven. By April he had been watching broken, ailing men come into the hospital for three months. And when they left, if they left at all, they weren't much improved. Not because nothing could be done for them, but rather because they were still facing such overwhelming shortages in medical supplies. Myers figured that at any given time, the death rate among them was about twenty-five percent. At that pace, none of them would be alive to see another year.

Word reached the camp on April 14 that President Roosevelt had died a day or so earlier. The strain of the past four years combined with his failing health made him yet another casualty of the war. On the heels of that announcement, a group of prisoners, mostly officers, were rounded up for transport to another camp. The scuttlebutt was that this group was headed for more coal mining duties in Manchuria by way of Korea. As always, both those going and those remaining behind wondered if things would be better in new surroundings. Given their past experiences, most POWs agreed that taking a chance on something new was pretty risky.

The firebombing over Japanese cities continued. The POWs anxiously watched the aircraft crisscrossing the sky over the camp, but thus far none of them had dropped any of their deadly eggs on the prisoners. They felt the bombs' impact anyway, though. The guards at the camp were building tremendous resentment against the POWs for the pounding the Home Islands were taking as a result of the American bombing runs. They readily took their anger out on the prisoners.

The brutality of the guards at Pine Tree Camp reached an extreme in the late spring of 1945. Prisoners were beaten and tortured regularly. One man who tried to escape was hung alive on a barbed wire fence. There, he begged for water and mercy over the course of several days before he died.

Myers saw men every day who had suffered gruesome injuries at the nearby coal mine, where men descended six thousand feet into its shaft to perform suffocating and harsh labor. The mines were still privately owned, and therefore privately run. These civilians, too, had a hateful attitude toward the Americans and often abused them more aggressively than the camp guards did.

One night a man fell into a sewage ditch and broke his leg. He was informed that until the leg healed, he would not have to go back down into the mine again. With the revelation that an injury meant no work, self-mutilation became a part of life at the camp. For Myers, trained in caring for the sick and injured, and witness to the horrors inflicted on the POWs by the Imperial troops, the self-mutilation was a new abhorrence the men were thrust into.

Myers treated men who had asked to have their arms and ankles broken by their fellow prisoners. If none was willing, they did it themselves. He saw other men who had taken battery acid from their mining headlamps and introduced it into their open sores. One man had deliberately stared at his welder's torch to flash-burn his eyes. Another set off a detonator in his hand.

In response to the increasing frequency of the requests, the camp soon had two professional bone crushers. For a fee, they would administer clean breaks. And while one of them asked a higher price, he included carrying the victim out of the mine as a part of his services.

The element that these men failed to consider ahead of time was that the doctors and corpsmen still had no supplies with which to treat injuries, accidental or self-inflicted. Men's hands, mangled from mining tools and coal cars, were never given antibiotics or any other medically proven treatment. All that was available was hot water, in which the injury was soaked to kill as many bacteria as possible. After that, Myers would tell them, it was in God's hands.

The number of men starving to death was holding at a fairly steady rate and kept the burial crews busy. As midsummer settled over Japan, the men at Pine Tree Camp struggled to stay alive and keep the flies away. Myers and Tarpy figured out that of the original group of 173 who had arrived with them from the *Brazil Maru,* 52, nearly thirty percent, had died since their arrival in Japan six months earlier.

Germany had surrendered on May 7, 1945, but the news never reached the prisoners at Pine Tree Camp. The Allies had called on the Japanese to surrender at the same time, but the man now in charge of Japan's third wartime government, Admiral Baron Kantaro Suzuki, ignored the Allies' ultimatum. This left the Allies with no choice but to continue the bombardment of Japan.

To prevent as many civilian deaths as possible, planes dropped leaflets over the targeted cities ahead of time, urging evacuation. From the middle of April to the middle of June, Allied fire raids hit the targets called the Big Six—the cities of Tokyo, Nagoya, Kobe, Osaka, Yokohama, and Kawasaki.

The night of June 20, 480 bombers flew over Fukuoka, destroying nearly a quarter of the city. Nine days later, 487 bombers dropped their loads on Moji, destroying more than a quarter of it. The prisoners at Pine Tree Camp heard the thunder and saw the flashes of the firestorm glowing in the summer night air. Given what they could see even from a distance, they knew that should they be hit, they didn't have a chance.

As June drew to a close, the island of Kyushu was rendered useless by Allied air supremacy. The currents of heat that arose from the conflagrations tossed the planes as they flew away from their bombing runs and actually tore helmets from the heads of crew members.

Meanwhile, American mining of Japanese ports was so intense, it completely overwhelmed the enemy's minesweeping force. After having sunk one minesweeper, an American P-38 pilot sent what was probably the war's most mellifluous message:

Saw steamer . . . strafed same . . . sank same . . . some sight . . . signed Smith.

As a result of both the bombing raids and Operation Starvation, the Allies' shipping blockade, Japan's five great ports were now handling less than one eighth of their 1941 trade. The secondary mode of transport, the rail system, had been reduced to twenty-five percent of its carrying capacity. Three quarters of the Japanese fishing fleet had also been destroyed. The country was so hard up for oil that their planes sat empty on the airfields. When the Allied bombs struck them, they didn't even blow up.

With a sudden and terrible reckoning, many in the Japanese government realized that not only was the country unable to defend herself adequately, but she wouldn't be able to feed herself into the next spring. Japan was on the verge of panic, plagued by disease and starvation. While the military factions of the government still insisted on keeping the Japanese people in the dark, Imperial diplomats were desperate to find peace with honor.

The diplomats secretly asked Sweden, Russia, and Switzerland to arrange a summit with the United States. When the government's military fanatics, still in the majority on the Japanese Supreme Council, heard mention of proposed peace talks, they responded with the threat that they would kill anyone who discussed it further.

The Emperor did make the request, on July 7, that the war be ended as soon as possible. But since the Emperor never spoke directly to them, and the message traveled through many levels of secretaries and assistants, the military leaders did not interpret the Emperor's words as a call for surrender. They opted to continue fighting, choosing annihilation versus disgrace and suicide versus surrender.

The Imperial fanatics at Japan's helm believed beyond a doubt that the United States' invasion of the Home Islands was imminent. They were unable to pinpoint an exact date, but they were certain now since the new President, Harry S. Truman, had spent his first three months as commander-in-chief becoming familiar with the invasion's strategies, that it would not be long before the evil white invaders arrived.

Truman had been vice president under Roosevelt for eighty-two days. During that time, he had been invited to the White House only once. Consequently, when he took office after Roosevelt died, he had little more knowledge of the ongoing war against Japan than did the American public. At the close of Truman's first cabinet meeting, Secretary of War Henry Stimson pulled him aside to disclose the details of a secret project that had been carried on since 1942 by a group of the world's top scientists. The secret project's code name was Manhattan, after the Manhattan Engineer District Office, the site where all of the research began.

At the outset of the Manhattan Project, Stimson explained to the stunned Truman, Roosevelt and Churchill had decided not to inform Stalin of its existence or its goal. Many members of both the American and British governments weren't convinced the Soviet chief was as much interested in world peace as he was in furthering his own agenda, so sharing sensitive information with him too early might have a deleterious effect on the project. Stalin did, however, have moles inside the Manhattan Project in the form of an exiled German scientist, who kept the Soviets informed as the project unfolded.

More than one hundred twenty thousand people had worked on the Manhattan Project between 1942 and 1945. They were located in thirty-seven different facilities at the cost of $2 billion. They called their final product the atom bomb, although co-creator Dr. Robert Oppenheimer affectionately referred to it as "the gadget."

The morality and cost of using such a destructive weapon were questioned throughout its development. Some scientists weren't certain that it could be prevented from destroying all life on the planet, even if its ground zero was thousands of miles away. On July 16, at 0529, those fears were allayed when the test bomb, code-named Trinity, was detonated at Alamagordo Air Base in the New Mexican desert. Even at twenty miles, observers felt the heat of the explosion on exposed skin, and they reported that the radiation level in the rising mushroom cloud was so intense it emitted a blue glow. The dress rehearsal had been a success.

The Allies, meanwhile, kept the pressure on Japan by continuing the B-29 runs. On July 17, fifteen hundred planes bombed Tokyo, taking off from the Okinawan airbase. To the south, another base had been established on Tinian, an island in the Mariana chain, but its purpose was not associated with the bombardment of Tokyo. Located fifteen hundred miles from Japan, it was home to the 509th Composite Group. This seventeen-hundred-man outfit had spent months honing their skills with high-level bombing test-runs in Utah before shipping out for the island base.

A total of four hundred B-29s were on the island, but a select group of planes had been kept secluded from the rest. These planes were outfitted differently and were kept near a specially constructed air-conditioned hut. On July 26, personnel at the hut took delivery of the materials needed to assemble the first atomic bomb to be used against an enemy, code-named Little Boy.

Concurrently, five potential targets for the bomb were being considered by a committee composed of American military strategists and governmental officials. The first site was the city of Kyoto, an urban industrial center with a population of one million. As the result of the destruction occurring in other areas of Japan, a large number of people and industries had been moved to Kyoto, which was one of Japan's intellectual centers.

Hiroshima was the second city being considered. It was home to an important army depot and was a port of embarkation located in the middle of an urban industrial area. It was a good radar target, but it was not thought to be a good incendiary target because of the city's proximity to rivers.

The third choice was Yokohama, another important urban industrial area that had so far been untouched by other bombing raids. Its major manufacturing activities included aircraft, machine tools, docks, and electrical equipment. It was also the site of oil refineries. As the damage to Tokyo had increased, additional industries were moved to Yokohama, but it was also home to the heaviest anti-aircraft concentration in Japan.

The fourth target choice was the arsenal in the city of Kokura. It was one of the largest arsenals in Japan, housing light ordnance, anti-aircraft, and beachhead defense materials. Properly placed, the bomb's blast could potentially damage not only the arsenal, but the surrounding urban industrial structures as well.

The least favored target was Niigata, a port of embarkation on the northwest coast of the island of Honshu. Niigata's importance was increasing as Japan's other ports were being damaged, plus machine tool industries were located there, as well as oil refineries and storage. But it was less significant when compared to the other target choices.

The final possibility was the Emperor's palace itself. The committee agreed early on that the palace should not be an initial target, but that information should be obtained about the advisability of making it the target of future atom bombs.

After hearing all the facts, and debating the pros and cons of each location, it was the recommendation of the committee that the first four choices for targets should be Kyoto, Hiroshima, Yokohama, and the Kokura Arsenal. When the committee presented the list to Secretary Stimson and President Truman, it was noted that Koyoto had also been Japan's former capital. As such, it had a significant place in the nation's history, and President Truman had it removed from the list. The discussion of possible targets for the atom bomb continued, and a decision was ultimately reached. Should it prove necessary to employ Little Boy, it would be dropped on Hiroshima, where it would wipe out not only the war industries but the headquarters of the Second General Army as well.

With the target for the atom bomb decided, the Allies sought to find peace with the Japanese once again. A meeting between President Truman, Churchill, and Churchill's successor, Clement Attlee, was held to draft a declaration calling for the unconditional surrender of the Emperor and his people. Named the Potsdam Declaration, it was presented to the Japanese government, which rejected it on July 30, 1945, as a mere rehash of earlier proposals.

It appeared that there was no other course available to end the horrible war that had dragged on so long and cost so many lives. On August 5, Allied planes dropped seven hundred thousand leaflets on the Hiroshima area, urging its citizens to evacuate the city immediately.

August 6 was a perfect summer day in Japan. The citizens of Hiroshima who had chosen to remain in town ignored the squadron of B-29s that cruised overhead. They had become used to the planes, which usually flew reconnaissance missions. At 0811, the ten-thousand-pound bomb was dropped. It was air-burst at nineteen hundred feet above the city to maximize destruction, and by 0815 hours, Hiroshima ceased to exist.

In the days that followed the bombing of Hiroshima, President Truman made a radio broadcast in which he told the Japanese people that the attack on Hiroshima "was only a warning of things to come." He told them to surrender or "face a rain of ruin from the air, the like of which has never been seen on this earth." The Japanese stubbornly refused to surrender.

Again military strategists and governmental officials discussed a course of action. The bomb's creators had a second weapon, code-named Fat Man, ready for use. In addition, they felt they could have a dozen more bombs ready by November, if necessary. Fat Man's target would be the arsenal at Kokura on the northeast coast of Kyushu, but warning leaflets had been dropped over all the target cities remaining on the list. Military intelligence surmised that there were probably camps housing Allied POWs in or near all of the remaining targets. But the importance of each of the chosen cities could not be disregarded.

Fat Man was originally scheduled for detonation on August 11, but poor visibility was predicted and the detonation was moved up two days to the 9th. Unlike the clear skies over Hiroshima three days earlier, Kokura was obscured by smoke and haze. The pilot spent ten minutes without sighting his aim-point, as his instructions were to bomb visually. He then proceeded to his second target, Nagasaki, farther south on the island of Kyushu, and dropped Fat Man at 1101 hours, detonating it at 1,650 feet.

At the news that a second jumbo bomb had been dropped on Nagasaki, an Imperial conference convened and the debate began about what step the Japanese should take next. Most of the Japanese military leaders were prepared to continue resisting. Others suggested that perhaps the terms outlined in the Potsdam Declaration should be reconsidered. The Emperor himself arrived at the conference shortly before midnight on August 9 and heard from both sides.

In the dark hours of the night, Hirohito reasoned that if continuing the war meant "destruction of the nation and a prolongation of bloodshed, then I swallow my own tears and give my sanction to the proposal to accept the Allied proclamation on the basis outlined by the foreign minister."

Although President Truman received word of the Japanese acceptance on August 10, provisos had been added to the peace agreement. It was several days before the Allies had made clear once again that they sought unconditional surrender. American military had informed the President earlier in the day that materials for a third bomb could be shipped to Tinian on August 13. It could be ready for detonation on August 17.

The third bomb was never needed. On the morning of August 14, Emperor Hirohito made clear to his cabinet that he accepted the peace terms originally laid out by the Allies. It was his intention, he said, to do anything to end the war and persuade the Japanese military to lay down their weapons.

The ministers suggested that perhaps the Emperor should address the nation directly with the news of the surrender. This was an unprecedented idea, and the decision was made for the Emperor to record the address. Upon listening to the tape, the ministers decided the quality was not clear enough for radio transmission and the Emperor was obliged to deliver his surrender speech a second time. The tape of this speech was held under lock and key until the moment of broadcast, because of the risk that a remaining military zealot would steal it.

At 1200 hours on August 15, the Japanese national anthem was played on radios across the war-weary Empire, and Hirohito spoke to his people for the first time. In the history of Japanese emperors, commoners had never heard them speak. Hirohito told his "good and loyal subjects" that they must "endure the unendurable and accept the unacceptable."

CHAPTER EIGHTEEN

★

Freedom and Old Glory

As they had for the Japanese people, the B-29s flying overhead had become commonplace for the POWs at Pine Tree Camp. When the air-raid sirens sounded on August 9, as they had almost daily ever since Myers arrived, the prisoners and patients who were mobile were herded into their flimsy bomb shelter. None of them thought the shelters would protect them from anything, but one of the men had discovered a hole through which he could watch the bombing runs. It provided great entertainment for the other prisoners when he later shared his observations with them. On this particular day, when he positioned himself to watch the action overhead, he saw something indescribable.

"A huge, pale gray cloud—looked like a big mushroom—just rose right up in the sky," he told the men in his barracks that evening. Myers and Tarpy listened to him intently.

"What do you think it was?" Tarpy asked. The question was followed by several weak hypotheses.

"Don't know," the first man said. "I think the Japs invented some kind of 'air island.' They're gonna use it to float arms and tanks and troops across the ocean to the west coast. I think they're gonna try to invade us before we invade them."

More discussion followed, none of it coherent, as they disagreed about what the prisoner had seen. They did agree, however, that whatever the thing was, it had gone away and nobody in the camp seemed to be the worse for it.

Had the bomb fallen on Kokura as it was originally scheduled to do, it would have almost certainly killed all of the POWs being held in southern Japan. There were prisoner casualties nonetheless. At the bomb's hypocenter in Nagasaki, three hundred and fifty American, British, Australian, and Indonesian-Dutch prisoners were killed instantly. A little over a mile from the hypocenter, the camp at Fukuoka #14 was completely destroyed, with between sixty and eighty POWs perishing. Five miles farther from the hypocenter, at Fukuoka #2, four men died as a result of the bomb blast.

One of the prisoners had a radio secreted away and he listened to the stories about what had occurred flooding the short-wave radio bands. The information traveled quickly between English and Japanese radio operators and, because of inconsistencies in translation, the bomb was being called names like "autonomic bomb" and "adam bomb." The most incredible detail of all was that so much destruction could come from just *one* bomb.

The war did not end at the stroke of noon on August 15, 1945, for the POWs being held in Asia. Almost immediately after the bombing, the faces and attitudes of the Japanese guards changed. Questions flew around the camp, most of them dealing with reprisals. How would the prisoners be treated now? If the Japanese were angry about the firebombing earlier, would they now be so incensed that they would kill the POWs without hesitation? The prisoners assumed that the Allied troops were not far off, and some had heard the disconcerting rumor that, in the event of an invasion of the Home Islands, the Japanese were going to drive the prisoners in front of them onto the battlefield, using them as human shields. Either that or the Japanese were simply going to massacre them all.

The fears were justified. Elsewhere throughout the Japanese Empire, camp officials continued brutalities even after they had heard the Emperor's speech. Prisoners were shot or beheaded or hacked to death in camps outside of Japan. For most of the seventeen thousand men being held in the one hundred and seventy-six camps throughout the Home Islands of Japan, though, a different scene transpired.

In Pine Tree Camp, the men got up at their usual times to fall out for muster and work detail, only to be told by the guards that there was no work that day. The Japanese gave a myriad of reasons: a cave-in at the mine, a cholera outbreak, the equipment was broken. The POWs were given the day off and then watched as officers burned records from the administrative offices by the armfuls. The *gunso,* sergeants, and other guards, who had spat ferocious tirades at the men for three years, were now whispering.

Finally, the words were spoken: *senso owari.* The war is over.

Myers and Tarpy awoke one morning several days after the official surrender to find that the Japanese had simply left the camp. Their quarters were empty, the supplies gone, the gates open. The enormity of being free after being captive for so long was something that took a while to sink in. Most of the men went about that day discussing what they were going to do when they got home. But all of them kept an air of caution about them, for fear that the war had not really ended and the Japanese might capture them once again.

The caution faded as soon as a plane appeared over the camp. It waggled its wings at the prisoners in the compound of Pine Tree Camp and flew off. Shortly more planes appeared, their pilots dropping seabags packed with their own belongings: shoes, socks, skivvies, messages, magazines, chocolate, and cigarettes. The first stage of the liberation, called "Operation Birdcage," had begun, which called for the Allied aircraft to locate the POW camps. Myers and Tarpy were about to be liberated.

Another wave of aircraft flew over the camp, dropping leaflets that instructed the prisoners to create the letters "PW" out of anything they had, as long as they could make it visible enough to be seen from the air. The leaflets also asked that the number of men in the camp be listed. The men used blankets and clothing held down by rocks, and spelled out the requested information.

The second phase of liberation, "Operation Mastiff," then began, the phase to resupply the desperately needy men. Packages began falling from the skies containing the things they needed most and had been deprived of the longest—food and clothes and medicine. To keep the contents of the packages somewhat together, the military used crates and barrels on pallets, some weighing as much as five tons, affixing them with parachutes. The huge B-29s dropping them were flying so low, the chutes never opened. The goods dropped from the sky and crashed through the roofs of the barracks and hospitals. They exploded on impact, the force either crushing the contents or extruding them. One man thought he'd been shot when in reality the "blood" he saw was only the contents of a jug of tomato puree.

As impossible as it seemed, the prisoners who had arrived at Pine Tree Camp aboard the *Brazil Maru* were once again being bombarded by their own military. They raced through the compound on stick-like legs, trying to avoid being crushed and, at the same time, collect the blessings they had missed for so long. Within a day a flight correction was made and the planes flew at greater altitudes so that the chutes would open properly.

The men in the camps had lost significant amounts of weight. Myers guessed he was down from his usual one sixty-five to around ninety pounds. One man in camp had lost 110 pounds, more than half of his body weight. Without a thought to the consequences, Myers watched the men gorge themselves on the newly dropped provisions just as they had done with the brown sugar aboard ship.

The military must have suspected the prisoners would have difficulty with the food. Soon new leaflets rained down, warning the prisoners not to overeat. After a protracted starvation diet, too much food too quickly could be fatal. Not all the men heeded the advice. When the Pine Tree Camp burial detail lay to rest their final man, he was a prisoner who died of overeating.

On August 27, Allied ships cruised into Japanese ports. American troops systematically went from camp to camp, liberating the gaunt, half-naked men. They arrived at Pine Tree Camp on September 1 and transported the prisoners to the Moji Harbor. There, the newly freed men boarded a small landing craft that took them out to the waiting hospital ship.

The POWs who were too ill or weak to walk were admitted directly to the wards for immediate treatment. Those who were ambulatory, including Myers and Tarpy, were taken to the decontamination ward. Their clothing was discarded and they took showers, the first they'd had in more than three years. The men were issued new clothing and examined by a medical officer to determine whether they could immediately begin the passage home.

Three years, eight months, and twenty-five days had passed since the Japanese first bombed the Philippines. Estel Myers was finally going home.

Five hundred miles northeast of the ship on which Myers was awakening to his first full day of freedom, the official surrender ceremony was taking place in the Tokyo harbor. The ceremony was scheduled for midmorning of September 2 aboard the 45,000-ton battleship *Missouri*. Scattered through the harbor were scores of other ships from the 3rd Fleet, American flags fluttering from them in the morning sun. The sailors aboard the ships were dressed in their whites; the Marines wore freshly pressed suntans.

An ordinary mess table draped in green baize cloth was set up on the ship's forward quarterdeck. On the table lay two sets of surrender documents—one in English and the other in Japanese.

At 0800 hours, the ship's band played "The Star Spangled Banner" and a detail raised an American flag, the same one that flew over the nation's Capitol building on the day of infamy in 1941. Hundreds of enlisted men and officers were already assembled, including Lieutenant General Jonathan Wainwright and British Lieutenant General Sir Arthur Percival. At 0815, Admiral Nimitz and General MacArthur came on board, followed thirty-five minutes later by the arrival alongside the *Missouri* of a small American ship. The vessel carried Japanese Foreign Minister Mamoru Shigemitsu and General Yoshijiro Umetsu, the Supreme War Counsel, who had threatened suicide rather than take part in such a degrading ceremony. With them were seven generals and admirals and three men formally attired in top hats, morning coats, and striped pants.

At 0859, MacArthur stepped up to the microphone a few feet from the table and addressed those assembled.

"From this solemn occasion, a better world shall emerge out of the blood and carnage of the past." He motioned for the Japanese delegation to come forward. At 0904, Foreign Minister Mamoru Shigemitsu signed the documents, officially ending World War II. After the Allies signed, MacArthur concluded the twenty-minute ceremony: "Let us pray that peace be now restored to the world and that God preserve it always. These proceedings are now closed."

Minutes later, those aboard the *Missouri* heard a rumbling which quickly grew to a roar. A formation of nine B-29 Superfortresses took shape, followed by several more formations. Other Allied aircraft appeared—Avengers, Hellcats, Corsairs, Helldivers, Liberators, Flying Fortresses, Billy Mitchells—nearly one thousand in all. They roared over the bay toward Tokyo in a final display of military power.

For Myers and the other men, their new freedom was similar to being awakened from a long nightmare, as if they were coming back from the grave. Since the Japanese were not bound by any of the conventions regarding POW treatment and had allowed practically no communication in or out of the camps, neither the military nor the men's families knew who had survived and who hadn't. As soon as they were able, the men sent word home.

Myers' letter arrived at his parents' home in Kentucky on September 16.

Dear Mother,

This is the first opportunity I've had in years to write and now that I have the chance there's more than I can begin to write. If you want to know about me I'll have lots of stories when I get there. I'm well and gaining weight very fast. After my little journey, which 1600 prisoners began and 300 survived, I weighed 104 pounds. I have gained enough strength and now I weigh around 140 so you can see how fast I'm coming back. . . .

Is Norma married yet? I'm afraid to try to write to her because four years is a long time and a lot of water has passed under the bridge. . . . I'm leaving Japan today on a destroyer. The only time I'll be happier is when I get home. It's been terrible. How is dad and all? Does Iola have any more children? I hope to see you all very soon.

Lots and lots of love, Estel.

P. S. We weren't allowed to have any pencils or anything in our possession so it's been a long time since I did any writing.

The doctors on board the hospital ship began the task of healing the prisoners' physical ailments without delay. Myers told the doctor examining him that during his more than three years of imprisonment he had suffered from dengue, ascariasis, chronic diarrhea, bronchitis, asthma, beriberi, pellagra, night blindness, malaria, and general malnutrition. He was still suffering from some of the diseases and had lingering aftereffects of all of them. When the doctor asked Myers if he had any particular complaints, Myers told him no. For a man who had suffered through the trials that Myers had, having no complaints seemed unusual to the doctor.

After the same type of interrogation of other former POWs and other incongruous answers, the doctors realized that the psychological ailments these men were suffering from would take much longer to heal than their bodies would. Each man reacted to his new freedom in a unique way, ranging from extreme elation to complete apathy. Some of the men couldn't talk enough about their experiences, while others preferred to sort things out in their own heads.

With the help of a former POW who was a chaplain, the medical staff aboard the hospital ship was able to help those who needed it over the rough spots of repatriation. The priest advised them to treat the POWs by following two pieces of advice. First, he told them not to give the men any obvious sympathy. They needed someone to listen, not pity them. Secondly, he told the crew to give lots of tender, loving care. This, he said, had been missed the most.

For Myers, dealing with healing and the readjustment to freedom would be managed in the manner most familiar to him. Myers was a man with strong character and a positive outlook on life. His faith in God, his love of family, and his sense of duty and honor were the things he held closest to his heart. They were what sustained him through his darkest hours as a prisoner of war and nothing was more important. And now that he tasted freedom, he had neither the desire to discuss the past nor the wish to complain about the present. He was only interested in the future.

On October 6, 1945, the USS *Catron* sailed under the Golden Gate Bridge into the San Francisco harbor with about seven hundred fifty repatriated men. Among them was Estel Myers. They shed tears unashamedly as they looked through the misty sunlight at the sign on shore that read simply, "Welcome Home!" By Treasure Island, another sign read, "Hi Mates, Well Done!"

Myers had come full circle. When he had embarked from Treasure Island in April of 1941, he was a young man, fresh off the farm, eager to find his place in a rapidly changing world. Since that time, he had traveled a distance that was equal to the circumference of the earth. He had earned the friendship of many men and the respect of others. He had seen places unlike any his family could ever imagine.

But Myers had also seen the apocalyptic side of mankind. Death, torture, mutilation—these were only words to describe the acts he witnessed. In reality, nothing could describe what depravity roamed the black abyss of his captors' souls. Estel Myers had looked into the belly of the beast and would be forever changed by what he had seen there.

Epilogue

There was no doubt in the minds of the American military and the American public that the Japanese were responsible for a great many atrocities during the years of World War II. The difficulty came in determining which Japanese were responsible and to what level. Unlike their Nazi counterparts, the trials in the Pacific often took much longer and often resulted in the guilty parties receiving no sentence whatsoever. The debate continues over why this was so, impeding efforts to bring closure to this terrible chapter in human history.

In order to facilitate legal proceedings, the Allies created three classes of war crimes and corresponding war criminals. "A" Class criminals were tried by the International Military Tribunal of the Far East in Tokyo. They were the highest-ranking officials in the Japanese government who were found to have direct knowledge of acts of incomprehensible barbarism or to have directly ordered such acts. The Allies then developed a list of more than three hundred thousand "B" and "C" Class criminals, stopping only because they realized they had to stop somewhere. In the end, only fifty-seven hundred were actually tried, the proceedings taking place in the areas where the crimes occurred.

The trials began shortly after the surrender was officially signed. On September 15, 1945, General Tomoyuki Yamashita, the "Tiger of Malaya" and the man from whom General MacArthur retook the

Philippines, was sentenced to death by an American military court in Manila. MacArthur procured Yamashita's seven-hundred-year-old fighting sword and had it sent to West Point for display.

The prime "A" Class criminal was General Hideki Tojo, who had served as prime minister, war minister, and home minister during the war. On September 16, 1945, weeks before his trial, he attempted suicide but failed. He recovered from his wound and was sentenced to death by hanging. The sentence was carried out on December 23, 1948.

General Masaharu Homma, the commander of the Japanese troops who captured the Philippines, was classified as another "A" Class criminal. He was executed by a firing squad in April 1946, a date that ironically corresponded with the date of the fall of Bataan four years earlier.

The two men responsible for the horror aboard the *Oryoku Maru, Enoura Maru,* and *Brazil Maru* were found guilty of multiple war crimes. On May 9, 1947, Lieutenant Junsabura Toshino, the ships' commander, was sentenced to death by hanging, while Shusuke Wada, the nefarious interpreter, got life imprisonment at hard labor.

The man who signed the surrender documents aboard the *Missouri,* Foreign Minister Mamoru Shigemitsu, was sentenced to seven years' imprisonment.

The final fate of Emperor Hirohito was by no means satisfactory to many Americans, who believed that as the chief of state of Japan he should have been tried, found guilty of war crimes, and subsequently executed. Following Japan's unconditional surrender, General MacArthur oversaw the occupation of the country for six years. During that time, the Emperor saved himself by agreeing to the de-deification of his position. In other words, Hirohito remained as emperor but surrendered his divine powers. Neither did he have any political powers, but took the position of a mere mortal figurehead. Since he had never exercised his powers as emperor in any way, political or divine, many have been left to wonder how fitting a punishment this was for a man whose country made 59,167 men and women prisoners of war, of which 23,559 died.

Hirohito and his family became the subjects of human-interest stories, in much the same way other royal families' lives are reported. He renewed his interest in biology and was published several times on the subject. On January 7, 1989, Hirohito died of cancer at his Imperial Palace, at the age of eighty-eight.

The saddest epilogue to World War II was the difficulty the ex-POWs have had in putting their lives back together. These men and women lost all of their innocence and a great deal of their hope. The nightmares they lived on foreign soil followed them home to their own bedrooms and remained with them for the rest of their lives.

Statistics abound detailing how many of our troops made it and how many didn't and what the percentage of survivorship works out to be. There were 23,317 Americans in all branches of service in the Philippines when the war broke out. About one thousand were killed in action. Four hundred, mainly men of the 19th Bombardment Group, escaped to Australia. That left 21,917 to become prisoners of the Japanese. At least 12,195 died as POWs for many reasons, but starvation was the primary cause of death for the great majority. The 9,732 survivors were repatriated. But what that 42 percent had lived through during the war was only the beginning of their trials.

Physically, more former POWs suffer from tuberculosis and cirrhosis of the liver than their peers who were not prisoners. They have a higher than normal incidence of cancer and heart problems. Their general state of health is average at best. They suffer from a laundry list of psychological difficulties. Studies of "prisoner of war syndrome" have shown it to be progressive and unpredictable. The long-term effects of starvation, malnutrition, maltreatment, disease, and mental stress can manifest themselves at any time. It is an unfortunate state of affairs that these men and women, who gave so much at the most pivotal point of the twentieth century, have had to live constantly with the consequences of their sacrifices.

As soon as Myers arrived back on American soil, he phoned his family from the naval base in Oakland, California, to let them know he was on his way home. A train took him from Oakland to Chicago, and another took him from there to Louisville. Since all

POWs were automatically given a one rank promotion, Myers arrived home as a Pharmacist's Mate First Class. In early November, he was honored along with other veterans in an Armistice Day parade in Louisville, and then reported to the naval hospital in Memphis for more examinations.

The hospital found him "mentally and physically qualified to perform all the duties of his rate" and recommended that "he be returned to full duty." He continued the prescribed rehabilitation and on March 13, 1946, was honorably separated from the Navy. Myers was awarded the American Theatre Medal, the Victory Medal, the Asiatic Pacific Medal, and the American Campaign Ribbon. He was presented with three bronze stars for "meritorious service as a Hospital Corpsman" during the hell ship ordeal. James Forrestal, Secretary of the Navy, made this commendation on behalf of President Truman on January 18, 1947:

> Myers made every effort possible to alleviate the suffering of his fellow prisoners and sustain their morale, despite his own intense suffering. Stouthearted and courageous throughout this perilous voyage, Myers by his outstanding fortitude and self-sacrificing devotion to his fellow men, served as an inspiration to all prisoners on board and upheld the highest tradition of the United States Naval Service.

His military chapter closed, Myers began rebuilding his personal life. As happened to many of the POWs, the girl he had left behind feared him dead, and married someone else. Myers met another woman, married her soon after, and their family grew to include seven children. His interest in medicine had been piqued during the war. He became a chiropractor and built a practice in the Louisville area.

Myers' spirit was willing, but like so many former POWs, his body had been weakened by years in Japanese prison camps. He developed bronchial difficulties one damp Kentucky winter, and the problem grew worse each year. Finally, in 1959, he packed up his family and moved to the sunshine and dry air of Phoenix, Arizona.

Although surrounded by his own family as well as those of his brothers Ken and Orville, Myers' physical problems continued. He suffered one heart attack and then two more, finally developing lung cancer. On September 12, 1973, Estel Myers died after suffering his fourth heart attack. He was fifty-three years old.

Friends and family alike marveled that despite the horrors he had experienced, he never complained about his lot in life. They remembered him having a ready smile, always being willing to help out a fellow human being. Myers wasn't a hero or a celebrity; he was more than that. He was a good man, one of the thousands who, between 1941 and 1945, made unfathomable personal sacrifices for a good cause.

After Myers' death, a letter surfaced that he had written to his children several months earlier. In it he listed what he felt would help them live happy and successful lives—things undoubtedly learned from his own life's experiences:

Believe with all your heart in God, country and family. Be truthful. Be loving, patient and forgiving with your spouses and children. Give an honest day's work in whatever you do. Believe in the Golden Rule. Be loyal and honest to your country; be a good American and thankful that you are one. I love you all. Remember papa.

Index